Managing Women

Managing Women

Disciplining Labor in Modern Japan

Elyssa Faison

UNIVERSITY OF CALIFORNIA PRESS
Berkeley · Los Angeles · London

University of California Press, one of the most distin-
guished university presses in the United States, enriches
lives around the world by advancing scholarship in the
humanities, social sciences, and natural sciences. Its activities are supported by the UC Press Foundation and
by philanthropic contributions from individuals and institutions. For more information, visit
www.ucpress.edu.

University of California Press
Berkeley and Los Angeles, California

University of California Press, Ltd.
London, England

Library of Congress Cataloging-in-Publication Data

Faison, Elyssa, 1965–.
    Managing women : disciplining labor in modern
Japan / Elyssa Faison.
        p.   cm.
    Includes bibliographical references and index.
    ISBN 978-0-520-25296-7 (cloth : alk. paper)
    1. Women textile workers—Japan—History.
2. Personnel management—Japan—History.   3.
Women—Employment—Japan—History.   I. Title.

HD8039.T42J313   2007
658.30082'0952—dc22   2007004263

Manufactured in the United States of America

16   15   14   13   12   11   10   09   08   07
10   9   8   7   6   5   4   3   2   1

This book is printed on New Leaf EcoBook 50, a
100% recycled fiber of which 50% is de-inked post-
consumer waste, processed chlorine-free. EcoBook 50
is acid-free and meets the minimum requirements of
ANSI/ASTM D5634–01 (Permanence of Paper).

*To my teachers, Professor Miriam Silverberg
and Professor Yamada Kōhei*

Contents

Illustrations

Acknowledgments

Many people and institutions have provided the intellectual, emotional, and material assistance necessary for me to produce this book. I would like to first thank David Ambaras, Andrew Gordon, and Patricia Tsurumi as well as several anonymous readers who read the entire manuscript and offered invaluable suggestions. Many other individuals gave feedback on the project even before a complete manuscript existed. Acknowledging them provides something of a genealogy of the book and a history of my professional life to this point.

While a graduate student at UCLA I benefited from the intellectual rigor and excitement generated in classes and conversations with Professors Benjamin Elman, Fred Notehelfer, Herman Ooms, Miriam Silverberg, and Mariko Tamanoi. I was fortunate to find myself surrounded by fellow students who believed that our individual work was part of a larger collective endeavor. Without the support and friendship of Michael Baskett, Haengja Chung, Eugenia Lean, Yue Meng, Hiromi Mizuno, Allison Sneider, Yuki Terazawa, and Rumi Yasutake, this book could not even have been conceived.

Eighteen months of dissertation research in Japan were funded by a Japan Foundation Doctoral Fellowship. While in Tokyo I was affiliated with the Ōhara Institute for Social Research as a visiting researcher working under the tutelage of the labor historian and former institute director, Professor Nimura Kazuo, whose critical eye and seemingly boundless knowledge about all written sources related to Japanese labor history helped guide me through the initial stages of the project. The Ohara Institute staff, especially Mikoshiba Keiko and Sadamori Takako, helped at every turn, initiating me into the institute's collections. While affiliated with the Ohara Institute, I simultaneously received mentoring from Professor Kawamura Minato at Hōsei University. My weekly meetings with Professor Kawamura and fellow students David Rosenfeld and Kim Kono, to discuss colonial and proletarian literature, gave me a fresh perspective on Japanese women's and labor history.

During my time in Tokyo and in subsequent visits to Japan for further research, I received invaluable help from Professors Fujime Yuki, Kamo Toshio, Kim Chan'jong, Kimura Masato, Koyama Hitoshi, Mizuno Naoki, Kate Nakai, Narita Ryūichi, Ōtsuki Katsusuke, Manfred Ringhoffer, Suzuki Akira, and Tomiyama Ichirō. They variously allowed me to sit in on classes they were teaching, acquainted me with the holdings of their university libraries or archives, gave me access to soon-to-be-published manuscripts, and in all cases shared their expertise and advice. The staff of the Shūyōdan head offices in Tokyo allowed me to spend a day with them looking over materials, as did the staff of the Kishiwada City Hall records and archives division. Katō Shūichi of Gozandō Publishing generously discussed with me the collection of Professor Hazama Hiroshi, which he was in the process of cataloging for its move to the International Research Center for Japanese Studies (Nichibunken) when I visited his offices, and permitted me to reproduce images from Professor Hazama's publications in the present book.

These later research trips to Japan were funded by several University of Oklahoma Junior Faculty Research Grants, Presidential International Travel Fellowships and Faculty Enrichment Grants, a grant from the Northeast Asia Council of the Association for Asian Studies, and a travel grant from the Yale Council on East Asian Studies, where I held a postdoctoral fellowship from 2003 to 2004 that enabled me to write much of the book.

I could not have had a more supportive environment for a first professional position than I did at the University of Minnesota, Twin Cities, where I spent a year teaching Japanese history and learning what it means to work with an engaged and welcoming community of colleagues. In particular, Anna Clark and Ann Waltner helped me get through my first year of full-time teaching while offering abundant opportunities to discuss and present my work to groups large and small. I am grateful for their continued support and friendship.

My colleagues at the University of Oklahoma have helped me in innumerable ways, including reading and commenting on my work, mentoring a junior faculty colleague, and offering camaraderie in abundance. I would especially like to thank Ray Canoy, Rob Griswold, Sandie Holguín, Cathy Kelly, Melissa Stockdale, and Sarah Tracy for helping me see this book to publication.

Other colleagues have also helped me in my research and professional life. Tak Fujitani read part of the manuscript at a crucial moment and helped breathe new life into the project. I have been privileged to know Carol Gluck, who has mentored me informally since I first had the idea of going to graduate school for Japanese history and has continued to assist me in my work and provide inspiration in the form of her own. From the time I first met him nearly fifteen years ago, Jonathan M. Hall has been a constant friend and a gentle critic. Dorothy Ko gave me sage advice when I needed it most. Lara Jacob and Dilip Menon have enriched my work and my life in countless ways and from seemingly countless locations around the globe. Ruth Barraclough, Barbara Brooks, Christopher Gerteis, Sally Hastings, Sharalyn Orbough, and Ann Walthall have all shared their comments on parts of this work.

My family has been a great support throughout the many years I have been engaged researching and writing this book. My mother has offered guidance and a steady stream of good energy. My father has read and commented on my work, and my two brothers have always somehow trusted that I would finish what I started. Most of all, my partner Zoe Sherinian has offered good humor and unbounded generosity of spirit through the daily successes and failures—some small and some large— that are part of any project of this duration. I thank them all for their love and encouragement.

Finally, a word about two people without whom this book could not have been written and to whom it is dedicated.

I met Professor Yamada Kōhei while taking one of his classes in Japanese political history at Nagoya University in 1988. He guided me in my research for over a year and continued to correspond with me after I left Nagoya, frequently sending me books and articles he believed might be of interest. Over the course of our nearly twenty-year relationship he has invited me into his home and made me a part of his family. He has introduced me to scholars in Japan I might otherwise not have been able to meet. His own scholarship on local politics has been inspirational. I am unspeakably fortunate to have him as a mentor and a friend.

I began working with Professor Miriam Silverberg when I entered the

Ph.D. program at UCLA in 1992. Her brilliant work on the cultural and intellectual history of Japan's interwar period, her insightful wit, and her political convictions have all served as models for me. I am grateful for everything she continues to teach me and for the opportunities her teachings have laid before me.

Introduction

Women or Workers?

"What is bringing about the destruction of the family system is the growth of industry together with the expansion of spheres of women's professional work."[1] This remark by social commentator Kawada Shirō in 1924 indicates some of the anxieties produced by increases in women's wage work in Japan since the turn of the twentieth century. At a time when industrial labor was regarded as potentially the most volatile of Japan's "social problems," female labor in particular threatened to undermine a newly imagined national moral order based on the family system.

This book examines the labor-management practices that grew out of these gendered expectations and how workers reacted to them, especially in the cotton-spinning factories of interwar Japan. Central to this project is an integrated analysis of gender ideology and ideologies of nationalism and ethnicity, which were used by industry and the state to discipline and control both a labor force *and* state subjects; in other words, creating *workers* went hand in hand with creating gendered imperial subjects. For this reason, the cultural meaning of labor-management practices and workers' responses to them must be evaluated in light of contemporary socially and culturally contested meanings of womanhood, Japanese and various colonial ethnicities, and the development of working-class subjectivities among women.

Industry managers actively constructed female factory workers as "women," rather than as "workers," inculcating moral and civic values as well as offering practical domestic training more consistent with the needs of housewives than industrial workers. This often took place through the corporate use of semistate organizations that had roots in the local improvement movement (*chihō kaizen undō*). This construction as woman rather than as worker reflected a strategy for containing union activities and strikes, since consciousness as a Japanese woman theoretically precluded the class consciousness of the worker. But it also demonstrated how femininity itself came to be used as a boundary marker within a swiftly urbanizing and industrializing modern society. During the early decades of Japan's modernity, major demographic, technological and social changes occurring simultaneously with imperial expansion created internal boundaries between a "traditional" countryside and modern urban centers in which the containment of female workers as women played an important role.[2]

I argue that the "womanly ideal" promoted by textile companies produced a counterdiscourse by female textile workers themselves, who sometimes acquiesced but at other times rejected employers' claims of parental benevolence and related demands for filial obedience. In the latter case, female workers found ways to define themselves as part of an industrial working class while maintaining their close ties to the agricultural economy and the affective ties of the countryside. Doing so, they simultaneously constructed "woman" in a way that allowed them to actively oppose management's disciplining techniques and to break free of the familial bonds imposed by both company and state rhetoric.

Finally, looking at colonial labor and the conditions of Korean and Okinawan female migrant workers to Japan's main islands, I demonstrate how the feminized bodies of Japanese women workers stood in contrast to the highly ethnicized bodies of colonial women workers, mirroring in industrial labor relations the highly fluid boundaries of inclusion and exclusion playing out among Japan and its colonies. While feminized Okinawan bodies marked a crucial site on the perimeters of Japan's colonial empire for contests over identity, I argue that within the factories of the Japanese metropole, ethnicity rather than gender stood as a privileged signifier precisely because "woman" in Japanese labor-relations had already been defined as "Japanese."[3]

Thus, within Japan's textile factories during the interwar period (1918–37), gendered, classed, and ethnicized constructions of identity underlay the historical trajectory of labor relations. The work of Andrew Gordon and other historians has demonstrated that policies and attitudes about Japanese male wage workers in the early twentieth century most often configured them as *classed* individuals.[4] This book argues that, in contrast, Japanese women workers in the textile industry tended to be *gendered* rather than classed and that the dominant construction of non-Japanese (Korean and Okinawan) female workers saw them principally as *ethnicized* workers.

This is not the story of the making of a working class along the lines of E. P. Thompson's classic of English history.[5] It does not seek the seeds of a working-class consciousness among factory women, nor does it suggest a struggle between earlier forms of artisan work and community and the new wage work of the industrial era. This is not to suggest that Japanese factory women at no time possessed a working-class consciousness, but rather that that consciousness was produced and manifested strategically as workers sought to define themselves in relation not only to their employers, but often more importantly to their families and the state. Contemporaries and later scholars pointed to the temporary nature of female factory labor as a significant factor in the failure of a vigorous and effective labor movement to develop in prewar Japan. But such arguments view women's wage work in an instrumentalist fashion and neglect the ways it was tightly tied to understandings about the modern ethnic nation and its particular forms of gender relations.

In Japan it was not working class men competing with women for jobs and status who made the most strenuous attempts to make the separation of the domestic and public spheres a reality; but rather, it was factory managers and owners working in conjunction with the state who sought to define womanhood as distinct from an identity as a wage laborer.[6] The state's motivations from the late nineteenth century onward were to achieve equality with the West by emulating Europe and the United States in terms of political institutions, industrial development, military strength, educational levels, and gender relations. These gender relations were predicated on a nuclear-family system of separate spheres and based on the image of Victorian womanhood. Thus, more than England or the United States, the Japanese state had a vested interest in promoting modern middle-class models of domestic womanhood, even as it depended on the wage labor of rural women and girls for the project of industrialization.

The promotion of these womanly values within the textile industry was inextricably tied to the development of labor paternalism and the rationalization of industry, both of which occurred in conjunction with recessionary trends in the local and global economies. Textile managers only gradually came to define their employees more as future wives and mothers than as workers in a process that spanned several decades. Early textile industrialists preferred to see female workers as an expendable resource, easily replaced by a large pool of ready labor recruited from the countryside. Two factors led to changes in this view. First, early discussions of a factory bill that would limit working hours and force the industry to provide certain safety and welfare measures launched a public debate over the treatment of workers. The rationale used by many bureaucrats and social reformers for implementing such protective measures included arguments that women's health and time for domestic work needed to be protected for the sake of the family. Such arguments were not peculiar to Japan, but had become commonplace in organizations such as the International Association for Labor Legislation.[7]

The second factor was a series of changes in Japan's economic environment that took place in the period after the First World War, which led industry leaders to embark on a strategy of rationalization. A string of recessions in the 1920s were followed by the worldwide Great Depression. Industry leaders moved to increase production through higher rates of efficiency and simultaneously took steps to attract and retain workers amid a contracting labor market. These factors taken together prompted some of the larger cotton-spinning companies to introduce their own welfare, educational, and cultural programs, along with other amenities including medical facilities. These became the backbone of paternalist policies in the cotton-spinning industry. They functioned first to indicate to the government and the international community that Japanese capitalists needed no regulations imposed upon them to maintain harmonious relations with labor, which would exist as a matter of course thanks to the benevolent practices of employers and the resulting good will of their employees. These paternalistic practices also offered to the parents of female workers the promise that their daughters would be well taken care of by the company, and would in fact receive training unavailable to them at home that would make them more attractive as brides once they left the factories to get married.

Among the female images shaping understandings of gender and family configurations in early twentieth-century Japan, the textile worker needs to be placed alongside the modern girl (moga), the housewife (shufu), and the professional working woman (shokugyō fujin) of the 1920s. The modern girl, the housewife, and the professional working woman have stronger associations with the urban environment and, by extension, with the modern. As I will demonstrate, however, female factory women occupied a position associated with both the modern urban factories and the "traditional" countryside from which the vast majority of them came.

The chapters that follow examine these issues of gendered paternalism, the importance of sexuality and its containment in the management of female workers, and the ethnically nationalized construction of the worker by taking up a variety of case studies that allow an exploration of the interweaving of these themes. Chapter 1 looks at women's wage work in early industrial Japan and the paternalist practices developed as a central part of management strategies. During the Meiji period (1868–1912), the textile industry emerged as a major source of foreign capital for the new state and a significant source of employment for Japan's first generation of women to engage extensively in wage labor. This chapter charts the history of the Factory Law and the development of paternalism in some of the largest textile companies. It elucidates the connections between an emerging national ideal of "good wife, wise mother," which was grounded in middle-class assumptions of education and leisure, and the growing demand for young women and girls to leave their rural families for work in the cotton-spinning and silk-reeling factories of the new industrial economy.

Chapter 2 focuses on the 1929 ban on night work for women and children and the sense of crisis the ban provoked among managers of female labor. The end of night work sparked concerns about the use of workers' free time, an increase in which managers feared would result in labor organizing and actions against employers or in immoral sexual activities. Managers' attempts to discipline textile workers in accordance with their construction as future wives and mothers intensified after the prohibition of night work. Company managers implemented new educational, cultural, and physical-exercise programs in order to direct every working and nonworking hour of their female employees. This shift toward bodily management signaled a new strategy by companies to combat labor organizing and the increasingly large and violent strikes of the post-Depression era.

Chapter 3 focuses on the Shūyōdan (Cultivation Association), a semigovernmental "cultivation group" that solicited the membership of women factory workers with the encouragement of their employers. The Shūyōdan was one of several such cultivation groups that inculcated docility and obedience to family and state in young women, and that was opposed by labor unions and by many workers for its coercive nature. Among the methods used to effect the kinds of bodily management promoted by textile companies in the 1920s and '30s, these kinds of cultivation groups became central to the intensification of bodily discipline and the social and civic discipline it accompanied. By 1929—the year the legal prohibition on night work in the country's textile factories went into effect—managers of the female worker–dominated textile industry were making membership mandatory for their employees. This was part of an orchestrated effort by industrial managers to mitigate union activism while simultaneously disciplining productive workers, inculcating a gendered imperial subjecthood and promoting a notion of service to the state. This chapter examines the kinds of techniques employed by the Shūyōdan to promote middle-class feminine virtues and the ways in which many workers refused complicity in such constructions.

Chapter 4 examines the 1930 Tōyō Muslin strike in which female employees walked off the job and eventually fought a street battle with the police and strongmen hired by the company. This strike involved not only employer and employees, but a wide range of actors, including left intellectuals, social reformers, union activists and organizers, workers, their families, the townspeople of Kameido (the Tokyo neighborhood where the factories were located), the state (in the form of local police), right-wing gangs, and the company itself. What was at stake for each of these social actors varied widely, but the rhetoric deployed by the protagonists reveals the way debates over womanhood, class identities, and the meaning of civil rights and national responsibilities were central to the standoff. An investigation of the work and writings of Tatewaki Sadayo, a teacher and activist who ran a school for factory girls in Kameido and supported them in the strike, and the proletarian writer Nakamoto Takako who had come to live alongside the workers and was imprisoned for her involvement in the labor actions of that year, places the strike in the context of Japan's early women's rights and Marxist movements. Both of these movements helped define the period of the 1920s and early 1930s. The Tōyō Muslin strike was eventually defeated, after a protracted letter-writing campaign by the company to parents and families of strikers, the citizens of Kameido, and to the women themselves. These letters addressed concerns about feminine morality (of both a sexual and filial nature) and placed the strikers clearly within a moral economy of familial relations that extended outward from natal home to company/employer, and finally to the state.

Chapter 5 explores issues of ethnicity, status, and citizenship in Japan's textile factories. Beginning in 1920, a number of mills began to employ increasingly large numbers of Korean and Okinawan women and girls. Partly this move was tied to wage-cutting strategies involved in the process of rationalization and as such reflected the globalization of Japan's capitalist system. But it also signaled company strategies for preempting labor conflict associated with the better organized and more demanding workers who traditionally came from Japan's countryside. This chapter offers a more detailed analysis of how ethnicity functioned in the construction of various "womanhoods" (Japanese and colonial) in the textile industry, and how the taxonomies of race, class, and gender produced through colonial policy and ideology were vital to such constructions. It examines companies, such as Kishiwada Cotton Spinning, that employed large numbers of Korean or Okinawan workers. It also investigates the development of organizations that worked closely with Korean textile workers, such as the assimilationist (and state-supported) Sōaikai and the oppositional Osaka Korean Labor Union.

Finally, the epilogue demonstrates that much continuity existed in the management of female factory labor during wartime and into the postwar era. By the early 1940s, the textile industry had almost totally collapsed, as the war cut off Japanese access to raw cotton and to foreign markets for finished goods. But textile-industry labor management provided a template for the state as it sought to mobilize women to work in the war economy. With defeat came the temporary resurgence of the industry, which for about two decades after the war was used to jump-start Japan's war-ravaged economy. Analysis of the Ōmi Kenshi Spinning strike of 1954 and Japan's Olympic gold-medal women's volleyball team of 1964, which was composed of female textile employees, help us better understand how postwar labor-management practices and the position of women in factory labor compared to the prewar situation. In both cases, much of the prewar emphasis on the cultivation of womanly virtues, a company work ethic, and service to the state persisted, but in a new context of expanded civil rights for women and the emergence of Japan as an economic power in the postwar world.

CHAPTER I

From Home Work to Corporate Paternalism

Women's Work in Japan's Early Industrial Age

When the Meiji state oversaw the opening of Japan's first government-run textile mill in 1872, its leaders had already decided that female labor would propel the early stages of Japan's industrial revolution. The government's part in initiating industrial development by funding and operating the Tomioka Silk Filature in Gunma Prefecture, and the strong role the state would play throughout the Meiji period (1868–1912) in directing the growth of capitalist institutions, ensured that the growth of industry could never be separated from the fortunes of the nation.[1] If the industrial *technologies* of the Meiji period reflected the goals of a nation aspiring toward "civilization and enlightenment," it followed that industrial *labor* should similarly reflect the patriotic nature of the project of industrialization.[2]

In the textile factories that fueled Japan's earliest and arguably most intense drive for industrialization, the vast majority of factory operatives were Japanese women and girls, ranging in age from approximately thirteen to twenty-five years old. In the silk-reeling factories women accounted for roughly 85 percent of all workers while in cotton spinning and weaving they made up 70 percent of the workforce, making Japan's early industrialization and capital accumulation dependent on the labor of rural women and girls. Their participation in the industrial project coincided precisely with the Meiji state's attempt to reenvision the parameters of Japanese womanhood and the place of women within the imperial state. As Japanese women's historian Koyama

Shizuko has demonstrated, the womanly ideal of "good wife, wise mother" (ryōsai kenbo) took hold as an organizing principle of female gender immediately after the Meiji Restoration (1868). "Good wife, wise mother" grew out of debates over women's education that began with the institution of compulsory elementary education for both males and females.[3] With this ideology as its anchor, the modern family emerged as a primary site for the mobilization of national citizens by a new, modern nation-state undergoing large-scale urbanization, industrialization, and militarization. For female industrial labor especially, the family became the site first of recruitment efforts and then of corporate control, as companies invoked the authority of male family members (who in most cases had signed the employment contracts on behalf of their daughters) to induce desired behaviors in their workers. In some cases this invocation came in the form of admonishments to work hard so as to fulfill their filial duty to their parents, but in more extreme cases (as we will see in chapter 4) fathers and brothers were asked to come to the factory to take in hand daughters and sisters who had decided to participate in strike activities.

Because middle-class assumptions underlay the feminine ideal predicated on the "good wife, wise mother" ideology, wage-earning women and girls working in factories (and thus cut off from the domestic sphere) embodied the tensions inhering in classed understandings of female gender throughout the early twentieth century. This became particularly true once the "good wife, wise mother" ideology was supplemented by the birth of the shufu, or "housewife," ideal. The housewife ideal emerged from the confluence of new configurations of family life and domestic space and the appearance of a bourgeois middle class around the time of the First World War. The housewife embodied the modern and scientific rationalism found in the study of home economics, which she practiced with single-minded dedication. But as part of the acquisition of her specialized knowledge of domestic management, she was most frequently a graduate of a girls' higher school, which Jordan Sand has described as the "true hatcheries of professional housewives."[4] Thus, the education and middle-class status required to attain the status of housewife and to be considered a true "good wife, wise mother" remained elusive for working-class women and for girls from poorer farming families.

Factory managers, concerned with disciplining Japan's first generation of industrial laborers to be productive workers, attempted to resolve tensions between gender and class by designating female textile labor a temporary condition and promoting the womanly values of motherhood and domesticity within the factory itself. This allowed them to offer to employees educational and cultural amenities that they framed as opportunities to become ideal (and presumably middle-class) housewives and mothers. A poor farming family might not be able to afford to send their daughter to the local elementary school, much less the girls' higher school that might make her into a "lady." But they could send her to work in a cotton-spinning mill that offered not only an attractive advance to the family, but also the hope that she might receive some basic education and training in the womanly arts. Such amenities were rarely offered during the Meiji period, but by the 1920s they had become a primary means of recruitment and retention for companies hungry for a stable workforce.

But in fact, many female workers did not leave the factory for marriage and a life of domesticity, but rather moved to positions in other better paying textile companies or else to new jobs in the service industry. A survey conducted in 1936 found that of 204 female workers who had quit work at large cotton mills to return home, 46 percent said they planned to go out and find employment in another cotton mill, and only 23 percent had gotten married.[5] In other words, the standard narrative propounded by contemporary commentators that viewed female factory work as a temporary form of employment overlooked large segments of the wage-earning female population. While many female workers may have worked only temporarily (for a few years) in any given company, they often moved to similar employment at another textile company rather than abandoning wage work altogether. There are no comprehensive statistics to indicate the number of women who did return home to their villages to marry after a few years of textile factory work. But the scattered surveys and oral histories that do exist suggest a wide range of paths chosen by former textile operatives. Some returned to the countryside and took up agricultural work, some moved from company to company for a number of years, and others settled in towns and cities nearby the factories they had quit to marry or to take up work as maids, shop hands, bar hostesses, waitresses, or prostitutes.[6]

Since before the Meiji Restoration, women from a variety of classes had engaged in home work (naishoku), or cash-paying "side jobs" that could be performed in the home in addition to unremunerated domestic work. Such work, which often involved sewing, embroidering, and other crafts associated with domestic life and identified as women's work, be-

Figure 1. This group of young women were among the first to come from Kagoshima Prefecture to work at a cotton-spinning factory in the city of Amagasaki in Hyōgō Prefecture in 1906. Courtesy of Unitika Museum.

came commonplace after World War I among women of the middle classes as well.[7] In fact, as increasing numbers of women entered the paid labor force in the 1920s, *naishoku* was encouraged by some social commentators as the form of "employment" most consistent with the "good wife, wise mother" philosophy that circumscribed women's roles within the home.[8]

Work in the form of *naishoku* did not challenge ideals of women as primarily mothers and household managers and had become acceptable for urban middle-class women as well as those from rural agriculturalist families. Industrial labor for women and girls in textile factories, however, took women out of the domestic sphere and simultaneously marked them as part of what journalist Yokoyama Gennosuke called the "lower strata society" (*kasō shakai*). Yokoyama coined the term *kasō shakai* to describe the working poor whose livelihoods (as well as their dire poverty) were a product of Meiji urbanization and industrialization. Those who fell into this lower strata included rag pickers, tenant farmers, male iron and steel workers, and female cotton and silk spinners in the newly mechanized textile industry (figure 1).[9]

FACTORY WORK FOR THE NATION

With Japan's rapid industrialization after the Meiji Restoration, the textile industry was responsible for bringing in large amounts of the foreign cash so desperately coveted by the Meiji leaders. Women and girls who customarily engaged in *naishoku* were recruited as low-wage laborers in silk and cotton–spinning and –weaving factories. Even before the turn of the century, the government had created a flourishing environment for industrial capital by selling to industry many enterprises that had been established and supported at public expense. From 1910 through the 1920s, textiles accounted for roughly 50 percent of industrial revenue.[10] The dying and weaving industries boasted a share of the industrial workforce equal to its share of revenue, with the majority of these workers being women (table 1).

The women who went to work in Meiji-era textile factories were exhorted by recruiting advertisements and employer-distributed educational handbooks to "work for the nation" and for the sake of their families.[11] In a formulation that would become commonplace throughout Japan's imperial period—from shortly after the Meiji Restoration to the end of the Pacific War in 1945, marked by colonial expansion and an emperor-centered state—nation and family, civic duty and filial piety, merged in a series of substitutions. Employers stood in for parents, so that respecting their will meant honoring one's natal family, and spinning silk or cotton for the nation meant honoring the emperor, patriarch of the national family. "Factory owners and managers think of you all as their own daughters" and "can be depended on even more than your real parents," promised one didactic tract for female factory workers.[12] Another reminded that "the reason you all work so hard from morning until night is in order to serve your country."[13] Publication of such works—many of them produced by industry associations—aimed to convince female textile workers of the importance of their contributions to the national polity (*kokutai*) and to simultaneously remind them that excelling at their work offered the sincerest expression of filial piety and reverence for their families.

As with many such works of the time, *Kōjo kun* (Instructions for Factory Girls, 1910) began with a preface explaining that simple language and *furigana*—the practice of including phonetic markers next to Chinese characters to make them more easily readable—had been used to make the book more accessible to the few female factory workers possessing the modest education needed to attempt reading it at all. Scores

TABLE I. JAPANESE NATIONALS EMPLOYED IN
THE TEXTILE INDUSTRY FOR SELECT YEARS
1906–1940

Year	Female	Male	Total	Percent Female
1906	639,200	246,200	885,400	72.2
1910	757,700	265,100	1,022,800	74.1
1915	723,000	290,500	1,013,500	71.3
1920	950,700	415,400	1,366,100	69.6
1925	933,800	466,100	1,399,900	66.7
1930	934,100	491,800	1,425,900	65.5
1935	1,030,600	509,800	1,540,400	66.9
1940	870,700	461,100	1,331,800	65.4

SOURCE: Adapted from Umemura Mataji et al., *Rōdōryoku* (Tokyo: Tōyō keizai shinpōsha, 1988), 204–205, 209, 211.

of texts from this period employed such stylistic modes as a form of pedagogy. Some included annotations at the top of the page with vocabulary words used in the text that girls might want to learn for use in writing letters home to their families.[14] Essentially a primer on nationalist history, civic duty, and the importance of the textile industry to Japan's future glory, this text employed a strategy of literally imaging female factory workers onto its narrative of military might and industrial triumph. Each of its forty-eight pages included separate photographs of three female workers lined up across its top, titled with their names, the names of the factories where they worked, and their locations. These factory workers, along with another 224 whose names and place of employment appear on the first pages of the book, had all received special commendations from the Japan Silk Association (Nippon Sanshikai).

The written text further emphasized this connection of the individual and the local with the fate of the national community, clearly articulating the official Meiji ideology of "rich nation, strong army":

> Until the Sino-Japanese War, Westerners treated Japan as a small country of barbarians; but since the Sino- and Russo-Japanese Wars, Japan has leaped in one bound to the ranks of the first-class nations of the world. . . . But if we consider it closely, simply being strong does not win the final battle. Together with strength, a country must have wealth. . . . In looking at the actual state of Japan, it is clear that despite the fact of an unbroken imperial line with the emperor at its head and with loyal servants below and strong soldiers who are the pride of their country, next to the leading nations of England, France, Russia, Germany, Italy and America, Japan is regrettably still a very poor country.[15]

The lucrative silk industry played a major role, the argument continued, in combating Japan's debt-heavy poverty by creating wealth for the nation by exporting to foreign countries. Dubbing the silk industry the "flower of the country" (*kuni no hana*) and the female workers within it the "flowers of the people" (*hito no hana*), this text linked female labor directly to those issues of greatest concern to the Meiji state: Japan's status within the international community, patriotic wars, national wealth, and the emperor system. In so doing, it also clearly identified the workers as ethnic nationals—a point that would become important for the development of labor-relations discourses with the influx of colonial labor in the 1920s.

GENDERED PATERNALISM IN THE MODERN FACTORY

Female textile workers generally lived in dormitories within factory complexes, which were often located long distances from their natal villages. The dormitory system circumscribed women's movements and in most cases involved elaborate systems of surveillance, including the employment of vigilant dormitory supervisors and a highly monitored pass system that restricted workers' freedom to leave the factory compound. The physical space of the compound itself was surrounded by high walls to mark off the industrial space from the outside world and to prevent escapes. Textile company owners and managers claimed to act as surrogate parents for the young women and girls under their charge. They provided (and often enforced) moral, civic and educational instruction for their "daughters" in keeping with these girls' and women's future roles as wives and mothers. And they insisted that any disagreements or discontent that arose between employers and employees be handled "within the family," with all parties respecting the hierarchies implicit in that structure. Similarly, disagreements *among* employees would be arbitrated by a benevolent company owner or manager as patriarch.

Companies readily took on this role as benevolent protector and increasingly adopted paternalistic recruitment policies and welfare institutions for employees. Amenities and other aspects of employer benevolence directed toward female workers emerged in the 1920s in response to a shrinking pool of labor from the countryside after the First World War and the intensification of competition among recruiters and employers in contracting and retaining workers.[16] Their reasons for working within contemporary discourses on Japanese womanhood rather than insisting on treating female operatives as generic workers were fourfold. First, companies found they could be more successful recruiting girls from rural families if they convinced workers' parents (who were often the ones making the final decisions about employment) not only that the girls would be well treated, but that they would be treated *like daughters*. The assumption of parental responsibility by the company (or its representative) suggested an understanding among company, parents, and the worker herself that female textile laborers were not only workers, but also future wives and mothers. As such, they would need to receive in the factory context the kinds of training in domestic arts (especially things like sewing and needlework) that they might otherwise have gotten at home. In fact, as the larger cotton-spinning companies expanded the scope of their educational amenities, they sometimes argued to rural parents that the training in womanly skills their daughters could receive in the factories was superior to what families would be able to provide on their own.

Second, creating a consensus that female labor was by definition temporary labor (that is, not a life career, but a short-term stop on the way to marriage and motherhood), companies could justify paying lower wages to women than men. Third, by using rhetoric consistent with dominant popular and state discourses on Japanese womanhood, companies tried to hold at bay accusations (made by Japanese social reformers as well as by international observers) of exploitation and maltreatment of their workers—accusations that became increasingly frequent as the twentieth century wore on. And fourth, company managers discovered that rhetorics of sexual morality tied to the dominant ideal of chaste womanhood served as a potent weapon against unions and labor organizing. By depicting female workers as susceptible to sexual corruption and simultaneously branding unions as evil outside influences, textile companies not only adapted to contemporary discourses of Japanese womanhood, but in fact used those very discourses to their advantage.

What I am referring to as "paternalism" is actually a concept derived from two closely related terms used by companies and by the state during the interwar period. Japanese policies of compassionism (*onjōshugi*—most often translated as "paternalism") and familism (*kazokushugi*—a term often used in conjunction with *onjōshugi*) focused on the management of female textile workers. Compassionism was from the beginning part of what Andrew Gordon has referred to as the "invented tradition" of Japanese labor relations, in which a timeless tradition of master-servant reciprocity was invoked as a blueprint for maintaining harmonious labor relations in a new age of industrialism.[17] Oka Minoru, a Home Ministry

Figure 2. Workers operate spinning machines at Tōyō Spinning's Sangenya factory in Osaka, circa 1920. Source: The Mainichi Newspapers.

bureaucrat and champion of Japan's Factory Law, summed up this philosophy of compassionism circa 1910, proclaiming that "in the future, our capitalists . . . will be steeped in the generous spirit of kindness and benevolence, guided by thoughts of fairness and strength. The factory will become one big family: the factory chief as the eldest brother and the foreman as the next oldest. The factory owner himself will act as a parent. Strikes will become unthinkable, and we can look forward to the increased productivity of capital—the basis for advances in the nation's wealth and power."[18]

Paternalist policies became more common among larger companies by the 1920s. A more competitive labor market and a series of economic recessions felt keenly among textile companies prompted changes in labor-management strategies, encouraging company owners to create incentives for workers to stay with them rather than move to another company or run away from the factory because of ill treatment.[19] Further, female workers influenced by Taishō-era (1912–26) democratic trends that included a vigorous women's movement and an active labor-union movement prompted demands for greater recognition of workers' individuality and personhood (*jinkaku*).[20] This decade also saw the emergence of a new form of what William Tsutsui calls "revised Taylorism" in Japan, marked off from its earlier incarnation by a dedicated attention to the "human elements" involved in making workplaces more efficient. By "human elements," Tsutsui refers to the policies of paternalism that were characterized by a "warm, familial and cooperative" relationship between employer and employee and the establishment of worker welfare facilities.[21]

Among the companies engaged in fostering such "warm, familial and cooperative" paternalist policies, none was more prominent than the Kanegafuchi Cotton Spinning Company. Founded in 1887 as a cotton-trading company, by 1889 the company had begun cotton-spinning production and by 1908 had entered the silk-spinning market. It was one of prewar Japan's largest and most successful textile companies, boasting 139,576 spindles and a capitalization of four million yen in 1902—twice the size of its nearest competitor.[22] With its first factory built in Tokyo, the company quickly expanded nationally by building additional factories and acquiring preexisting ones through mergers and acquisitions of smaller textile firms. By the time paternalist practices started to be developed in earnest in the industry, Kanegafuchi Spinning was positioned to be a leader in these new forms of labor relations. Indeed, one of the company's most important prewar leaders authored many of the key features of prewar paternalist practice.

Mutō Sanji (1867–1934) guided the helm of Kanegafuchi Spinning (hereafter Kanebō, as it was known for short) for nearly twenty-three years, from 1908 until his retirement in 1930.[23] He put into place a set of labor-management practices that became legendary throughout Japan's textile industry, and he was chosen to be part of Japan's first delegation to the International Labour Organization in 1919. Company labor practices during this time of sustained industrial growth assumed an ample supply of disposable labor and emphasized aggressive and increasingly far-reaching recruitment efforts over policies of retention. Runaways and worker attrition due to accidental death or illness had been treated by companies as a matter of course in the second decade of the twentieth century, but by the mid-1920s tactics had changed, spearheaded by this new policy of paternalism launched by Kanebō and imitated by other cotton-spinning companies that offered new amenities to attract and retain workers.

In official histories of the company, Mutō's interest in paternalist policies are often attributed to the great wellsprings of compassion and humanist impulses of the man himself. His son, who eventually followed in his father's footsteps to become president of Kanebō in 1947, has written of his father's tendency to valorize the underdog, offering as an example of his humanism the elder Mutō's insistence on calling the family's servant "Miss Maid" rather than simply "Maid," presumably restoring to her some of the dignity otherwise lost as a result of her position.[24]

In the year Mutō became company president (1921), Kanebō boasted a wide range of amenities for its over 2,800 female and close to 640 male employees. Educational facilities were the highlight of the offerings, with male workers at the main factory in Tokyo able to take advantage of up to two year's worth of supplemental education in the form of classes in ethics (*shūshin*, a kind of civics instruction), Japanese language, basic mathematics, and English. Kanebō's more numerous female employees could attend the Kanegafuchi School for Girls, which was designed to take young workers up through the six-year compulsory elementary education. Or, for those who had already finished their required elementary education and showed promise in their studies, the company offered courses through its School of Practical Learning for Girls in a wider range of subjects, including ethics, Japanese language, mathematics, geography, history, science, and home economics. In addition, girls could opt to take a three-year special course that taught them the modalities of proper Japanese womanhood. Subject offerings included sewing, housework, and etiquette and promised students the skills that would enable them to make good marriage matches and successfully manage their future households.

The supplementary educational opportunities offered to girls and young women working in the textile industry served several important purposes. In addition to providing an incentive in the form of educational opportunities and bridal training that these poor rural girls who endured low-paid and difficult factory work might not receive by staying in their villages, these curricula served two additional purposes. One of them was to manage worker free time, a management concern that grew after the abolition of night work for women and children went into effect in 1929. Such time management, it was believed, might effectively preempt labor organizing and the possibility of labor unrest. The second purpose was to promote a newly imagined middle-class vision of Japanese womanhood among female employees who were expected to marry and leave the company within a few years of their initial employment.

Part of the reason for the difference in educational facilities for males and females—in addition to the company emphasis on treating female employees more as women and future mothers than as labor—has to do with their relative ages and educational background upon entering the company. While girls as young as fourteen commonly came to work as operatives for the larger textile mills, and just under half of the girls employed by Kanebō had not finished their elementary education, males who were concentrated in the dyeing sections of Kanebō's operations tended to be somewhat older and to have at a minimum completed their elementary studies. Age, of course, was not the only factor involved in the lower educational level of females: despite the laws that since the turn of the century had required an equal elementary education for both boys and girls throughout Japan, many of the poorer farming families that sent their daughters to work at the mills could ill afford to do without their daughters' family labor, much less pay the fees required to send a girl child to school. Boys, on whose future earning power the families relied, were at any rate more likely to be in compliance with the law than their sisters.

The gender-specific nature of Mutō's efforts to formulate a new system of labor relations based on the concept of compassionism at Kanebō is evident not only in the specific educational opportunities offered female workers, but also in the architecture of the factory itself. The gates and high walls surrounding working, living, educational, and entertainment facilities acted as spaces of containment designed to offer protection and safety together with surveillance and control. Parents deciding to take a cash advance and sign a contract handing over their daughters for a period of indentured servitude were often convinced to do so after hearing descriptions of the factory's many amenities, and the precautions taken by the company to keep their charges safely locked away from the many dangers—often presumed to be sexual—that lurked just outside the factory gates. Employees at Kanebō were encouraged to purchase color postcards from the company store to be sent home to anxious relatives and neighbors. These postcards depicted the newness of the factory buildings, smokestacks signaling the modern nature of the important work undertaken by the sender. The dormitories, dining halls, nursing facilities, lecture halls, and factory shop floors all were part of Mutō's paternalist policies that took women and girls as their primary object.

Among those profoundly influenced by Mutō's formulation of paternalism was the labor consultant, author, and publisher Uno Riemon

(1875–1934). The founder of the Industrial Education Association (Kōgyō Kyōikukai), Uno gained prominence as a consultant and labor-management theorist first in his hometown of Osaka and then nationally. The series of pamphlets and books published by the Industrial Education Association—many of them authored by Uno—circulated among factory managers at all levels, in nearly all parts of the country. Uno is perhaps best known for the nationalism inhering in his insistence on recognizing the "beautiful customs" of paternalist labor practices as evidence of "Japanese uniqueness."

In his 1915 *Shokkō yūgu ron* (On the Good Treatment of Factory Workers), Uno argued that as a late-developing nation Japan had mostly factory workers who were single, young girls from the countryside and who were forced by their circumstances to live a collective, unfamily-like life in factory dormitories. But these potential negatives were related for Uno to two major advantages in the Japanese system. First, he argued that even amid industrialization and development, the loyalty and pliability inherent in the Japanese national essence (*kokuminsei*) had remained unchanged. And second, the factory dormitory system offered the possibility of harnessing this preexisting national essence in the service of harmonious industrial relations.[25] To do this, Uno believed that companies needed to re-create the elements of family life their employees had given up in coming to work in the factories. This re-creation meant the cultivation of good womanly virtues such as chastity, filial piety, and obedience—all qualities that could be used in the promotion of harmonious industrial relations. Or, as Oka Minoru put it in the passage cited earlier, "The factory will become one big family . . . [and] strikes will become unthinkable."

As part of his efforts to promote the cultivation of devoted daughters/workers in Japan's textile factories, Uno published a volume titled *Kōjo risshindan* (Stories of Factory Girls Getting Ahead, 1910). More of a hagiography of women workers who demonstrated filial piety and persistence in the face of adversity than a primer on industrial relations, *Kōjo risshindan* offered examples of "model factory girls" who Uno believed possessed those qualities most desirable in a female factory worker. The easy-to-read personal histories probably appealed to young readers, many of whom may have recognized something of the hardships of their own lives in these "true stories."

Shimazaki Takiko from Fukui Prefecture, Uno's "model factory girl #1," worked for the Teikoku Seima Company at their Ōtsu Seihin factory. Readers learned by looking at the description under Takiko's photographic portrait that her primary traits included "obedience, an admirable depth of filial piety, trustworthiness, and a willingness to help new hires." They would learn also that Takiko had displayed in her room the Chinese characters for the word *kannin* (endurance); that she regularly sent money home to her family (including her sick mother); and that she had also managed to save up an admirable sum of money for herself in preparation for becoming a bride.

Another model factory girl described by Uno, Watanabe Makie, decided not long after the death of her father to find work at a factory and hired on with Kanebō. Her two sisters, mother, and younger brother joined the company too. She was eleven years old at the time. Soon Makie's mother, who was getting old, and her young brother returned to the countryside so as not to leave their village home empty, and Makie and her two sisters continued to send money to them from their earnings. Makie's eldest sister became ill and died at age eighteen, leaving the two remaining sisters to work even harder to provide for their old mother. Upon the engagement of her younger sister, Makie bestowed upon her everything she owned, including precious hair decorations, as a parting gift. Finally, still working at Kanebō, Makie decided to pursue an education and eventually graduated from the higher elementary school at the factory.[26]

This tale of an exemplary Japanese woman worker depended on the exemplary conditions Uno believed existed at factories like Kanebō, even before such companies had implemented the more extensive welfare programs that would appear in the 1920s. These were places where workers could earn enough money to send home to ailing parents if they worked diligently, and where they could take advantage of company schools to better themselves through education. In fact, after publishing *Kōjo risshindan*, Uno undertook the writing of a five-volume series on model factories. As he put it in the preface to one of the volumes, "just as people need role models, so do factories."[27] Four of the five model companies featured in his series were textile companies employing mostly women—one of them was Kanebō.

These stories of self-sacrifice and filial piety—deeds made possible thanks to the benevolence and opportunities bestowed by the textile companies—present examples of *risshin shusse,* or "getting ahead," for women. Indeed, the very title of Uno's *Kōjo risshindan* (Stories of Factory Girls Getting Ahead) made the connection explicit. *Risshin* (also read as *mi o tateru*) referred to "raising oneself in the world," while *shusse* (or *yo ni deru*) referred to "going out into the world" to seek one's

fortune. The combined term *risshin shusse* gained wide currency immediately after the Meiji Restoration as a new generation of young men
(with encouragement from the government) took up the slogan in their
quest for advancement in the new society.[28] While *risshin shusse* for men
emphasized education and personal achievement, in these texts aimed at
female factory workers, "getting ahead" for working-class and rural
women took selfless dedication to natal and national family as its
measure.

The elements that went into the development of labor paternalism in
Japan emerged in the early twentieth century in response to the first
phase of Japanese industrialization and the specific conditions of Japan's
labor market.[29] Many scholars have pointed to these elements of prewar
labor paternalism as the precursor to the systems of lifetime employment
and seniority-based wages that emerged after the war, policies that have
only recently begun to be abandoned by Japanese corporations plagued
by the recession in force since the economic bubble burst in the early
1990s.[30] But the idea and practice of labor paternalism has always been
highly gendered, applying to women in the prewar period and men in the
postwar. Further, the term "compassionism" meant something vastly
different in 1920 than it did in 1970. Compassionism for Mutō Sanji and
for Uno Riemon referred to a set of practices targeting temporary female
labor in Japan's textile mills. By 1970 Japan's textile industry had all but
been abandoned, and the predominantly male industries such as auto
and steel forced a reconfiguration of paternalist practices to emphasize
the cultivation not of filial daughters, but of family wage-earning male
heads of households.

THE FACTORY LAW

At the same time that didactic texts admonished female factory workers
to work selflessly for the nation and for their families, a fierce battle was
being fought among government bureaucrats, textile industry leaders,
and social reformers over what measures the state should take to safe-
guard workers from the excesses of industrial capital and to protect the
nation from the kinds of social conflict that had plagued England after
industrialization. The debates over how to construct and implement factory legislation in Japan that would allow industry to develop at a rapid
pace, but that would also address domestic and international concerns
for the welfare of workers, often focused on the textile industry and the
conditions of the women who worked in it.

Textiles remained crucial to the Japanese economy even after the post-1895 growth of heavy industry, and as the number of female factory workers increased through the 1930s, policy makers, bureaucrats, journalists, and social critics came to see female workers not only as necessary contributors to the national economy, but also as potential vehicles for social unrest, disease, and the corruption of public morals. R. P. Dore has succinctly summarized the arguments of Soeda Jūichi, at the time a senior civil administrator in the Ministry of Finance, who articulated the concerns of a generation of bureaucrats and politicians as he spoke out in 1896 in favor of factory legislation: "The advanced countries have recognized the need for legislation for four reasons: bad conditions weaken the health of children and potential mothers, hence of a country's soldiers and hence of her defensive power; bad conditions breed epidemic diseases; the promiscuous mixing of the young of both sexes leads to moral deterioration; resentment against maltreatment leads to labour problems, and generalized social conflict."[31] For Soeda then, national interests lay in the protection of motherhood (which he linked through a series of relations to the defense of the nation), the physical health of the national body, the sexual/moral constitution of the populace, and the containment of labor. Female gender, sexuality, bodies, and labor unrestrained and unprotected, he asserted, could—and perhaps would—inevitably lead to the downfall of the nation. As we shall see in the chapters that follow, Soeda's concern for the sexual integrity of factory workers motivated many of the labor-management policies that would be adopted by textile companies in the interwar period.

The preparations for drafting a factory bill, a process that spanned thirty years and more than a generation of bureaucrats, included the commissioning of studies to address just such issues of public health, public morals, and public unrest. And female factory workers, deemed most at risk of physical and psychological disease, became the central objects of official and scientific investigation. As part of their research efforts the government commissioned several major studies, including the three-volume report *Shokkō jijō* (Conditions of Factory Workers). Published in 1901, this report derived much of its methodology from Yokoyama Gennosuke's book-length exposé of conditions among Japan's "lower strata."[32] Dr. Ishihara Osamu's studies of tuberculosis among women factory workers, also commissioned by the government, warned that rates of infection among female operatives were reaching epidemic proportions and threatened to decimate the countryside where many of these girls returned home to die.[33] And following the lead of the ministries, local governments of the cities where migrant workers (from various parts of Japan) and immigrant laborers (especially from Korea) settled surveyed their living and working conditions meticulously as part of public-policy efforts to minimize the social unrest believed likely to follow such significant demographic changes.

The many surveying efforts of the 1920s and 1930s generally followed the model established by the Social Bureau—set up by the Home Ministry in 1922 to oversee labor and welfare matters—which documented factory conditions, strikes, immigrant labor, and unemployment compensation.[34] Very quickly, major metropolitan governments such as those in Tokyo and Osaka moved to create their own Social Bureaus, which conducted scores of surveys and issued similar reports at the local level.[35] These reports and the surveying techniques with which they were associated attest to the ways in which the female factory worker and her fate were, right from the time of her appearance in the industrial workplace, a national concern of grave proportions.

The thirty years of parliamentary and bureaucratic debate that went into producing and later implementing the Factory Law have been treated extensively as labor and political history in a variety of sources.[36] But the mass of national and local government studies and surveys, industry reports and recommendations, and commentaries across the political spectrum debating the law in the print media can also be read as part of the process of reifying and universalizing newly established middle-class values that had strictly coded normative categories of gender and sexuality as their linchpin. The product of competing discourses that went far beyond debates over industrial management, labor relations, and worker protection, the Factory Law and the tortuous route of its passage and implementation testify to the degree to which the "labor problem" was infused with the rhetoric of gender.

The Factory Law had its beginnings as early as the 1880s, when it was conceived as a manufacturers' rather than a workers' protection law, with provisions that would guarantee industry a steady flow of labor power.[37] It developed out of an industrial policy aimed at reproducing a sound labor force in a society where the threat of tuberculosis remained a significant public health crisis.[38] Despite its passage in 1911 after decades of wrangling between politicians and industry leaders, and among the various bureaucratic factions charged with drawing up the bill, the law did not go into effect until 1916. And because its passage came only as a result of concessions made to big business, the regulations included exceptions that in some cases seemed to go against the very spirit of the law. For example, the new law set maximum working hours at twelve per day, but the silk industry was exempted from the twelve-hour rule and allowed to have operatives work fourteen-hour shifts. The cotton industry was permitted to continue using two alternating twelve-hour day and night shifts despite earlier legislative attempts to abolish night work that had inspired many of the arguments for protective factory legislation in the first place. In 1909 the Japan Spinners Association had strongly opposed a provision in an earlier version of the law that would have abolished night work beginning ten years after its passage as submitted to the 26th Diet in 1908, and their opposition effectively forced the government to withdraw the bill. The government rewrote the offending language to allow night work to continue for fifteen years after passage of the Factory Law and finally won the cotton industry's support.[39]

But even after enforcement of the law began in 1916, many believed it was not enough. Pressured by the International Labour Organization, the government revised the Factory Law in 1923, with the revisions not going into effect until an imperial edict ordered them implemented on June 5, 1926. These revisions tightened a number of provisions and restricted some of the exemptions from the previous version. As a result, as of July 1, 1929, the textile industry was finally prohibited from allowing women and children under the age of sixteen to engage in night work between the hours of 10:00 P.M. and 5:00 A.M.[40] But once again the powerful cotton lobby successfully negotiated a less rigid standard for itself, and the cotton industry was granted a special extension to allow night work to continue one hour later than the 10:00 P.M. stipulated in the law.

The history of the prohibition of night work can be read as the story of Japanese labor-management relations, wherein the weakness of prewar organized labor made it dependent on international pressure, the good will of so-called liberal bureaucrats, and the rise of party politics to effect real change for workers in the form of protective factory legislation.[41] But the rhetoric used by those party to the law's passage points to another story involving more than just a struggle over competing economic interests. While factory workers themselves had for years decried mandatory fourteen- and sixteen- hour workdays as unhealthful at best and inhumane at worst, for factory owners and managers, shortening work hours for female factory workers raised questions about how they would spend their nonworking hours and what the implications would be for public morals. As we shall see, arguments in favor of a law prohibiting night work begat counterarguments that increased free time generated by the decrease in work hours would result in a further decline in the moral standards of young women factory workers. These women workers, so the counterarguments went, were particularly susceptible (because of their supposed low educational level, immaturity, youthful lusts, and putative predisposition towards sexual adventurism) to the overtures of young men whom they might encounter outside the protective walls of the factory dormitories. Such a position went hand in hand with the paternalism that offered educational and welfare facilities for the betterment of employees and sought to cultivate them as proper wives and mothers of the future.

CHAPTER 2

Keeping "Idle Youngsters" Out of Trouble

Japan's 1929 Abolition of Night Work and the Problem of Free Time

In 1929 the last of the provisions of Japan's Factory Law (passed eighteen years earlier) went into effect after years of delays and deferments. Beginning that July, women and children under the age of twelve could no longer legally engage in work between the hours of 10:00 P.M. and 5:00 A.M. The abolition of night work prompted heated debates among factory managers about "proper use" of the increased "free time" (*yoka zenyō*) created by the new regulations. The problem of free time had been discussed before 1929, but after the end of night work it became a critical issue for the textile industry, motivating managerial decisions on everything from worker health to worker education and completing a shift in priorities among textile industry leaders that had begun with the introduction of paternalist practices. By the end of 1929 the emphasis on corporate consolidation (which had been largely realized) had changed to a focus on the control of individual workers through the regulation of time and bodies.

The attention paid to the issue of free time in the cotton mills reflected a broader concern for the management of all workers' off-hours as part of a plan for social regulation, but this concern manifested itself in particular ways when applied to female labor. Employers' expectations that the end of night work would increase the amount of factory girls' unsupervised time led to the development of programs meant to foster the ideology of "good wife, wise mother" first promoted systematically in the early 1920s by larger cotton-spinning companies, like Kanegafuchi Spin-

27

ning, that offered significant amenities as part of their paternalistic labor policies. Management consultants in the post–night work era suggested that companies intensify their efforts to create modern housewives of their employees by training them in home economics and offering reading rooms and libraries for their use. As part of a new emphasis on the scientific management of workers and their physical fitness, calisthenics programs were introduced, specifically tailored to the needs of factory women. Not all of the reactions to the ban on night work, however, were based on a sense of opportunity. Factory managers charged with protecting the chastity of the employees they sometimes referred to as "daughters" feared most of all that free time would lead to sexual depravity, and thus the breaking of the company's compact with parents who had put their girls in the company's care. The possibility of workers getting pregnant while working at the factory—or worse, turning to prostitution—motivated much of the extra worker programming offered after July 1929.

The distinction made during the 1920s and 1930s between free time (*yoka*) and leisure (*goraku*)—two concepts that were closely related and often appeared together—revolved around the close relation of the former term to wage-earning or salaried work. As the social researcher Ōbayashi Munetsugu explained in his 1922 treatise on leisure in Osaka, *goraku* (the word he used to translate the English word "recreation") indicated time used freely in the pursuit of play, social interaction, or cultural training.[1] *Goraku,* then, pointed to activities taken up for enjoyment, while *yoka* referred simply to time not spent on salaried or wage work. Because of its associations with wage work, *yoka* suggested the specter of the working masses engaged in unspecified (and therefore uncontrolled) activities, and efforts were made to study, delineate, and thereby manage it. Textile companies countered the negative possibilities of *yoka* by offering (and sometimes coercing) their own activities for employees during their off-work hours. The kinds of activities offered to the female employees of some of the larger textile concerns—such as calisthenics, cultivation-group membership, training in flower arrangement and tea ceremony—reflected at once efforts to inculcate a gendered national subjecthood and to frustrate attempts at labor organizing and collective action.

During the period when night work was still a common practice, female factory workers typically worked alternating weekly night shifts, usually from midnight until noon the next day. These twelve-hour shifts would then be replaced by the noon to midnight "day shift" after a shift and a half break. In her memoirs, the cotton spinner turned labor activist Yamanouchi Mina described a typical experience working the night shift in 1913, when she first went to work at Tōyō Muslin in Tokyo. Yamanouchi recounted her days as a twelve-year-old who worked twelve-hour night shifts with only one-hour rest period per shift. The girls, she said, would try to keep themselves awake as they worked by singing:

> Two, three in the morning
> Even the plants and trees get to sleep
> But can't I be sleepy?
> If a cotton-spinning girl is a human
> Then flowers will bloom on dead trees on the mountain[2]

Seventeen years later such complaints over the physical and emotional tolls of the system were still being registered by female factory workers, as 167 of them named night work as the most distressing aspect of factory work (ichiban tsurai koto)—by far the largest number of similar responses—in a survey of muslin factory operatives published in the 1925 inaugural issue of the journal Jokō kenkyū (Research on Female Factory Workers).[3]

NIGHT WORK AND THE RATIONALIZATION OF INDUSTRY

The rationalization of Japan's textile industry was part of a global trend. Nationally, the movement reached its peak in 1930 with the creation of Japan's Special Bureau on Industrial Rationalization; but as with industrialization itself, the drive for rationalization had its origins in the West. Organized efforts to promote industrial efficiency had begun in America as early as the 1890s with Frederick Taylor's championing of scientific principles of work organization based on his famous time and motion studies.[4] In 1914 Henry Ford instituted the five-dollar, eight-hour workday for his automobile-industry employees to ensure their adherence to new standards of time discipline, augmenting Taylor's scientific-management methods with organizational strategies encompassing the entire production process.[5]

Although American Fordist and Taylorist principles launched the international movement to reform business, the term "rationalization" was first applied to industrial-efficiency efforts when German business and government interests coined the term Rationalisierung after the First World War to describe a series of trends comprising new and theoretically more effective systems of industrial production and organization.[6]

Germany, an early rationalizer enamored more of Fordist models of production and consumption than of Taylorist management principles, began rationalizing industry as a strategy to combat the severe inflation caused in part by World War I, and in response to the increasing threat to the domestic capitalist system posed by internal and external forces set in motion by the Bolshevik Revolution in Russia.[7]

The Japanese government and industry paid careful attention to German efficiency efforts, but they were not the only ones. The successes of the German rationalization movement in evidence by the end of the 1920s prompted the National Industrial Conference Board in the United States—in an ironic inversion of origination claims—to study the implementation and efficacy of German methods in order to apply the approach to American industry. Americans thus reimported Germanized visions of Fordism, transfigured in the process of migration to Europe into more centralized systems of rationalization.[8] The crucial difference between the earlier American efficiency efforts and the later rationalization movement of the Germans lay in the organizational relationship between government and industry and the emphasis on corporate combinations, or cartels. As the (American) National Industrial Conference Board report explained: "Rationalization, or putting reason into industry, is understood in Europe to refer to the organization of technical processes in individual establishments and the co-ordination of these units in various co-operative forms to regulate production and distribution. It thus includes all that is known in the United States under the term of scientific management, but it goes beyond this into the problems of economic organization and combination."[9] This problem of the relationship between government and industry animated Japanese interests as they searched for models upon which to base their own rationalization efforts.

Japanese businessmen and politicians paid close attention through the 1920s to German rationalizing efforts and in 1930 modeled their Special Bureau on Industrial Rationalization on a similar German office launched nine years earlier.[10] The bureau comprised a joint effort between government and business charged with regulating industry in order to make it more profitable, just as the Reich Board for Economic Efficiency had been established as a cooperative effort between big business and the Weimar government.[11] In one of its first actions, Japan's Special Bureau on Industrial Rationalization drafted the Law to Regulate Essential Industries, which at its inception covered nineteen industries including silk and cotton. Promulgated in 1931 and in effect for the next ten years, this law created cartel agreements among the major industry players, in theory ceding to the government the final word on the addition or removal of companies from each trust.[12]

But in fact, the Law to Regulate Essential Industries was more an attempt to regulate a system of combinations already in existence. In Japan's cotton industry the process of cartelization had begun as early as 1882 with the founding of the Japan Spinners Association, and the consolidation of cotton interests continued at a rapid pace between the Sino-Japanese and Russo-Japanese wars.[13] With more than eighty cotton-spinning companies in the 1890s, the industry underwent a process of amalgamation such that by the 1910s five companies claimed ownership of nearly half of all spindles and produced 68 percent of cotton cloth output.[14] Japan's major banking institutions, many with separate ties to one or more of these cotton-spinning concerns, financed this period of growth via mergers and buyouts, augmented in some cases by capital investment in equipment and new technology. World War I had forced a cessation of spinning-machine imports, resulting in the development of imitation and original machines nationally, which in turned spurred domestic production.

The "Big Five" cotton companies included Osaka Cotton Spinning (founded by the famous entrepreneur Shibusawa Eiichi), Mie Cotton Spinning, Kanegafuchi Cotton Spinning, Settsu Cotton Spinning, and Amagasaki Cotton Spinning. Between 1897 and 1905, Kanegafuchi, Osaka, and Settsu had swallowed up sixteen smaller companies among them, and by 1904 each of these companies had at least doubled their spindlage. By the start of the First World War, Shibusawa had concluded a merger of Osaka and Mie to form Tōyō Cotton Spinning, and Amagasaki and Settsu had merged to form Dai Nippon Cotton Spinning.[15]

Thus, by the time the Law to Regulate Essential Industries went into effect in 1931, the process of rationalization as consolidation had largely been completed, and cotton-spinning companies shifted their emphasis to another front: the rationalizing of worker activities. Nothing had more of an impact on this process than the prohibition on night work that went into effect on July 1, 1929.

As public awareness of the conditions involved in night work grew throughout the first two decades of the nineteenth century, the movement to abolish such work legally gained momentum. The movement to abolish night work in the textile factories began in the 1880s, along with the earliest negotiations over factory legislation during the 1890s. Even as the public outcry over the practice had grown in intensity throughout

the first decades of textile production in Japan, cotton-industry leaders'
opposition to restrictions on night work scuttled innumerable drafts of
factory legislation, delaying passage until 1911 when the new Factory
Law—which would not go into effect until five years later—immediately
drew criticism for its failure to abolish night work.[16] Industry proponents
of the practice had argued in various ways for its necessity. One school
of thought contended that the abolition of night work would result in a
decrease in production, which would allow India to retake the Chinese
market in cotton yarn. Another faction had argued for the relevance of
night work as a "unique Japanese custom." According to this line of rea-
soning, Japanese workers did not yet possess the skill or discipline of European factory workers and therefore needed longer working hours in
order to reach a similar level of production.[17]

By the time the abolition of night work finally did go into effect in
1929, it did not deal much of a blow to the industry, which had had time
to prepare for it and which in a time of economic depression could use
the new regulations to its advantage by intensifying labor, lowering
wages, and laying off workers.[18] Nishikawa Hiroshi has argued that, in
fact, rationalization and a shift to producing smaller quantities of higher-
quality goods for export (rather than the large quantities that had allowed for earlier capital accumulation—quantities still being produced
by Japanese factories in semicolonial China) made night work financially
unnecessary in the cotton industry.[19] Indeed, over the course of the
decade leading up to the abolition of night work the number of spindles
assigned to each worker more than doubled.[20] Thus, while fewer bodies
were in use, those bodies that were employed experienced an intensification of their own relationship to the process of production.

"IDLE YOUNGSTERS FIND THEIR WAY INTO TROUBLE"

With productivity levels at least stabilized by these new rational management practices, supervisors of female labor in the textile industry focused their attentions not so much on how to make up the lost labor time
that the abolition of night work would bring, but rather on the "proper
use of free time" (yoka zenyō) created by the new regulations prohibiting
work between the hours of 10:00 P.M. and 5:00 A.M. Four months before
the abolition went into effect, a group of factory managers gathered for
a symposium sponsored by the Nittōsha publishing company to discuss
the effects of the impending changes on labor and personnel management.
Founded and run by labor-management consultant Ishigami Kinji, the

company Nittōsha published *Jokō kenkyū* (Research on Female Factory Workers), a trade publication produced by and for textile-industry managers. Ishigami, a former textile-factory supervisor and the protégé of Uno Riemon (discussed in chapters 1 and 3), acted as editor in chief of the journal and contributed dozens of articles to it throughout its ten years of publication. He believed in training, education, and discipline (the words he used were *shitsuke, kunren,* and *kun'iku,* respectively) as part of a holistic approach to the management of workers. He sought throughout his career to order classifiable and individuated bodily techniques as a means of rationalizing textile-industry personnel administration.

Along with Ishigami, the textile-company representatives who took part with him in the 1929 *Jokō kenkyū* symposium made clear their desire to monitor and direct the entirety of workers' lives using rationalist models that accounted for each hour of a worker's daily activities. As one participant stated,

> At our company we have calculated free time (not including sleep and rest time) to be seven hours. Two of these go to meals, bathing, and laundry, and the remaining five are pure free time. So we thought long and hard about how those five hours should be used. If you look at the way most companies do things now, three hours generally go to what is called "health preservation" [*hoken*], including leisure and recreation; two hours are spent on study, the arts, and training [*gakushū, gigei, kun'iku*]. However, these concrete activities are undertaken differently in different companies.[21]

The importance of the various activities that were to fill a worker's free time pointed to management's concern to shape workers as whole people. As Aihara Takeo, a personnel manager at Fukushima Cotton Spinning's Sasaoka mill, observed in a *Jokō kenkyū* essay outlining the direction management should take in the post–night work era, "In order to make an outstanding product, one needs to make people—that is, factory people—into persons of character [*jinkakusha*]."[22]

The Osaka Social Bureau study published in 1923, *Yoka seikatsu no kenkyū* (Research on Free Time Life), took as its object of study the use of free time *and* various leisure activities available to male teachers, merchants, bank employees, and other company employees. Its editors related in the first pages their concern that unmanaged free time could result in social disorder: "There is the saying, 'idle youngsters find their way into trouble' [*shojin kankyo shite fuzen o nasu*]. But not only among children does the wasteful use of free time have bad consequences. There are statistics that demonstrate that in America 80 percent of all crimes are committed during free time [i.e., during nonwork hours]. In any event, there is a very intimate connection between the problem of free time and the problem of culture."[23] The Osaka Social Bureau study investigated the various ways in which male workers in Osaka spent their free time as well as the facilities that were available to them, including parks, museums, restaurants, and brothels.[24] But for female factory workers, the options were at once more limited and more tightly controlled.

Ishigami Kinji's introduction to the special issue of *Jokō kenkyū* inaugurating the mandatory abolition of night work encapsulated the views of the managers who contributed to the journal in the several months after the law went into effect:

> The factory managers' epoch-making establishment of the law abolishing night work went into effect on July 1. A number of factories implemented the new law as policy before this date, but even those that opposed it must follow the directives of the Factory Law beginning this month. This being the case, from now on there will be in effect a total abolition of night work throughout the country resulting in major reforms in personnel management. . . .
>
> [Also] . . . workers should take advantage of this opportunity to improve their lives with respect to their own education, and must make an effort to use their newfound free time [*yoka*] wisely. This is indeed the intent of the law.
>
> However, in order for workers themselves to put this time to its best use, the appropriate guidance regarding the responsibility of instructional management is necessary. Just as a conductor drives a train steadily on its track, so should the personnel manager/conductors carefully steer the free time of the female factory workers.[25]

Ishigami invoked the image of the train—perhaps the most important symbol of modern industrial progress—as a metaphor for labor-management relations in the textile mills, casting management-conductors as benevolent leaders whose duty was to establish the proper course and to make sure it was followed. In Ishigami's narrative the abolition of night work appears as a voluntary gesture on the part of industry officials. The appropriate response on the part of the workers who have received such benevolence included individual efforts at self-improvement that entailed a rigorous surveillance of one's own use of time.

Of course, crediting the companies of the textile industry with the establishment of the law abolishing night work constituted a self-congratulatory act with no basis in fact; but Ishigami's admonition that female factory workers "must make an effort to use their newfound free time wisely," hinted at one of the most oft-repeated cries of personnel managers over the next several years: that workers' proper use of free time created by the end of night work was fundamental to the continued success of the textile industry itself.

Discussions in the journal *Jokō kenkyū* regarding the abolition of night work positioned management concerns in terms of the maintenance of workers' health and public morals and focused attention on training and education, particularly in the areas of civic duty and the domestic arts. Managers construed the end of night work not as an ameliorative measure meant to ease the chronic fatigue and the health-related problems that such long working hours produced, but as a threat to workplace discipline and even to the moral character of the employees in their charge. Even as Ishigami Kinji acknowledged that health should be a supervisor's first concern related to managing the newfound free time of female workers, he remarked a month after the prohibition went into effect (repeating the proverb used by the authors of the Osaka report, Research on Free Time Life) that "the abolition of night work has meant an extra two or three hours [a day] of free time for female workers, and of course it will not do to have them sit idly about in the dormitories gossiping. As is often said, 'idle youngsters find their way into trouble.' "[26] The specter of juvenile delinquency raised here went hand in hand with managerial fears of successful labor-union organizing and strikes against the companies, all of which motivated management's desire to regulate the daily routines of workers in their entirety.

PRODUCING CONSUMERS

One way managers found to regulate these daily routines was to provide instructions and training in basic household management. This was part of a broader trend within the industry of cultivating employees as young Japanese women rather than managing them explicitly as workers. As part of this project of producing workers who would be informed consumers, workers were to be instructed, wrote Ishigami Kinji in his journal, how to comparison shop. He noted that often they purchased socks, footwear, hand towels, and soap at the company store, judging each product only by its looks. "It is necessary for these female factory workers who will be housewives in the future to be able to evaluate products according to price and quality."[27] Rationalization conceived as a national project should reach every corner of daily life, and consumer practices must be regulated to fit the needs of a depressed economy that depended on the thrift and savings of female household managers.[28]

Carefully controlled consumption and the education of proper wifely virtues received enthusiastic industry support. But a different set of values—those associated with women's economic independence and decadent forms of consumption, embodied especially by the new working woman (*shokugyō fujin*)—demanded much more careful control and circumspect surveillance. Popular journalism, especially women's magazines, quickly became the primary vehicles for the dissemination of these new values, as compulsory education meant that more and more working-class women (and men) possessed at least the most basic reading skills.[29] The problem of literacy was fraught with hidden dangers for managers who on the one hand disseminated both factory regulations and the values of filial piety and womanly virtue through company newsletters and brochures, but on the other hand recognized the tremendous power of women's magazines aimed at a mass audience to influence the desires and aspirations of their employees.

As one personnel manager warned his colleagues in a Nittōsha-sponsored symposium, "By today education has progressed to the point where there isn't one female factory worker who can't read a newspaper, and most of them can pick up and read a women's magazine when they want." Another participant summed up the group's arguments thus: "Women generally believe everything they read in women's magazines, and don't know how to take it critically. They can be incited by these articles, or confused by contradictions, and they look at the economic issues that get brought up there. Movies and music, including Western jazz, can also incite them."[30] The title of this symposium, "Rōdō sōgi o chūshin toshite" (Focusing on Labor Strikes), makes it clear that the "incitement" of this warning is clearly the incitement to engage in labor actions. That factory managers would point to wages, movies, and music as having the greatest power to "incite" workers to strike suggests a slippage between the economic (wages) and what Miriam Silverberg has called the culture of "commodified eroticism" signaled by references to "Western jazz."[31] Women's magazines included articles on working women, cinema, music, politics, and sex, offering information to literate factory workers about Japanese modern life to which their employers preferred they remain unexposed.[32] Such magazines often featured stories glorifying the decadent and dangerous *shokugyō fujin*—that liberated figure of self-sufficiency who was smart, slender, and urbane—who had found her way into department stores, clerical positions, and the popular imagination after the economic boom created by the First World War.[33] Thus, as managers hastened to implement new training programs in their factories, they remained wary of fostering the democratic impulses associated with mass literacy.

A Social Bureau report published in *Jokō kenkyū* in 1931 investigating the establishment of factory facilities and programs geared toward the proper use of free time in the post–night work era found that the availability of reading materials and libraries demonstrated the least improvement, especially when compared to athletics and educational programs.[34] This finding hardly seems surprising given managerial views on women's magazines and their potential to instill in female factory workers "unreasonable" expectations about wages and a consciousness of their position in society. Unlike reading material, athletic and educational programs could be more easily directed toward the needs and aims of management because their content could be carefully controlled.

MANAGING MORALITY

The instruction offered by the cultivation groups and other factory programs intended not only to provide female factory workers with guidance in achieving respectable womanhood and the limited degree of literacy required to do so, but also to prevent the fall into sexual depravity to which working-class girls from poor families were thought to be so susceptible. The journalist and social researcher Yokoyama Gennosuke had juxtaposed the image of the female factory worker as ideal wife and mother with the specter of her sexual impropriety as early in 1899. In his famous analysis of Japan's newly emergent "lower strata society," he took an early stand against night work for women and girls, not only on the grounds that it could ruin their health but also because it promoted sexual promiscuity: "It is my belief that such scandals are a result of various opportunities abounding within the factories, but night work provides the setting for such scandals to take place. Just as falsehoods and crimes of all sorts in the world occur when ordinary people are asleep, so are crimes committed within the factories at night when the watchful eyes of supervisors can be eluded and at places where lights are dim."[35] But elsewhere he deplored the domestic deficiencies of female factory workers whose training neglected the skills they should possess as "ladies": "Factory girls can reel cocoons or spin cotton threads, but many of them cannot do needle work. Some of them cannot dress their own hair. Nor are they able to even cook meals! It is truly unfortunate that the work and life of factory girls in textile mills lead them to become cripples who cannot perform the work expected of grown-up ladies."[36]

Thirty years after Yokoyama voiced his concerns for the chastity and femininity of women working in the textile industry, the sexual corruption into which female factory workers could so easily fall still sat uneasily beside the image of wifely virtue fostered by company managers. Where Yokoyama had blamed lapses of sexual propriety on the practice of night work, Ishigami Kinji blamed them on the *absence* of night work. Since the abolition of night work, female workers had more free time on their hands, he argued, and to the extent that they had a lot of free time they tended to leave the factory more often: "Under these circumstances it is more likely for them to be involved in sexual situations, and since problems of public morals involving men and women continue to occur with great frequency in recent days, for people such as factory dormitory supervisors who oversee female factory workers, these circumstances are quite worrisome."[37]

The concern for "public morals" betrayed a preoccupation with the problem of female sexuality not limited to members of the managerial class, but encompassing a wide array of social reformers, politicians, and social scientists. The operative social, state, and corporate consideration regarding the sexuality of working-class women in the 1920s and 1930s was containment. Labor-management policies aimed at women workers focused considerably on the maintenance of chaste bodies that also exhibited the characteristics associated with a particularly Japanese form of femininity. Containment of women's sexuality was deemed crucial because the countryside was believed by many to be an environment that produced lax sexual morals. Women and girls come to work in textile factories were susceptible to depravity, many thought, for three reasons: first, they came from environments in which they had not received adequate disciplinary training in chastity and virtue; second, upon leaving their families and villages, they also left behind what few social institutions had existed to keep them from untoward behavior; and third, the (now nearby) modern city offered temptations beyond what rural migrants could possibly resist.

Historians of labor, and of gender and sexuality in industrializing America and Europe, have pointed to the associations made throughout the nineteenth century between female wage labor and sexual morality. Jeffrey Weeks has noted that in Britain "the fundamental problem as conceived by the middle-class moralists was the effect of industrialisation and urbanisation, and in particular factory work, on the working-class family and the role of the woman within it," and Joan Scott has argued that political economists in France "focused attention on women workers because they seemed to reveal something of the problematic of urban/industrial development, especially its moral dimension."[38] In Japan, similarly, the project of industrial modernity was continually haunted by the specter of the fallen woman, and women involved in wage work were seen as those most likely to fall. Furthermore, rural women were considered especially vulnerable to the corrupting influences of the processes of modern industrial capital.

Several discussions related to female sexuality and the moral corruptibility of female factory workers found in the journal *Jokō kenkyū* suggest that textile-factory managers played a leading role in the project of containment that sought to isolate "woman" as a stable category for the articulation of national and corporate goals.[39] Contributors to the journal advocated the "cultivation of womanly virtues" as part of factory-sponsored curricula and as a duty of all factory overseers who had day-to-day contact with operatives, "especially," as one author put it, "since most of them in three or four years' time will have become housewives and mothers."[40]

It was the implied placement of the female worker, through her very name (*factory* woman), within the space of the factory that accounted for her inherent corruptibility—a manifestly corporeal susceptibility inhering not in the nature of her person, but in her bodily placement within factory walls located in close proximity to the decadent influences of an outside world marked urban, male, and predatory. Poverty, lack of education, and a home life that neglected training in middle-class social values may have been believed to have set the stage for moral fallibility, but as statistics from social reformers like Hosoi Wakizō consistently reminded their readers, the "fall into sexual depravity" (*daraku*) was usually set in motion by contact with modern urban forces through the permeable space of the factory. Images of the fallen women already populating urban spaces abounded in the popular press and the popular imagination. Especially remarked upon were the independent modern girl and the *shokugyō fujin*, or "working woman," whose jobs in the new department stores and clerical offices put these unmarried women in constant contact with men who were not relatives or neighbors, and whose lifestyle factory managers worried that their female employees would emulate.[41] Consequently, factory-sponsored efforts to protect chastity through the cultivation of proper morals played an important role in the containment and naturalization of female sexuality.

A symposium titled "Jokō no sei ni kan suru mondai" (Issues Relating to the Sex of Female Factory Workers) published in the July 1929 issue of *Jokō kenkyū* offers a telling picture of the ambivalence and anxiety produced by the location of women in factory spaces. The symposium began with a discussion of the definition of *sei*, or sex, which the journal's editor in chief summed up by invoking the equally ambiguous term, *fūki mondai*, or "the problem of public morals." The conversation among company managers and personnel administrators that followed construed factories as dangerous sites in a sexual economy threatened by the entry of large numbers of women into the industrial workforce. Factory manager Okamura Genkichi began the discussion noting that temptation (*yūwaku*) was "the biggest problem." The problem of temptation, he argued, came from outside the factory; therefore, factory girls should not be let out of the compound. This was "not to restrict their freedom," he said, "but rather to protect them."[42]

What, then, constituted these grave temptations lying outside the factory gates? Another symposium participant, Ogame Tsuneta, described them this way:

> In the cities . . . there are many incitements to temptation. There are people from the countryside and working people, in addition to cafés, restaurants, ice sellers in the stores during the summer, and the temple festivals. The allure of going to such places is great, and the evil influences available are increasing. For this reason it is not sufficient to simply warn or admonish our employees, or to only warn and admonish the local people. Rather, since such an approach would be so open-ended and since the situation is so complicated that warnings might not always be effective, we must work hard to supervise sex.[43]

Here the supervision of sex could be achieved only by the careful surveillance (and, we presume, physical containment, since warnings are not enough) not only of young female employees whose individual activities demand constant monitoring, but of "the local people" as well.

A factory manager from Gōdō Woolens Company, participating in another journal symposium concerning the free time of female factory workers, painted the contrast between city and country in equally stark terms. Responding to a colleague's call for more factories to build gardens on their grounds for the health and welfare of their predominantly female workers, Satta Tadashi remarked that operating a factory located in the countryside made the management of female labor much easier: "There are no tempting stores or places of entertainment to draw one in, so that one can fully immerse oneself in gardening. But the cities are trouble. It only takes one step outside the [factory] gates, and the evil atmosphere is enough to tempt the heart of a factory girl."[44] But did the policing of sex become necessary only once a worker stepped through the factory gates and outside the confines of the contained site of industrial production? The liminal status of the factories, in which rural women and girls manipulated the machinery of modern industrial production, meant that the threat to the stability of the categories of "woman" and "female sexuality" necessarily existed within as well as without. While the modern city offered the temptations associated with the "erotic-grotesque-nonsense" that characterized the urban culture of 1920s Japan, the interior space of the factory could also harbor dangers of a sexual nature.

Before the abolition of night work, bureaucrats, managers, and social critics seemed more likely to implicate the dormitory system itself in the corruption of public morals. In 1917 Oka Minoru, the Home Ministry director who oversaw the passage of the original Factory Law, condemned the more highly monitored spaces within the factory for lapses in sexual morality:

> There are few factory workers who engage in immoral behavior who commute from home. But the morals [fūki] of those factory girls who live in dormitories attached to factories that are in the cities, or in areas where there is a large concentration of factories, are generally speaking quite loose. . . . Of course it is not always the case that they come from villages where there are good public morals. In the villages and townships [gunson], when a girl once loses her virginity the result is that a new family is formed and that is how the affair ends. However, in factory areas unchaste women end up falling into a life of decadence. For that reason we should be especially wary of the results of the kind of immorality that goes along with the factory organization.[45]

The reference to new families formed out of the loss of a woman's virginity likely pointed to the village practice of yobai, or "night crawling," in which young men would visit the homes of young unmarried women to have sexual relations with them. Usually if a woman became pregnant as a result, the couple would marry. The practice of yobai (which continued in some rural areas up until the 1950s) ignored the emphasis on monogamy and the injunctions against premarital sexual relations that were part of the modern state's efforts to appear civilized and enlightened. Its prevalence throughout the countryside made the sexual morals of the rural population suspect in the eyes of many bureaucrats, social reformers, and industrial managers.[46]

Oka's identification of the villages as the source of lax morality also resonated with many Meiji-period taxonomies of factory-worker personalities that pointed to family social class and occupational background as well as regional origin as determining character.[47] But this lax morality at least occurred in the context of social networks that provided clear consequences for premarital sex: the offenders would be married and the offence thus rendered meaningless. The factory environment had no such customary ways of dealing with nonnormative sexual behavior, thus making its geography—everything within its walled boundaries, but especially the dormitories—especially dangerous.

MORAL DECAY AND SEXUAL PERVERSION

Proletarian writers, as well as factory managers, focused on the sexual morality of factory women as they sought to depict the evils of the capitalist state and inspire the masses toward class consciousness. Hosoi Wakizō (1897–1925), most famous for his best-selling journalistic account of the working and living conditions of cotton-spinning women titled *Jokō aishi* (The Sorrowful History of Female Factory Workers), began his writing career as an author of proletarian fiction. From a poor family and having worked as a factory hand in the cotton mills since the age of thirteen, he was uniquely situated to understand conditions in the textile factories. Hosoi joined the early labor union (the Yūaikai) while in his early twenties, attended a union-sponsored "labor school," and became interested in literature.

Hosoi's proletarian fiction, written before *Jokō aishi* but published only after his death in the years immediately following the success of his nonfiction work, evinces a concern with female sexuality and points to the ways that the figure of the female factory worker could be deployed in literary texts to signify the excesses of the capitalist system. His "Aru jokō no shuki" (Notes from a Female Factory Worker) used first-person narrative to let us into the life of Hayashi Masayo, a fictional factory worker in Nagoya who we learn has become as corrupt and decadent as the capitalist factory that produced her.[48]

Masayo is literate, sexual, consumerist, and interested in independence both financial and emotional. She reads books and magazines, likes restaurants and new clothes, and lets herself be taken out by male factory employees whenever she can get a day off work. The city appeals to her. There is nothing for her in the village. In many ways she reflects the decadence of the urban modern girl who flaunted tradition and reveled in hedonism. Rumors of promiscuity circle around Masayo at the factory after she returns wearing a new kimono bought for her by a male coworker with whom she has just spent several days in Kyoto. She is restricted to the factory compound for a month by the dormitory supervisor for taking too many days away from work, and when her father gets word of her affairs with men, he instructs the company to send all her wages directly home to him, thus cutting off her financial lifeline to the world outside the factory gates. In response, Masayo refuses to work, hiding in the dormitory all day reading books and magazines while her boyfriends sneak food to her. Upon hearing that her father plans to come to the factory to bring his incorrigible daughter back home, Masayo thinks through her options. She could simply go back to work, succumbing to the restrictions placed upon her by father and employer; but it would not be worth it, she decides, to work all those hours for the mere ten yen a month she would be allotted for spending money. She could go home with her father; but there she would be treated like a maid and would have to watch over her younger brothers and sisters and do all the housework. She would have no money of her own, and most of all, she would not be able to engage in love affairs (ren'ai). So the only option left, she decides, is to run away from the factory and her father out into the city of Nagoya.

Once settled on this last option, Masayo decides that if she is going to run away to a city it might as well be Tokyo, a place she has never visited but which she has read about in books and magazines. Without any kind of plan for what she will do once there, she collects her savings and leaves for the capital. Toward the end of the story we find Masayo back at a cotton-spinning factory, this time in Tokyo, having lied her way into a female supervisor position. Immediately upon her entry into this new environment she finds herself the object of male attentions and concludes her story, saying that "once again, I had fallen in among the female factory workers." For Hosoi, this falling was inevitable, as the factory ruins women, making them decadent, selfish, and immoral.

Another carefully monitored sign of moral decay attributed particularly to female factory workers existing not *despite* the containing walls of the workshop and the dormitory, but rather *because* of them, was the so-called unnatural (*fushizen*) practice of same-sex relationships. In his 1921 book *Jokō no shitsukekata to kyōiku* (The Training and Education of Female Factory Workers), Ishigami Kinji admonished factory and dormitory supervisors against certain habits that would be "disruptive of public morals in the factories." Along with suggesting prohibitions on the "unnecessary direct contact between male and female operatives" and warnings to workers not to dress garishly or obscenely (*inbi*), he also recommended that managers not allow the girls to sleep in the same bedding. All of these precautions were meant to prevent what he called "sexual perversion," or "abnormal sexual desire" (*seiyoku no ijō*).[49]

Ishigami's book was not the only one to identify the factory space as uniquely apt to produce unwanted homosexual (*dōseiai*) relationships and other so-called sexual abnormalities.[50] The social psychologist Komine Shigeyuki, who wrote prolifically on the medical, social, and psychological reasons for suicide, claimed that same-sex double love suicides (*dōsei jōshi*) were almost unheard of among people from the middle classes. Among women, he wrote, same-sex double love suicides occurred almost exclusively among the working class, especially domestic workers, café waitresses, factory workers, and prostitutes.[51] And in *Jokō aishi* (The Sorrowful History of the Female Factory Workers), Hosoi Wakizō listed several perversions produced by factory-based industrial capitalism, including homosexuality, increased incidences of masturbation, and what he referred to as a form of "neutered" or "sterile" psyche (*chūseiteki shinri*). This latter perversion, he explained, referred to women who had worked at the factory and lived in the dormitories for years and who had lost all desires, not only sexual desire but also the desire for money:

> If one devotes one's body to total abstinence, then one characteristically becomes gradually cut off from the bonds first of sexual desire, then of other desires. There are quite a number of unmarried women, overmature [*ranjuku*] women over the age of thirty, living in the [factory] dormitories. These women earn money and send it back home or put it into savings, but they do not spend it. . . . No matter where you go, you will find generally around 10 percent of this kind of Karel Capek robotlike female worker in every factory. They have become completely neutered [*chūseiteki*].[52]

Here Hosoi related sexual desire to economic consumption. Listed among a group of perversions clearly associated with sexual activity (masturbation and homosexuality), he explained only the category of "neutered psyche" in terms of the uses of money rather than the uses of the body. This slippage between sexuality and economics points to an often unconscious link made regularly by managers, government, and social commentators, connecting industrial efficacy to the sexual constitution of the nation as rendered through the individual bodies of its citizens.

Hosoi was quite clear to specify that the same-sex love occurring among women and girls in factories did not stop at just mutual admiration on a spiritual level, but went so far as what he called "extreme physical acts."[53] But as we have seen, the participants in the 1929 roundtable discussion on sex education published in *Jokō kenkyū* were much less willing to implicate the factory system—and by extension their own management practices—in the production of sexual expressions that fell outside the parameters of a nationalized chaste womanhood.

The *Jokō kenkyū* symposium on sex education highlights the degree to which the supervision of sex among female factory workers had became part of the rationalization of individual workers' bodies by 1929. The conflict of impulses motivating discussions of female sexuality in the textile mills had by this time located female mill workers between the countryside and the city as an ambivalent site of both progress and corruption. This country/city divide became crucial not only in the discourse on sexuality, but also in medical discourses on disease and hygiene, which felt a similar impact from the prohibition on night work.

FACTORY CALISTHENICS FOR WOMEN

From the time the first textile factories began operations, the physical well-being of workers made up a central focus for concerns about industrial modernity and its potential effects. Women workers, whose poor health might endanger the race (*shuzoku*, or *minzoku*, depending on the author) as they gave birth to a new generation of national citizen-subjects, were a special object of investigation. Women and girls, supposed to be more vulnerable to disease and physical weakness, served as a critical and potentially deadly link to the entire national population. As migrant laborers working under unhealthful conditions, they could and did contract deadly diseases, especially tuberculosis, often returning home to the countryside having been cast off by their employers after growing too weak to work.[54] Workers sent home under these conditions might in turn infect their families and the people in their villages.[55]

As presumed future mothers, most arguments went, female factory workers could put at risk the next generation of national citizens. The women's rights advocate and author Hiratsuka Raichō, in an essay titled "Haha ni naru jokō no mondai" (The Problem of Female Factory Workers Who Will Become Mothers), implored her audience to consider the broad social implications of allowing factory workers to toil under such poor and unhealthful conditions: "The breaking of their minds and bodies does not stop just with them, but affects the future of the nation (*kokumin*) and the race (*shuzoku*). It is not simply a question of human rights, social ethics, or humanity, but as regards the state it is a question of great import not to be dismissed, and one that is infinitely more complicated and rife with contradictions than the labor problem at large."[56]

Later, Sakura Takuji wrote a follow-up to Hosoi Wakizō's widely read exposé of the "sorrowful" lives and working conditions of female cotton spinners and made a similar, if more detailed, observation: having to sit on low stools, hunched over and with their pelvic areas exposed to the cold, many female factory workers become stoop-backed, and even sterile. Hundreds of thousands of female factory workers returning home in poor health bear children who, because of the physical condition of their mothers as they were developing as fetuses, could hardly be considered whole persons. This danger of reproducing a generation of physically and mentally unfit children, he suggested, was "the gravest problem facing us as citizens today."[57]

Putting the problem of female labor in such nationalist terms reflected the anxiety produced by the confluence of women, factory work, disease, and motherhood, and the state itself expressed interest in researching the connections among these categories. In 1910 the Ministry of Commerce and Agriculture commissioned Ishihara Osamu, a medical doctor trained at Tokyo Imperial University in the field of public hygiene, to undertake a major study of tuberculosis, its causes, and the possibilities for its prevention. The female factory population became the central focus of his work because of the high incidence of lung disease among textile workers. Ishihara's studies investigated not only incidences of infection and mortality in the factories, but followed ailing workers back to their villages to track the outcome of their illnesses, thus offering a scientifically based corrective to the endemic underreporting of tuberculosis by the textile companies. Intended as one of several research initiatives that would provide data for the Home Ministry bureaucrats busy drafting the country's first factory bill, Ishihara's studies were finally published in 1913, two years after the final version of that bill became law.[58]

Reminders that female factory workers must be considered not simply laborers, but future mothers of the national citizenry came frequently from textile-industry officials. A Fukushima Spinning official noted in 1929 that according to Ministry of Education statistics, the number of women attending higher schools nearly equaled the number of women working in the silk and cotton mills. "This means," he remarked, "there will be two types of women, both of whom will be becoming mothers: one with education, and the other without." Female factory workers, he concluded, did not need a formal education, but they should all have domestic training, which would include training in childcare and home economics.[59] Meanwhile, Ishigami Kinji noted that the health benefits associated with the abolition of night work were important for female factory workers, because as women they were the "number-two citizens" (*dai-ni kokumin*) of the nation, and they would become the mothers of the "number-three citizens" (fathers presumably being the "number-one" citizens).[60]

While concerns for women's reproductive capacity and their role as mothers and household managers persisted, companies' roles in promoting womanly virtues and the content of gendered instructional discipline had shifted to accommodate industry's desire to monopolize the off-work hours of their employees. Likewise, where the earlier period of textile-industry development had been marked by attempts to contain a tuberculosis epidemic, by 1930 strategies for managing health focused on nutrition, caloric intake, sleeping habits, and exercise, signaling a new attention to the management of individualized bodies. Workers previously considered disposable had come to be seen as a capital investment.[61]

Especially after 1929, the rationalization movement inflected a shift in perceptions of working women, giving a new emphasis to physical exercise, or calisthenics, as part of the management of female labor. While earlier attention to health issues had focused on disease and its potential to spread from factory workers into the general population, by 1929 the emphasis on the disciplining of individual bodies focused attention on factory-sponsored exercise programs. A Social Bureau survey of 206 textile factories showed that by early 1931 over 90 percent had some type of physical-education program for their workers. Most of these programs fell under the general heading of "national citizens' calisthenics" (*kokumin taisō*), but some included basketball, volleyball, ping-pong, or traditional Japanese dancing activities.[62] The drive to implement such programs stemmed not only from considerations of worker health, but increasingly pointed to systematic efforts to contain a growing labor movement.

The disciplinary effect of such exercise programs had a different impact on women than on men. As one female factory worker lamented in a letter to the editor in the union-affiliated magazine *Rōdō fujin* (Working Woman), men could get out of doing calisthenics by leaving the factory after work for home, but factory women were trapped because they lived in dormitories: "The men who don't like it simply leave, but we women are severely scolded by the dorm supervisor, so even though we complain, we all must line up in the yard."[63]

Women were also subject to exercises designed to cultivate womanly virtues in a way that did not happen analogously for men. One form of exercise employed commonly as part of cultivation-group activities and known as the dust-rag dance (zōkin dansu) combined the rationalized form of calisthenics with a mimicry of the housewifely duties of the womanly ideal. In this exercise cum domestic chore (discussed in more detail in the following chapter), workers were ordered down on their knees to scrub the hallways under the "one, two, one, two" commands of a superior.

In March 1929, before the abolition of night work, Ishigami Kinji weighed in on the issue of factory exercise programs. When asked if physical education should be included as one appropriate way for companies to manage the off-work time of female factory workers, he responded in the negative: "Unlike female students, female factory workers are fatigued by long hours at work. Physical education is appropriate for female students, but for female factory workers recovery from hard work is the most important thing."[64]

But by July 1930, Ishigami had become an advocate of physical education for female factory workers, no doubt swept up in the fever of calisthenics programming that had accompanied the abolition of night work. In his preface to a set of exercise instructions put out by the Labor Science Research Institute, he reversed his earlier dismissal, but maintained his insistence that such programs must be implemented with the explicit recognition that the labor done by female factory workers made their exercise needs different from those of the rest of the citizenry:

> Recently the sports fever that has been on the rise in society at large has also swept over factory workers, and as all types of sport and competition have become popular, factory leaders have implemented semicompulsory "citizens' calisthenics" [kokumin taisō] and other forms of regulated physical exercise. This has been a welcome phenomenon for the sake of physical education as well as spiritual training. However, while such sport is fine for average young people, the female factory workers who work in spinning and weaving factories—who have incompletely developed minds and bodies due to work activities, and for whom everyday labor consists of mechanical industrial work—cannot be treated the same as average youth. It must be recognized that this kind of work proves an obstacle to their growth.[65]

The solution, then, would be a system of calisthenics specially formulated to address the physical and spiritual needs of female factory workers. Instead of national citizens' calisthenics, Ishigami advocated factory calisthenics—an exercise regimen tailored to address the specific conditions of factory work.

The implementation of factory calisthenics programs and the arguments in favor of them bespoke a growing trend among managers in the textile industry to combine their earlier and abiding concerns about health and hygiene with new efforts to adopt Taylorist efficiency techniques. While one specialist on worker health concluded that "from a theoretical point of view, factory calisthenics are a natural product of industrial rationalization," the form and content of factory calisthenics could be viewed as not only a *result* of the rationalization of industrial production and the consequent physical and mental impact such changes had on workers, but as *part of* that process itself.[66]

Female workers themselves recognized the correspondence between worker body and machine promoted by company rationalization strategies, although workers' experiences of it sometimes led them to precisely the strikes and labor actions that managers hoped to avoid through increased rationalization. The proletarian writer Nakamoto Takako, who lived alongside the women workers of Tokyo's Kameido district, rendered these correspondences between bodies and machines as the starting point for collective action in her short story "Shokufu" (Weave):

> The three women returned to the shop floor, each to her own machine. Saki and Fujino stood together cleaning one of them. They swept up the fine threads that had gathered all over the interlocking zigzag of gears and levers, from pedals and cranks underneath the machine, and from the concrete floor upon which it rested. They wiped off the machine and oiled it. Having become so accustomed to using it, they felt that this machine was a part of their own bodies. Cleaned and oiled with such care, it glistened with a black radiance.[67]

In this passage a common relationship to the industrial machinery that provides their livelihood, and which they feel as "part of their own bodies," provides a basis for community. By the end of the story, the three workers themselves form the core of a "well-oiled machine," as all the female factory workers on the shop floor tacitly decide to turn off their machines to protest the poor treatment of one of their fellow workers.

The new rationalization as applied to women's factory labor meant that earlier concerns for female chastity that sought to foster spiritual or personal growth and virtue among young women had now turned to the maintenance and control of the female body and its daily activities. The concern for the public morals of female factory workers persisted, but the focus of such concerns shifted to the minute and manageable details of everyday life: how workers dressed, what they ate, their sleeping habits, and their leisure activities. The paternalistic benevolence characteristic of an earlier management style, while not wholly lost, became reconfigured as rational business practice and claimed the mantle of the modern discourse of science.

Factory managers did not, however, act alone in their attempts to produce ideal workers who would also be ideal Japanese women and national subjects. Semigovernmental cultivation groups were also crucial in these efforts, as we will see in the next chapter.

CHAPTER 3

Cultivation Groups
and the Japanese Factory

Producing Workers, Gendering Subjects

Attempts by cotton- and silk-spinning companies to cultivate a particular kind of female worker closely paralleled efforts by other state and nonstate actors to mold different demographic groups into appropriately gendered loyal imperial subjects. Social reformers sought to educate women, abolish prostitution, and contain juvenile delinquency, while a host of organizations worked to reform the countryside.[1] The project of disciplining female factory workers involved the intersection of all of these concerns. Largely undereducated and hailing from rural and often impoverished villages, female workers were also perceived to be dangerously close to falling into prostitution or other forms of social delinquency. To combat the negative forces of illiteracy, poverty, and poor morals (combined with the unwholesome seductions of the modern city noted in the previous chapter), vigorous interventions had to be made once a girl came to live and work at a textile company. Among the organizations involved in female worker training, education, and reform, none were more important than the cultivation groups that got their start as rural improvement associations during the Meiji period. Tracing the genealogy of such groups is crucial to understanding how they perceived their mission among female factory workers and why they were invited wholeheartedly into the factory gates by company managers and owners by the 1920s.

Cultivation groups proliferated throughout the countryside immediately following the Russo-Japanese War, which ended in 1905 in a Japa-

nese victory that signaled the country's emergence as a significant imperial power. These organizations were promoted by the state, whose bureaucrats threw their support behind cultivation groups they believed
could help foster a strong national spirit, aid in the economic development of an agrarian sector seen as backward, and quell the potential for
rural unrest. Among them, the Seinendan for young men and the Shojokai for young women are perhaps the best known. A third cultivation
group, the Shūyōdan founded in 1906 just after the war, began as a rural
young men's cultivation group, but by the 1920s had set up branches especially for female factory workers in textile companies. All of these organizations shared in the goals of the state and Japan's industrial concerns to promote the strengthening of the economy and the creation of
a unified national identity.

Discussions of *shūyō,* typically translated as "cultivation" or "self-
cultivation," by definition concern the individual. But *shūyō* as practiced
and promoted by cultivation groups that began to appear in the late
Meiji period made self-cultivation central to efforts to create and maintain a national community and to integrating individual interests with
state interests. Cultivation groups linked and mobilized these state and
local interests in a rapidly urbanizing and industrializing environment.
The groups formed at the intersection of a broad intellectual and popular movement promoting personal betterment, and the movement for
local improvement (*chihō kairyō undō*) that grew out of government initiatives targeting the rural population as a site of potential unrest. Cultivation groups such as the Seinendan, the Shojokai, and the Shūyōdan
took the individual as their unit of reform, but ultimately sought to place
that individual within a broader national framework. Focusing on re-
suscitating earlier forms of *kyōdōtai,* the cooperative village community
associated with Tokugawa agricultural life, most took rural youth as
their object of reform until after World War I, at which time these organizations expanded their mission to include the "cultivation" of factory workers, both male and female. By examining the way *shūyō* was
defined by key figures in this movement, looking at several examples of
cultivation groups and finally investigating the efforts of one of them—
the Shūyōdan—as it began to engage female factory workers, we can see
how cultivation—as a means of linking the individual, society, and the
state—held gendered and classed meanings.

The notion of cultivation as a self-directed means of betterment was
crucial to the ideology of cultivation groups, and *shūyō* itself became a
buzzword both in intellectual circles and in popular magazines from

1910 through the 1920s. The social historian Tsutsui Kiyotada has argued suggestively that *shūyō* was the "mass culture" counterpart of *kyōyō*, the version of self-cultivation that characterized the elite culture of the Taishō period.[2] I would argue further that where *kyōyō*-ism represented a movement that sought the perfection of the social world through the removal of the individual from politics, the *shūyō* movement was from the beginning one that tied private interests to a broader sociality and to the interests of the state. This strong connection among the individual (engaged in self-cultivation), society, and the state in fact best characterizes *shūyō* as a phenomenon of the 1920s and 1930s.

Nitobe Inazō, the renowned boys' higher-school educator and translator of Japanese culture to the English-speaking world, popularized the concept of *shūyō* in three books first serialized in the male-oriented youth magazine *Jitsugyō no Nihon* (Business Japan). The first of them, a best seller titled simply *Shūyō* that appeared in 1911, sparked the imaginations of a mass audience of young men:

> The rules of cultivation [*shūyō*] I am explaining here do not have as their goal the receiving of applause from the world nor the doing of difficult things nor the production of brave and heroic conduct. Wealth, honor, and fame ought not to be the goal of cultivation. Rather, instead, you ought to aim at being satisfied within your heart, no matter how poor you are. You ought to aim at being happy by yourself, no matter how much you are slandered. You ought to aim at feeling good fortune in the midst of adverse circumstances. You ought to aim at passing through the world with thanks, no matter what. These are the objects of the cultivation I am proposing.[3]

Shūyō, then, was different from the Meiji-era slogan *risshin shusse*, or "getting ahead" and "going into the world," which had as its audience the elite young men of the immediate post-restoration generation.[4] Rather, as Earl Kinmonth has argued, "the purpose of cultivation [*shūyō*]" for Nitobe "was to make the discontented individual happy with the status quo."[5]

The importance of individuals finding self-satisfaction and happiness even in the face of adversity appeared also in the writings of Tazawa Yoshiharu, for whom *shūyō* meant an entire physical and spiritual personality dedicated to community and to state. For Tazawa, a key figure in the Seinendan movement and its leading ideologue, *shūyō* played a central role in the mission of that organization: "The aim of our country's Seinendan is general *shūyō*, foundational *shūyō*, for full-fledged members of society [*shakaijin*]. In other words, cultivating a national people [*kokumin*] who will develop healthy bodies, train strong wills, have a cheerful outlook, polish a gifted mental disposition—these are the goals of the Seinendan's *shūyō* activities."[6] In Tazawa's vision of *shūyō*, then, the individual cultivated bodily and spiritual traits in order to become part of the social body and to serve the nation-state. Tazawa juxtaposed his notion of general or foundational *shūyō* against more specific forms of cultivation such as military training, in which the Seinendan also engaged. His understanding of *shūyō* and the cultivation of national subjects focused on the rural youth who formed the base of Seinendan membership and who were the target of the local improvement movement in which the Seinendan played a significant role.

Just as the notion of cultivation had different implications for the masses than for the elite, it also had different implications for women than for men. For a newly emergent literate lower and middle class of women who were both producers and consumers of the new mass culture, popular journals and magazines offered practical advice on how *shūyō* could improve their sense of self and quality of life.[7] Barbara Sato has noted in her analysis of the impact the Taishō-era "*shūyō* boom" had on a reading class of Japanese women that "the term *self-cultivation* encompassed a variety of different meanings, evoking connotations of 'character building,' 'moral training,' and 'spiritual and cultural growth.' "[8] But even while the *shokugyō fujin*—the "working woman" who became a nearly ubiquitous feature of Japan's cultural landscape after World War I—embraced *shūyō* as a means to get ahead in the world, to improve herself, and to participate more fully in modern life, the print media emphasized forms of self-cultivation that foregrounded conservative notions of gender conformity.[9] Indeed, for Yamawaki Fusako, the first director of the Dai Nippon Rengō Joshi Seinendan (All Japan Federation of Girls' Youth Groups), *shūyō* was a crucial part of young women's educational lives precisely because it emphasized highly distinct roles for men and women. *Shūyō*, Yamawaki claimed, was the means by which young women should become good wives and wise mothers, thus fulfilling their duty to the family as household managers.[10]

Among women working in factories, too, *shūyō* training emphasized filial piety and the cultivation of morally upright wives and mothers who, after producing cotton and silk for the nation, would reproduce healthy and obedient imperial citizens.[11] For working-class women, the impulse toward self-cultivation often derived from compulsory employer programs aimed at creating a workforce less prone to militant activism. Employer-directed *shūyō* efforts attempted to replace the desire to organize collectively with an ideology of duty to family, company, and nation. As will be discussed below, female factory workers subject to institutionalized cultivation training often resisted the values of moral purity and maternal domesticity promoted through the cultivation groups, and in essays and letters submitted to union and women's publications they expressed their resentment of the coerced nature of such disciplinary strategies.

The concept of *shūyō*, then, meant more than simply the self-cultivation of the individual. It served to link the moral individual to society and the state in classed and gendered ways. Nitobe's vision of *shūyō* as "being satisfied within your heart, no matter how poor you are" and Tazawa's vision of the cultivation of (male) national subjects marked *shūyō* as a project for the masses. *Shūyō* for both middle- and working-class women emphasized the duties of wife and mother. One of the major means by which such *shūyō* ideology proliferated among variously classed and gendered groups was through cultivation groups that emphasized education and spiritual training.

THE SEINENDAN AND THE NEW IMPERIAL SUBJECT

Cultivation organizations such as the Seinendan (Young Men's League), which emerged as powerful social forces after the Russo-Japanese War, linked the concerns of a rapidly expanding imperial and newly industrial state to what many saw as the "organic" and quintessentially communitarian values and structure of Japan's agricultural society. The Seinendan was the largest and most well-known of the *shūyō* organizations. It traced its history to the young men's societies organized locally throughout the country and known during the Tokugawa era (1600–1867) as *wakarenjū,* or *wakaishūgumi.* The *wakarenjū* or *wakaishūgumi* groups from which the Seinendan developed operated autonomously throughout the Tokugawa period and typically mandated membership for all male village youth between the ages of fifteen and twenty-five. In their ideal form, such organizations served the dual purpose of inculcating communitarian values and community-sanctioned forms of masculinity in a homosocial environment, and constituting a permanent body of village members able to undertake various forms of practical community service. Youth groups offered mutual support and discipline, operated fire and crime prevention patrols, and organized and celebrated festivals of the local Shintō shrines and Buddhist temples. Thus, from their inception, they offered to the communities that sustained them both practical service and the reproduction of social values in a configuration based neither on individual volunteerism nor on direct state control, but rather on a community-based culture of social obligation and mutual aid.[12]

But state and local officials at times also saw these male youth groups as a source of crime and social disruption. Bands of young men sometimes used their collective power within the village to engage in extortion, robbery, and various forms of petty crime.[13] By the late Meiji period rural youths were of particular concern. Those who had completed the six years of elementary education required by the state and who (for financial or other reasons) would not continue their education at the middle-school level, but who were not yet old enough to be conscripted for military service, became an especially vexing demographic. With no formal schooling to keep them occupied, these teenaged youths became a source of concern for village elites, who looked to the state for solutions to the problem of social unrest.[14]

While the Meiji state inherited concerns about unruly rural youth gangs, it also discerned the potential of village young men's associations to be used as tools to mobilize a new citizenry to work for the goals of a modern, industrial state. After Japan's victory in the Russo-Japanese War in 1905, officials from the Home Ministry sought to place rural youth groups under the control of local authorities. These efforts were part of the broader, state-directed local improvement movement, which attempted to produce a coherent national identity among the rural population and to strengthen the state's economic position by concentrating administrative power among local officials, who in turn took directions from the central authorities. As historian Kenneth Pyle has noted, the state's focus on the countryside as the target of improvement—rather than the urban centers that were arguably the locus of industrial change—sprang from an ideology in which "the countryside came to be thought of as embodying and preserving the essence of what was historically Japanese," as well as from the fact that four-fifths of the country's population still resided in the countryside by the turn of the century.[15]

In 1915 the government unified male village youth groups, by this time known as Seinendan, into a loose national network under state direction, giving it an independent administrative identity. In this year, also, the Home Ministry and Ministry of Education issued a directive to prefectural governors to "publicly appreciate" the work of these organizations and also issued standardized codes of organization and operations to be observed by all the local Seinendan branches throughout the country.[16] The motivation for organizing and unifying the Seinendan in 1915 was the government's desire to mobilize young men and prepare them for military conscription after the outbreak of the First World War, taking the military drills of the German youth associations as its model.[17] One of the effects of organization under state direction was that what had originally been a movement based in agricultural villages spread to the cities, widening its scope and becoming national in character.

It was, however, the construction of the Meiji Shrine that fully mobilized organization of the Seinendan on the national level, dedicating local groups and their members to the service of the imperial house through their collective labor. Plans to erect a shrine in Tokyo dedicated to the memory and deification of the deceased Meiji emperor were announced in 1915, and from 1919 to 1923 some three hundred local Seinendan groups composed of over sixteen thousand members came to Tokyo to work on the construction of the buildings of its inner and outer gardens.[18] Tazawa Yoshiharu, having been appointed to the bureau overseeing construction of the shrine, was instrumental in getting Seinendan labor involved in the actual building of the site. The Japan Young Men's Hall Foundation was established in 1921 using contributions from local Seinendan groups across the country, and by October 1925 the Young Men's Hall (Nippon Seinenkan), which stands among the outer gardens of the Meiji Shrine, was completed.[19] Where service to local Shintō shrines had long been part of Seinendan activities, participation in the erection of the Meiji Shrine complex in Tokyo imparted to local youth a national consciousness with strong religious overtones based on the Shintō faith and worship of the emperor.[20] And the construction of a hall within the sacred grounds dedicated expressly for use by the Seinendan symbolized the familial relationship of Japan's male youth to the imperial house-as-state: a relationship in which filial sons rendered service, love, and loyalty and the patriarchal ruler offered protection, benevolence, and approbation.

Thus, the nationalism fostered by the Seinendan combined "love for the soil," or local pride and loyalty, with patriotism and devotion to the emperor. That is, *shūyō dantai,* or cultivation groups such as the Seinendan, acted as vehicles for the integration of particularistic local interests with the universalism of state interests embodied by the emperor. Cultivation groups accomplished this by supporting the central elements— "the imperial myth, the religious tradition of ancestor worship, the social structure of the family system, and the customary heritage of folk morality"—that went into linking the *ie,* or "family," with the *kuni,* or "nation," in order to produce a mythology of the family-state (*kazoku kokka*).[21] That is, the Seinendan acted as an extension of the *kyōdōtai—*

the cooperative village community associated with Tokugawa agricultural life—performing service to the state through the process of building up local communities.[22]

"FACTORY GIRLS ARE FILIAL GIRLS":
THE SHOJOKAI AND FEMALE FACTORY WORKERS

At precisely the moment that government officials moved to incorporate
male regional youth groups in a national network, those same officials
took steps to create parallel organizations for women. The state-directed
Shojokai Chūōbu (Young Women's Association Central Office) opened
its doors in April 1918.[23] While its explicit mandate was to provide supplementary education for all unmarried girls except those in middle
school, the Shojokai had as its main goal the production of wifely counterparts to the young men of the Seinendan.[24]

The male social reformer and Shojokai ideologue Amano Fujio described
supplemental education as first and foremost a means for young women
from farming villages to receive training in becoming a proper helpmate and
spouse. Even those young women who possessed a formal elementary education, he suggested, would need supplementary education in order to
meet the high expectations contemporary society placed upon wives in
terms of literacy and cultural attainment.[25] The practice of cultivation for
the young Japanese women of the Shojokai, then, foregrounded indoctri-
nation into the cult of "good wife, wise mother," as well as incorporation
into the social fabric of local communities through cooperative projects.

Both boys and girls receiving formal schooling beyond the elementary
level were subject to different (and differently classed) sets of disciplinary
strategies from those used to cultivate rural youth and workers. Middle
and higher schools were often located in prefectural capitals and other
cities, situating their pupils in urban environments requiring different
kinds of reform than those provided to youth who were the object of the
local improvement movement. Accordingly, Seinendan members theoretically included all the male youth of a village except those attending
higher schools.[26] Likewise, the Shojokai strove to enlist as members all
the girls of any given locale who had not left the village for work or
schooling. In the case of girls, factory workers constituted the majority
of those no longer living at home (and hence unavailable for Shojokai recruitment), while the number of girls attending normal and higher
schools would have been much lower than those having left the village
for work.

The supplemental education typically offered to both male and female members of cultivation groups—the provision of which the Shojokai designated as its principal mission—focused on efforts to impart to them a social sensibility (*shakaiteki jōshiki*) and to increase their usefulness as citizens of the imperial state and as industrial workers.[27] Particularly for young women less apt to complete compulsory elementary education than boys if they came from poor families, supplemental education offered training and instruction in areas of practical use. For young members of the Shojokai, such education consisted of training in the womanly arts (*fudō no kenma,* or "polishing the way of woman") and in sewing and household management.[28] In addition to training sessions on sewing, cooking, handicrafts, etiquette, child rearing, and nursing, local Shojokai also engaged in moral reform activities, field trips, book and magazine circulation, cooperative savings, visits to the elderly, sympathy and congratulations visits, picnicking events, and sports meets.[29]

Nearly from their inception, female regional youth groups like the Shojokai evinced an active interest in the problems of female factory workers as part of their efforts to discipline young rural women as wives and mothers ready to serve the imperial state as family managers and reproducers. But by leaving their villages to engage in wage work, female factory workers had seemed to move out of the reach of rural reform efforts aimed at young women and girls. Recognizing this weakness in its organizing abilities, the Shojokai's central office first began paying attention to the problem of female factory labor in 1919, the same year that the International Labour Organization (ILO) convened its inaugural meeting in Washington DC. Japan's official participation at the first ILO convention had intensified debates at home about what constituted Japanese labor relations and particularly about the status and role of organized labor within those relations.[30] The position of the Shojokai with regard to female factory labor reflected the tensions in society at large in an era when the specter of class revolt embodied in the "labor problem" perhaps best reflected a more generalized fear of what popular books and magazines—as well as government documents—referred to as the "social problem."

The first references to female factory workers in the pages of *Shojo no tomo* (Girls' Friend), the serial publication put out by the Shojokai's central office, appeared only months before Japanese representatives joined labor leaders and politicians from around the world as part of the first ILO meetings. The editorial staff of the magazine opted to use the slightly older term *kōjo* (an inversion of the characters for "female" and "industry") rather than the more common *jokō* to signify "female factory workers," in part because of the negative nuance the word *jokō* had assumed in the wake of large-scale industrialization and the new forms of social stratification that it had engendered, and in part to take advantage of a slogan that depended on the word's use with a homonym. Shojokai ideologue Amano Fujio had coined the phrase *kōjo wa kōjo*—"factory girls are filial girls"—a slogan that came to characterize Shojokai policy with regard to female factory labor and that pointed to the organization's role in helping to cultivate filial behavior in female factory workers who Amano feared might otherwise forget their allegiances to family and to native place.[31]

Issues of filial duty and love for native place were central themes for Amano and for the Shojokai more generally in its mission to cultivate young village girls and their sisters and neighbors who had gone to the factories to work. Indeed, in some respects female factory workers offered a perfect model of filial duty and sacrifice as they endured the travails of factory work so that they might earn money to send home to support the families from whom they had been separated.

But the family relations associated with filial piety could be experienced by female workers themselves in highly contradictory ways. The unproblematic narrative—repeated so often by social reformers, management consultants, and union leaders alike—of the young factory worker gone to the city to earn money to send back home to her suffering family could become a very different story of those workers' relationships to their families and to the factory when told in the words of the girls themselves.

In one of the many songs female factory workers composed and sang for themselves and for each other, a young girl lamented her estrangement from her parents and the conditions she endured in the factory.[32] This counting song from the 1920s consists of fifteen verses, out of which I have provided the first five. I have indicated the first line of every verse in Japanese, each of which begins with a word or word part that is homophonous with the words for the numbers one through five (*hitotsu, futatsu, mitsu, yotsu, itsutsu*). Italicized words in the translation indicate the English meanings of the Japanese homophones. The first line is repeated in English translation, followed by a translation of the rest of the verse:

1.
Hito mo shitaru yama no naka
In the midst of mountains *everybody* knows,
Where the sound one hears is the sound of waterfalls
One finds the Fuji Cotton Spinning Company of Suruga

2.
Futaoya somuite kitabachi ni
I came here as a punishment for defying my *parents*.
Now I toil at Suruga,
Never to defy my parents again.

3.
Mina-san Suruga e kuru toki wa
People come to Suruga,
Thinking they will save money,
But one cannot make any money here.

4.
Yoru mo nenaide yagyō suru
We don't sleep at *night,* we work the evening shift.
Our life spans are shortened.
All of us are wretched, all.

5.
Itsuka okuni no futaoya ni
Someday I'll tell my parents back home
The bitter tale of the factory;
And move us all to tears.[33]

Such counting songs were often used as didactic tools for children and
adolescents, but frequently the individuals singing them felt free to use the
melody and change the lyrics to suit their own expressive needs. Use of the
counting-song form as a mnemonic device to remember the lyrics aided in
the transmission of such songs among female factory workers, who might
continue to modify and personalize the lyrics each time they sang a song.[34]

In this song a young woman goes to work at a cotton-spinning factory not as a form of filial piety, but as punishment for having not displayed enough reverence and obedience to her parents in the first place.
Her banishment takes her to a factory at Suruga, "in the midst of mountains everybody knows." This line indicates the liminality of the factory,
situated between city and country, both modern and traditional, in a
place that is part of the speaker's native home and yet somehow separated from it. Suruga and the factory itself become sites of deception, familiar and foreign at the same time, with workers duped by recruiters
into thinking they will make more money than is actually possible and
made to endure grueling night shifts and physically exhausting work.

The concerns voiced in the song became, in magazine articles appearing in *Shojo no tomo,* more about the moral and physical integrity
of the women who worked in the factories than about the circumstances
that had brought them there or the capitalist system that dictated their

living and working conditions and the wages they received. In his own essays, Amano played upon prevalent narratives of physical decay and moral corruption among female factory workers, citing lung disease and "sexual diseases" as particular problems. Shojokai members, he suggested, should send factory workers letters from home, since women and girls who feel themselves forgotten by their home villages often fall prey to temptation and seduction (*daraku*). Such letter writing should be done collectively, as a regular part of moon viewing and other celebratory village gatherings. Occasional care packages of fruits and other familiar remembrances from the village, together with special Shojokai-sponsored group visits to the factories, would serve to keep female factory workers connected with their communities at home.[35]

Amano's description of the kinds of activities in which Shojokai members should engage on behalf of their factory "sisters," and the spirit with which such activities should be undertaken, sound strikingly similar to the kinds of patriotic service women were frequently called upon to perform for soldiers at war. Care packages for soldiers sent by women affiliated with local branches of the Shojokai, the Fujinkai (Ladies' Association) and other patriotic women's groups, contained practical items such as towels and writing paper, along with copies of local newspapers and foods that might remind them of their native region in much the same way that the Shojokai sought to send comforting words and longed-for tastes from home to bolster the spirits of factory women. In this, both military men and factory women were seen to be working toward the strength and prosperity of the *kokutai,* the "national polity."

In his contributions to *Shojo no tomo,* Amano addressed his audience of Shojokai readers not as factory workers or potential factory workers, but as the "sisters" of those less fortunate young women who operated the spinning and weaving machinery of the modern textile industry. The familial reference drew upon the discourse of the family-state (*kazoku kokka*) to indicate that all subjects working for the good of the imperial state were part of a single Japanese family headed by the emperor. More than that, it pointed to the likelihood that many of those sent to work in factories were indeed the sisters, cousins, neighbors, and friends of Shojokai members still living in the villages.

Amano believed that the Shojokai should expand their role to the factories, citing the case of the Shojokai local branch of Kusu Village in Ōita Prefecture, which arranged for thirty female factory workers to be given a day's leave from work (presumably without pay) to attend one of their meetings, as an early example of direct factory sponsorship of Shojokai activities. Shojokai leaders, he believed, should make a regular practice of visiting and inspecting factories, lecturing on topics such as the labor problem, the social problem, the Factory Law, the "evil ways of the city," and the "evil teachings of the factory." Shojokai in the villages should hold "welcome home" parties for the factory workers when they came back to the village for New Year's holiday, and farewell parties when the time came to return to work. In all of these undertakings, the Shojokai placed itself as a protector of female factory worker interests insofar as it identified them as part of the rural countryside subject to potentially polluting influences of modern machinery, the industrial process, and urban life.[36]

To further its mission of factory intervention on behalf of young women of the countryside, the Shojokai opened its first factory-affiliated branch at the Hoshigatani factory of the Fuji Gas Spinning Company in 1920. Established as a "cooperative self-governing [kyōdō jichi] gathering," the organization took as its goal the development of exemplary women who would collectively "help each other, research the needs of daily life, and while raising the level of knowledge and ability about such things, [would] cultivate the womanly arts and improve morals" in a womanlike (onna-rashiku) fashion.[37]

In November 1926 the Home Ministry issued a directive designating joshi seinen dantai, or "girls' youth groups," as official cultivation mechanisms meant to improve the character and health of young girls and shape them as kokumin, or national citizens. This directive constituted a more rigorous effort toward the unification of a disparate network of girls' youth groups into a centrally administered body. Finally in April 1927 Yamawaki Fusako became the first director of the newly established Dai Nippon Rengō Joshi Seinendan—the All Japan Federation of Girls' Youth Groups—which claimed a membership of 1.5 million, spread out among thirteen thousand separate groups operating throughout the country.[38]

These changes closely followed trends in the male youth organizations. The Seinendan Chūōbu (Seinendan Central Office) first established in 1915 became the Dai Nippon Rengō Seinendan (Federation of Young Men's Leagues of Japan) in 1924, finalizing the consolidation of "autonomous" local units into a national framework that, despite the Seinendan's status as a private organization, was largely directed by the state.[39] But where the state and its agents represented local units of the Seinendan as organic compositions, spontaneously formed throughout the country through an insuppressible racial instinct, the origins of the female equivalents to these male youth groups were more clearly grounded within the history of Meiji state-building efforts.[40]

"LOVE AND SWEAT"

In addition to the Seinendan and Shojokai, other *shūyō* organizations emerged that remained outside the formal bureaucratic structures of the state, but still maintained close ties with government agencies and personnel. Out of these groups, which included organizations such as Kibōsha, Nogikō, and Shokugyō Shūkyōya, the most influential and longest-lived was the Shūyōdan. A 1933 article by Akamatsu Tsuneko appearing in the union magazine *Rōdō fujin* (Working Woman) named these organizations as prominent among the kinds of reformist cultivation groups (what she termed "official reactionary groups") that the Sōdōmei (Japan Federation of Labor) opposed for their antiunion philosophies and tactics.[41] The Labor Section of the Home Ministry Social Bureau reported in 1931 that out of all cultivation groups with a factory presence, the Shūyōdan claimed the highest degree of representation, followed by the Kibōsha, the Hōtokukai, and the Shojokai.[42]

The Shūyōdan, however, got its start as a rural youth group for males and only later moved into the industrial arena. Formally incorporated one year after the end of the Russo-Japanese War, it had much in common with the Seinendan that already claimed a substantial organizational network across the country. The movement took as its motto "love and sweat" (*ai to ase*), an abbreviation for longer terms meaning "all-encompassing human love" (*dōhō sōai*) and "letting one's sweat flow and disciplining oneself" (*ryūkan tanren*). The Shūyōdan oath composed by founder Hasunuma Monzō made clear that *shūyō* as practiced through love and sweat was bound to a form of sociality that emphasized discipline and collective effort:

> People awaken! Awaken and return to love
> A life without love is darkness
> Praying together, let us become close to all the people
> Until there is not a single person in conflict in the places we live
>
> People get up! Get up and return to sweat
> Without sweat society is corrupt
> Praying together, let us work with all the people
> Until there is not a single neglectful person [*okotaru mono*] in the places
>   we live[43]

"The places we live" (*sato*) points to the rural village communities that made up the *kyōdōtai*. Love and sweat here refer to harmony and hard work, values that Hasunuma believed were central to a nation's success. Hasunuma's oath, like the communal body itself, appears to transcend historicity, even though its composition served an organization thoroughly modern in form and function. The historian Harry Harootunian's observation that "appeal to the folk body fetishized 'natural' social relationships in the paradoxical effort to find an alternative to the commodity form and its propensity to 'objectify' social life" was reflected in the ideology, structure, and practices of Hasunuma's Shūyōdan, which took the communal body as its central organizing principle.[44]

Moving beyond its origins as a male regional youth group, the Shūyōdan by the 1920s had expanded its mission to become one of the best-represented cultivation groups with branches operating in textile factories. The regional youth group function continued to be a mainstay of the organization until the end of World War II, but its activities among the almost exclusively young female populations of workers who resided in factory dormitories required that different strategies be developed to discipline female factory workers as workers and as part of the national community. Where the state had seen fit to develop the Shojokai as counterparts to the Seinendan—the latter organized to produce young men as national citizens, the former organized to produce good wives and wise mothers ready and able to assist young Japanese men in furthering state goals—the Shūyōdan by the early 1920s had moved toward combining these efforts in a single organization.

In its efforts to promote a strengthened vision of the national citizen who would be molded spiritually and physically through education and discipline, the Shūyōdan was, like the Seinendan and Shojokai, part of the *kyōka undō*, or what Sheldon Garon has called the movement for "moral suasion," of the early twentieth century.[45] Instead of mandatory membership and communal living in a clubhouse like the Seinendan, the Shūyōdan employed training retreats (*kōshūkai*), which consisted of rigorous discipline in physical endurance and moral purity, including national citizens' calisthenics (*kokumin taisō*) and purification ceremonies (*misogigyō*), lectures on filial piety, cleaning rituals, and the singing of patriotic and uplifting songs. These training retreats provided the staple of Shūyōdan activities from its inception as a male regional youth group through its expansion into the realm of industrial worker reform.

The religious character of the Shūyōdan complemented its nationalist goals of forging a unified and disciplined population of young men (and later women) dedicated to the emperor and the *kokutai,* or "national polity," and Shintō practices underlay some of the key disciplinary strategies used by the organization. Not unlike the Seinendan, the Shūyōdan sponsored frequent shrine visits in order to render visible and promote through practice the unity of imperial-state and local interests.[46] Where participation in the building of the Meiji Shrine mobilized the Seinendan, and the construction of the Young Men's Hall gave it purpose, the Shūyōdan relied most heavily on the ascetic practice of *misogigyō* as a catalyzing and unifying event in the lives of its male members. In this Shintō ritual, participants would wash the sin and impurities from their bodies in the cold waters of a river as a gesture to the gods.

While Shintō underlay the Shūyōdan's fundamental message of emperor worship, Buddhist teachings also played a significant role in Shūyōdan activities and in the development of the group's spiritual message, and many of its training retreats took place at Buddhist temple complexes.[47] The organization's official thirty-year history refers continually to Hasunuma's reformist impulse as part of a "holy war," and the process of "rebirth" or being "born again" through a kind of charismatic conversion constituted a central element pointing, it was argued, to the efficacy of cultivation group practices:

> Upon participating in only one training retreat, the mysterious fact of people being reborn [*ningen ga umare kawaru*] has appeared. People who have always been critical become "doers." Those who were mercenary become dedicated to service. Those who were introverted become extroverted. Those who only saw the dark side of society begin to see the bright side. And there are so many others that they cannot even be counted. People return to their hometowns and their schools ready to turn their experience into reality, and begin to create model schools, model villages and model factories.[48]

These, then—the schools and villages of its original mission, and by the 1920s the factories of Japan—would be the sites where this rebirth or renovation was most needed and would have the greatest impact.

By 1921 the Shūyōdan joined in an educational effort with the two-year-old Kyōchōkai (Industrial Cooperation and Harmony Society) to make its first moves into the industrial realm. The key figure here was Tazawa Yoshiharu, mainstay of the Seinendan movement and Shūyōdan council member who had recently been appointed one of three new managing directors of the Kyōchōkai. It was Tazawa's experience with social education that had made him an attractive choice for the Kyōchōkai position, and he swiftly put that experience and his connections with various regional and youth groups to work for the organization. One of his first major initiatives for the Kyōchōkai was the establishment of workers' training courses (*rōmusha kōshūkai*) modeled on Shūyōdan retreats, the first of which had been offered in 1915.[49] The workers' training retreats, which followed the disciplinary method of the earlier Shūyōdan training meetings, marked a shift in emphasis from the reform of the countryside to the disciplining of industrial workers.

This application of Shūyōdan strategies to the industrial sector coincided with a new concern on the part of the organization with the cultivation of women and the structure of the family. As an official history of the organization lamented:

> Activity by these pure youth who underwent a baptism of love and sweat appeared in every region, and especially notable was a movement of awakening to the people of their native towns. But the more these pure young men devoted themselves to love and sweat, the more their disillusionment grew. In most households [*katei*], what they were trying to accomplish was not understood. Neither did the people of the village share their passion. . . . Without any roots in the household and without any understanding in the towns and villages, their movement started and stopped, stopped and started, until finally it vanished without a trace.[50]

The key to laying down "roots in the household" and "understanding in the villages," it became clear, would have to be the cultivation of not just young men, but entire families.

As Nishikawa Yūko has argued persuasively, throughout Japan's imperial period (and indeed, she argues, beyond), the family constituted the basic unit upon which the nation-state was founded.[51] There were in fact two families, or as Nishikawa puts it, two coexisting family structures that shaped both private life and the life of the state until 1945. The older *ie* system consisted of an extended family, which in its aristocratic samurai form had become the legal standard for family configurations as set out in the Civil Code of 1898. The *ie* system, however, was gradually being replaced by a newer form based on a nuclear family model, the *katei* (home), which developed as part of changing demographic patterns wrought by industrialization and urbanization.[52] Thus new concerns with the family—and the newer, more urban *katei* in particular—on the part of the Shūyōdan bespoke a recognition that forms of social management based on village communitarianism would have to find different strategies in order to continue to mobilize urban industrial workers as imperial citizen-subjects.

In 1922 the Shūyōdan sponsored its first household cultivation meeting (*katei shūyōkai*) in Osaka, an event in which everyone in a (male) Shūyōdan member's family was to participate. Most of the factory worker members were heads of households who claimed that what was needed in the cities where they worked was not so much neighborhood reform as household improvement (*katei kaizen*). In a gesture of cooperativism that pointed to the importance of "cultivation" for women as well as men, one of the principles of this family cultivation meeting came to be that the men would take on certain aspects of home work and childcare in order to give the women sufficient time for cultivation training.[53]

In 1926 the Shūyōdan took its new emphasis on the changing nature of the Japanese family and initiated new programs that spoke directly to families through women and through industrial workers of both sexes. In quick succession beginning in May of that year, the organization held the first of its training courses for the Yokosuka Naval Arsenal (a program that spelled the beginnings of a close working relationship between the Shūyōdan and the Japanese Imperial Navy), the first Tokyo Women's Training Course designed to cultivate female leaders in communities and in industry, and the first training course given by the Shūyōdan for employees of Hitachi.[54] Other firsts for this year included the founding of the Shūyōdan's Manshū Rengōkai (Manchuria Federated Association) and the translation into Korean of the text "The Shūyōdan Spirit," punctuating longstanding involvement by the organization in cultivating settlers to the colonies, as well as colonial subjects.[55]

The first training course for women took place in 1925 in Hyōgo Prefecture as part of a local initiative by the Women's Bureau of the Shūyōdan's Hyōgo-ken Rengōkai (Hyōgo Prefecture Federated Association). The success of the several women's training courses hosted in Hyōgo and others sponsored by the Shūyōdan's Kanagawa-ken Rengōkai (Kanagawa Prefecture Federated Association) prompted personnel in the head office to launch the publication in 1927 of *Shirayuri* (White Lily), a twenty-six-page magazine for women put out four times a year. By 1929 the head office in Tokyo decided to sponsor its own women's training courses throughout the country. The first took place in August on the grounds of Enryakuji Temple atop Mount Hiei in Kyoto. Over 500 women from all over the country applied and 214 were chosen to participate in the four-day retreat led by Takeuchi Uraji from the head office.[56]

At about the same time the Shūyōdan moved into the industrial arena, offered its first formal courses for women, and expanded its presence in Japan's colonies, other changes were taking place in the organization's leadership composition. The Great Kantō Earthquake of 1923 and the fires that ensued destroyed most of Tokyo, including the majority of the Shūyōdan's assets located there. Possessing from its inception a strong vision of nation and a dedication to building national strength through the cultivation of national citizens, the Shūyōdan had early on attracted the attention of bureaucrats, politicians, and industrial leaders. In the wake of the earthquake the state stepped in, donating a new location and thirty thousand yen from the Home Ministry for the reconstruction of the organization's Tokyo assembly hall. Though maintaining its private, nongovernmental status, the Shūyōdan invited Upper House member Hiranuma Kiichirō to assume leadership of the organization in 1924 (although founder Hasunuma would remain a driving force), cementing ties with the government and opening the door to further cooperation with state agencies.

Conservative politician, Upper House member and future prime minister Hiranuma Kiichirō was a dedicated nationalist. In May of the year he took the helm of the Shūyōdan, he helped found the right-wing Kokuhonsha (National Foundation Society), which emphasized the unique religious character of the Japanese state and supported a mission of expansion in Asia.[57] Under Hiranuma's leadership, the Shūyōdan answered requests by the Tokyo municipal administration to help in the postearthquake reconstruction effort by erecting simple housing developments known as *kan'i shukuhakushō*—further evidence of the organization's move toward urban industrial concerns.

But Hiranuma was not the only influential figure to become involved with the Shūyōdan in the mid-1920s. In 1925 the renowned industrialist Shibusawa Eiichi accepted an invitation to become chairman of the newly established Shūyōdan Kōenkai (Shūyōdan Booster Society).[58] Shibusawa had already played a significant role in the organization's history as part of a team of Kyōchōkai leaders who worked with the Shūyōdan in 1921 to organize factory-worker training retreats. Shibusawa had, from the time of its founding, taken a leading role in the Kyōchōkai, which denounced the militant tactics of labor unions, but which also opposed a hierarchical management style based on the philosophy of paternalism.[59] One of prewar Japan's premier industrialists, Shibusawa helped found throughout his career as an entrepreneur over five hundred companies, including Osaka Spinning and Mie Spinning, two of the largest cotton textile concerns in Japan.[60] Osaka Spinning—Japan's first major cotton-spinning company—owed much of its early success to its day/night two-shift system, which kept machines running twenty-four hours a day. In 1886 the company furthered its commitment to employing women and children in night work when it introduced electric lighting from steam-powered dynamos into its factories, improving the safety conditions of night work.[61] The influence of the country's leading industrialist, Shibusawa, and one of its most well-connected politicians, Hiranuma, served to reinforce the state-centered and probusiness posture of the Shūyōdan.

As part of its industrial efforts, the Shūyōdan opened branches in textile factories throughout the 1920s, effectively creating female branches of what had previously been an all-male rural youth group. By 1929 the Shūyōdan had opened retreats exclusively for women that proposed the same mission and consisted of essentially the same activities that the earlier all-male retreats had offered. It was not so much in the fundamental organization of the Shūyōdan as in the way Shūyōdan strategies were adopted in conjunction with other programs in the textile factories of early Shōwa Japan that a particular gendering of labor and of citizenship began to emerge.

INDUSTRIAL MANAGEMENT, THE SHŪYŌDAN, AND THE GENDERING OF NATIONAL CITIZEN-WORKERS

In 1927, Uno Riemon, founder of the Industrial Education Association (Kōgyō Kyōikukai) and renowned consultant on industrial relations, published one volume of his book series on model factories based on his visit to Tōyō Spinning's Himeji factory earlier that year. He had been invited as one of over two hundred special guests to attend the opening ceremony for the factory's new Shūyōdan branch organization. So impressed was Uno with the training program of the Shūyōdan that operated at this site that he titled his lengthy manuscript *Kan'ai no reika ni kagayaku mohan kōjō: Tōyō Bōseki Himeji kōjō* (Tōyō Spinning Himeji Factory: A Model Factory where the Divine Light of Love and Sweat Shines Brightly).

Born in 1875, the son of a rural doctor in Shiga Prefecture, Uno Riemon enjoyed only a modest formal education and as a young adult trained himself in literature and economics. He began writing for a magazine aimed at worker education in Osaka in 1901 and while there began the investigative factory inspections to major textile companies like Kanegafuchi Spinning for which he would become famous. Four years after beginning his journalism job, Uno returned home to help his mother who had become ill after the death of her husband. Uno and his younger sisters all worked as factory hands to support the family during this period, and as a result of exposure in the cotton-spinning mill where they worked, both his sisters contracted tuberculosis from which they died a short time later.

Having experienced firsthand the life of a factory worker, and having lost his sisters to the disease that infected so many women who worked in cotton- and silk-spinning mills, Uno only deepened his commitment to the field of labor reform and worker education—while in politics he favored compassion and conciliation rather than agitation and union activism.[62] He returned to the publishing world and by 1909 had founded the Industrial Education Association, an influential publishing and management consulting organization. In 1923 at the height of his career, he joined the Japanese delegation to the ILO as its labor representative.[63]

Uno is an important figure in the history of labor-management relations, not only for the impact his writings had among industrialists, but because he envisioned a form of labor-management relations unique to Japan, rooted in the particularities of what he saw as the Japanese national essence that supposedly made Japanese workers more docile and obedient than their Western counterparts. In order to capitalize on these national traits, Uno sought to devise a method of labor management that treated workers in their entire life-environment and not simply on the shop floor.[64] Uno believed, according to historian Sugihara Kaoru, that because most female factory workers lived in dormitories that could be monitored constantly, "therefore there existed the possibility of management intervention in the pattern of their whole lives, not just during working hours but all the time."[65] In the Shūyōdan slogan of "love and sweat," he believed he had found a most appropriate form of *shūyō* training for workers—especially women—who lived collectively in factory dormitories.[66]

But Uno was also a nationalist, and in the Shūyōdan agenda he saw the perfect combination of management and national interests. Not only could the principles of "love and sweat" be taught and applied with the utmost rigor and to the greatest effect to highly monitored female factory workers resident in dormitories, but those principles were part of a program that took the *kokutai,* or "national polity," as central to its philosophy.

When Uno received an invitation, along with over two hundred other specially invited guests, to attend the opening ceremonies for the Tōyō Spinning Himeji factory's new Shūyōdan branch in 1927, he suspected immediately that the trip might prove valuable to his labor-management consulting business. The new branch had come about through the efforts of a twenty-one-year-old *sewagakari* (a female manager who oversaw or "cared for" female workers) at the plant named Okumura Kiyoko. Okumura had attended the first Shūyōdan Hyōgo Prefecture women's training course two years earlier and began to implement some of the organization's practices—such as calisthenics and formal morning and evening expressions of gratitude (*rei*)—among the women and girls who worked under her supervision. Managers at the factory apparently liked what they saw and invited the Shūyōdan in to start a branch.[67] Although Uno had never heard of the Shūyōdan before, he eagerly boarded an express train to Himeji from Osaka. The consummate modernist when it came to all sorts of technology, not just industrial, Uno pulled out the camera he usually carried with him once he arrived and began taking pictures of the day's events.[68]

The afternoon began with a procession of invited guests onto the grounds located inside the walls of the factory complex. Uno joined Shūyōdan founder Hasunuma Monzō, a representative of the organization's president Hiranuma Kiichirō (who could not attend), and the president of Tōyō Spinning in a special viewing area shaded from the April sunshine. After all the guests had assembled facing the neat rows of nearly two thousand newly inducted Shūyōdan members—nearly all of them women and girls—a twenty-minute program of national citizens' calisthenics began. Male Shūyōdan leaders who had come to Himeji from the *honbu*, or "headquarters," for the clearly rehearsed event stood in front of each column of women workers. Dressed in white shirts, dark pants, and white *hachimaki* headbands, they led the women in their white aprons in a military-like drill of warm-ups and abdominal and aerobic exercises (figure 3).[69]

At precisely four thirty the calisthenics program ended and Uno and his colleagues were directed to a large building to observe *bika sagyō*, or "beautification work." In the "great hallway" of one of the company's large dormitory buildings, one thousand female factory workers (according to Uno's estimate) crouched on hands and knees in rows of five, moving up and down the hallway, singing the Shūyōdan song, and cleaning the floors with the dust rags they held firmly in both hands (figure 4). This exercise continued for half an hour, during which time Uno snapped photographs of the women's work from different angles. The visitors—impressed both with the discipline of the young women and the brightness with which the wooden floors shone after their cleaning—adjourned for dinner promptly at five o'clock.

The opening ceremony itself, held after the preliminary exercises and

Figure 3. All of the nearly four thousand employees of Tōyō Spinning's Himeji factory take part in national citizens' calisthenics as part of a Shūyōdan ceremony. The leaders of each column of workers are men, dressed in white shirts, dark pants, and *hachimaki* headbands. Behind each male leader, columns of female workers over one hundred deep wear factory uniforms consisting of dark work dresses with white aprons and caps and obediently follow the drills being shouted from the podium at the front of the yard. Originally from Uno Riemon, *Kan'ai no reika ni kagayaku mohan kōjō Tōyō Bōseki Himeji kōjō* (Osaka: Kōgyō Kyōikukai shuppanbu, 1927); reprinted in Hazama Hiroshi, ed., *Nihon rōmu kanrishi shiryōshū, dai-2-ki, dai-9-kan: Uno Riemon chosakusen; Mohan kōjōshū* (Tokyo: Gozandō shoten, 1989). Courtesy of Gozandō shoten.

the guest dinner had finished at five-thirty, included remarks from the head of the new Himeji factory branch of the Shūyōdan; the singing of the "national song" by all in attendance (presumably the *Kimi ga yo*, the unofficial national anthem of Japan); a special reading of the Imperial Rescript on Education, various announcements and congratulatory addresses from the group leader (*danchō*), the company president, and invited guests; a recitation of the Shūyōdan oath; and finally, the singing in unison of the Shūyōdan song.[70]

Uno described with complete approval what he termed the thorough "Shūyōdanization" of workers at Tōyō Spinning's Himeji factory. Shūyōdan programs at Himeji complemented other programs already in place, including special facilities for mothers and their children; a "developmental education" program that included lessons in ethics, company

Figure 4. "Beautification work," otherwise known as the "dust-rag dance," performed by dormitory residents employed at Tōyō Spinning's Himeji factory. Originally from Uno Riemon, *Kan'ai no reika ni kagayaku mohan kōjō Tōyō Bōseki Himeji kōjō* (Osaka: Kōgyō Kyōikukai shuppanbu, 1927); reprinted in Hazama Hiroshi, ed., *Nihon rōmu kanrishi shiryōshū, dai-2-ki, dai-9-kan: Uno Riemon chosakusen; Mohan kōjōshū* (Tokyo: Gozandō shoten, 1989). Courtesy of Gozandō shoten.

history, factory organization, safety education, and "the meaning of life;" a "housewife development" program where women workers took lessons in a special room modeled on a typical family kitchen; and a factory poster campaign for which the company hired a cartoonist to draw posters promoting frugality, cooperation, and self-cultivation (figure 5).[71]

The gendered effects of cultivation training concerned Uno in one area in particular: while he completely approved of national citizens' calisthenics for both men and women, exercise (*undō*) more generally was especially critical for male factory workers. In factories that only employed a small number of male operatives who were mixed in with a large female population (as was the case in most large textile concerns), those men ran the risk of becoming women (*joseika suru*) and losing their manliness (*otoko-rashisa*). Declaring that "exercise is the fire that forges personality [*jinkaku*]," Uno warned that "dangerous beliefs, unhealthy thoughts, and illicit sexual desires are only the product of youth who hate sports [*undō*]" and praised companies like Tōyō Spinning for

Figure 5. A poster promoting self-cultivation that would have been displayed in the dormitory or cafeteria buildings at the Tōyō Spinning Himeji factory. The text reads, from the upper right: "Shuyō / You eat three meals a day without fail / But try to eat a side of good books too! / Otherwise you'll become a malformed person." And on the bottom: "Open wide and eat up! / The same is true for boys." The title of the book showing from the bowl is *Reigi sahō* (Etiquette). Originally from Uno Riemon, *Kan'ai no reika ni kagayaku mohan kōjō Tōyō Bōseki Himeji kōjō* (Osaka: Kōgyō Kyōikukai shuppanbu, 1927); reprinted in Hazama Hiroshi, ed., *Nihon rōmu kanrishi shiryōshū, dai-2-ki, dai-9-kan: Uno Riemon chosakusen; Mohan kōjōshū* (Tokyo: Gozandō shoten, 1989). Courtesy of Gozandō shoten.

raising the funds to offer such activities as baseball, winter skiing, and horseback riding to their male employees.[72]

For women, however, Uno believed that the dust-rag dance (*zōkin dansu*) in conjunction with national citizens' calisthenics (*kokumin taisō*) offered much more appropriate forms of exercise. The dust-rag dance seems to have encompassed three elements of *shūyō* for women that Uno highly approved. First, as physical exercise its form was purely feminine, without any of the masculine hardness Uno associated with the sports he advocated for male workers. Second, it replicated a domestic activity—that of scrubbing the floors of a home—in which Uno believed all female workers should be given training. He saw female factory workers strictly as temporary labor, most of whom would return to the countryside to marry "after two or three years." As such, they needed training in the kinds of domestic activities that would help them to become engaged to be married and to enter successfully into their husband's family with all the skills required of a household manager and homemaker. Third, the dust-rag dance embodied the essence of the Shūyōdan motto of "love and sweat," requiring selfless dedication in the face of painful (and seemingly pointless) collective labor. This particular activity—associated with the Shūyōdan and undertaken only by factory women who were also dormitory residents—produced in a particularly feminized form the same ascetic ritual purification for women as did the practice of *misogi* water ablution for male members of the Shūyōdan.

What most historians of Japanese labor who have studied Uno as an influential promoter of paternalist policies overlook is that his philosophy of labor-management relations based on unique national traits was devised and applied almost exclusively using female textile labor as a model. Further, Uno's holistic management approach relied from the beginning on the same notions of bodily discipline—including supplemental education, ritualized calisthenics, and moral training—that virtually all the major textile companies would adopt in the wake of the abolition of night work and the intensification of rationalization in 1929. In promoting the use of cultivation groups such as the Shūyōdan that offered moral training, calisthenics programs, and reading programs to increase literacy, Uno offered a blueprint to textile companies and factory managers of how to rationalize their labor force in ways that addressed more than simply quantitative understandings of a labor market that could be manipulated through layoffs and plant closures. It was in large part because of Uno and his Kyōchōkai colleagues' promotion of the Shūyōdan and organizations like it as a means of promoting labor-management

conciliation, and thus as a way to avert strikes, that so many of their programs flourished in factories from the late 1920s onward.

THE DUST-RAG DANCE AND WOMEN'S OPPOSITION

Cultivation-association programs, then, were designed both to monopolize and manage workers' free time *and* to provide disciplinary training
in the domestic arts and the proper expression of femininity. But the lessons provided by cultivation associations were not always so clear as
managers intended. One silk-reeling worker indicated the contradictory
messages that could be had from cultivation-group training versus company training received on the shop floor.

In an essay titled "Jokō no te" (The Hands of a Female Factory Worker),
which appeared in the leftist women's journal *Hataraku fujin* (Working
Woman) in 1933, Ichikawa Kinuyo explained how the woman worker's
hands, subjected continuously to hot steam and boiling water as they reeled
silk thread, became rough and red and chapped to the point of bleeding:

> There seems to be no end to the cuts on these soft, festering hands that
> look as though they had themselves been boiled. The Shūyōdan teachers
> would often tell us that to allow these treasured hands given us by our par-
> ents to get cut is unfilial. I wonder if this is so. Perhaps it is. When the com-
> muting workers return to their homes in the evening, their parents must
> worry when they see their hands. But even if we try to be careful not to get
> cut while reeling, [the factory managers] are always shouting, "Efficiency!
> Efficiency!"[73]

This passage demonstrates how the various strands of factory rationalization could at times impinge on one another. Here, the rationalization
of *work* (identified by the factory managers' shouts of "Efficiency!")
competes with Shūyōdan efforts to rationalize workers' *lives* through
training and practice in filial piety. The Shūyōdan in this instance aided
the company in maintaining good relations with the families who provided the mills with labor by instilling in employees a sense of moral duty
and filial piety that made it each individual worker's responsibility to
avoid giving her parents cause for worry. The system of moral and civic
discipline, then, not only established guidelines for the proper use of nonwork time, but also shifted—from the companies themselves to their
workers—the onus of demonstrating to families back home the efficacy
of the corporate system of paternalism.

But the Shūyōdan and its methods were not accepted without opposition on the part of the factory women who were forced to join them.

The journal *Rōdō fujin* (Working Woman), the organ of the women's bureau of the national Sōdōmei union, featured over a dozen articles between 1929 and 1933 opposing Shūyōdan activities in the factories as antiunion and antiworker. With titles such as "Shūyōdan o taikōsu" (Opposing the Shūyōdan) and "Shūyōdan no kamen o hage!" (Pull Away the Mask of the Shūyōdan), these submissions written by female union activists used the same terminology factory owners often employed to describe unions—*mashu,* or "evil influence"—in order to describe the activities of the Shūyōdan.[74]

In some places factory branches of the Shūyōdan were called the White Lily Society (and the organization's magazine for women was also named *White Lily*). One unhappy member had the following to say about their purpose:

> Meetings are opened with the following words: "The aim of the Shūyōdan is simply to engender the gracefulness of the white lily." But these are superficial words. Clearly their scheme is actually to make us obedient like sheep and unable to say anything. . . . I believe it is not an exaggeration to say that the Shūyōdan is a poison that seeks to remove the backbone of us workers. At this time when the companies are afraid of the power of the growing numbers of union members, they are posting inside the factories posters that say, "Membership in groups should not be coerced," and they are implicitly prohibiting union organizing. Yet at the same time, openly during work hours, the head of the White Lily Society goes about preaching to our sisters and compelling membership in their society.[75]

Especially in the several months immediately preceding the abolition of night work for women in July 1929, contributors to *Rōdō fujin* complained bitterly about companies' policies of forcing compulsory membership in the Shūyōdan. Union members viewed the Shūyōdan as an organization brought in by the capitalists in order to stem the tide of growing class consciousness among workers, and in internal documents the companies did not hesitate to admit this was true.[76] In the pages of *Rōdō fujin,* formal essays decrying Shūyōdan tactics written by leading union activists and announcements of anti-Shūyōdan agenda items for union meetings sat side by side with poetry submissions such as the following, titled "Shūyōdan o warau" (Laughing at the Shūyōdan):

> The Shūyōdan that deceives the workers
> always nagging "cultivation"
> taking us to a temple
> telling us to become Buddhas
> makes us laugh[77]

In other words, Shūyōdan efforts to instill moral virtue through religious appeals and the organization's practice of taking workers to visit Shintō shrines and Buddhist temples seemed pointless exercises to many workers.

The dust-rag dance in particular elicited the wrath of workers subject to Shūyōdan disciplinary strategies within the factories. Many complained that after a full day of work in the factory, they were then required to perform the *zōkin dansu*, lining up in columns of four and singing the company song as they moved up and down the hallway cleaning the same area for thirty minutes straight. More often than not, such a cleaning ritual would be followed by a rigorous round of national citizens' calisthenics performed to the beat of a taiko drum.[78]

In a 1930 essay the Sōdōmei activist and principal editor of *Rōdō fujin*, Akamatsu Tsuneko, critiqued the factory calisthenics programs so admired by Uno Riemon. Where for some observers such programs fostered "physical education and spiritual training," Akamatsu attributed the "sports fever" in factories to three factors. First, calisthenics programs, she claimed, sought to make workers forget the pain of work life, especially the low wages and intensity of labor. Second, sports distracted workers from thinking about labor unions and the proletarian political movement. And third, sports programs were a way for companies to adopt a human face in the wake of wage cuts and work intensification brought on by industrial rationalization.[79] In other words, for Akamatsu the *shūyō* practices represented by sports and calisthenics programs stood less for the promise of self-cultivation than for the repression of forms of sociality not tied to the communitarian values of the *kyōdōtai*.

Shūyō as promoted by cultivation groups such as the Seinendan, the Shojokai, and the Shūyōdan linked individual cultivation practice to social harmony and dedication to the state. Individuals were to cultivate their own *jinkaku*, or "personality," through rigorous physical activity, spiritual reflection, and acts of mutual cooperation. Improved individuals working through mutual cooperation in their own communities would foster harmony in their villages, cities, and workplaces, and this in turn would promote "the advancement of the imperial state."

Changes in society and the economy after World War I led to an expansion of cultivation groups beyond their original concern with rural male youth to an interest in cities, workers, and women. The 1918 Rice Riots, in which women played a central role, initiated a democratic movement that would last through the 1920s. As heavy industry replaced textiles as the driving force of the industrial economy throughout the 1920s, and as more men entered the industrial workforce, union membership and strikes increased in number. The burgeoning women's movement saw institutional growth through the founding of a (middle-class) women's suffrage group, the New Women's Association, in 1920, and the communist women's Red Wave Society the following year. At the same time, women were moving into clerical and service positions associated with the urban new economy in increasing numbers. These fast-paced changes set the stage for the organization of the Seinendan under government auspices, efforts by the Shojokai to become active in textile factories, and the cooperation of the Shūyōdan with the Kyōchōkai in organizing its first worker training courses.

The Shūyōdan advocated a vision of civic discipline and national allegiance not limited to the *naichi*, or Japanese home islands, which marked the boundaries of metropolitan Japan. Local Shūyōdan branches operated throughout Korea by the 1920s, and the organization celebrated New Year's Day 1933 by opening a Cultivation Hall in the capital of the newly established puppet state of Manchuguo (Manchuria). Shūyōdan activities in Manchuria included educational efforts aimed at settlers to Manchuria from Tamagawa, as well as promotion of the state ideology of *gozoku kyōwa*, or "harmony among the five races" of Japanese, Koreans, Chinese, Manchurians, and Mongolians.[80]

By 1936 Hasunuma Monzō's Shūyōdan claimed two hundred thousand members throughout the Japanese empire and over one thousand local branches.[81] As part of a broader trend of national mobilization that intensified throughout the 1930s and 1940s, Shūyōdan activities exemplified efforts to train and educate textile industry employees both as productive workers and as gendered national subjects—categories increasingly valued by the state as it moved further toward war. Young women were to not only produce the silk and cotton threads for export needed to modernize the economy, but should maintain their ties to the countryside, train themselves in the "womanly arts," and equip themselves to enter the next stage of their development as imperial citizens by becoming dutiful wives and mothers.[82]

CHAPTER 4

Sex, Strikes, and Solidarity

Tōyō Muslin and the Labor Unrest of 1930

In August 1929—exactly one month after the prohibition on night work went into effect—Tatewaki Sadayo opened the Workers' School for Women (Rōdō Jojuku) in the Kameido district of Tokyo. The school would become an important training ground for many women who would take leading roles in a strike at Tōyō Muslin in September of 1930. Just as corporate policies were being redirected toward a focus on individual worker discipline through educational efforts aimed at "cultivation," workers at Tōyō Muslin were similarly realizing that the battle against the forces of capital would involve the intellectual, political, and bodily disciplining of female textile operatives. Female factory workers formulated and deployed a counterdiscourse to the bodily control of workers, sought by company managers as they rationalized the workplace, using some of the same strategies but for different purposes.

The activist and literary work of Tatewaki Sadayo and the proletarian author Nakamoto Takako—two women intellectuals who played key roles in events leading up to the strike—were informed by a modern notion of bodily discipline, constituted partly in response to corporate rationalization policies that sought to train female workers in a physical and spiritual morality based on an ideal of Japanese womanhood. Many of the female workers who took leadership roles in the strike attended the Workers' School for Women, a small school run by teacher and women's labor activist Tatewaki. Tatewaki's school sought to instill in working women a proletarian consciousness, rather than to cultivate the state ideal of "good wife, wise mother." Through her literature and her activism, Nakamoto also worked with the factory workers of Tōyō Muslin in creating and embodying an image of the woman fighter, in contrast to the housewife ideal promoted by corporate rationalization policies.

TATEWAKI SADAYO AND THE WORKERS' SCHOOL FOR WOMEN

Twenty-five-years-old the year she founded the school, Tatewaki Sadayo (1904–90) had been interested in education since her days as a student at Shimane Prefectural Normal School for Girls and had been engaged in left-wing politics and activism since abandoning her native Shimane for Tokyo in 1924. In lieu of continuing her formal education in Tokyo, she commuted regularly to a library in Ueno where she read voraciously, supporting herself by working in a tofu seller's shop. She met Orimoto Akira—a young student and labor activist who introduced her to the writings of Karl Marx—while working at a beer hall in Hongo, the area of Tokyo home to Tokyo Imperial University and many of its radical male students.[1] They married in 1925 and moved together to the worker enclave of Kameido, where Tatewaki dedicated herself to labor activism and the women factory workers of Tokyo.[2]

Tatewaki wasted no time in taking on leadership roles within the workers' movement. Her husband became a member of the "moderate" legal proletarian party, the Japan Labor-Farmer Party (Nihon Rōnōtō), and Sadayo was a founding member and later secretary of the All-Japan Women's Federation (Zenkoku Fujin Dōmei). When that organization merged with the more radical Proletarian Women's League (Musan Fujin Renmei) to form the Proletarian Women's Federation (Musan Fujin Dōmei) in 1929, Tatewaki, along with Sakai Magara (the daughter of the well-known socialist activist and writer Sakai Toshihiko), stood out as one of its most prominent figures.[3]

It was during this time, while a leader of the All-Japan Women's Federation, that Tatewaki more than likely got the idea for starting her school for women workers that would prove so influential during the Tōyō Muslin strike. Before moving to Kameido she had occasion to visit the Tokyo Imperial University Settlement House—a student-led project that had evolved out of postearthquake relief work and that sponsored one of the most successful labor schools in Japan at the time. Her husband, Orimoto Akira, had been involved with the radical student group Shinjinkai that had founded the settlement house in 1924, a year after the Great Kantō Earthquake.[4] The settlement house's labor school announced its mission with the slogan, "Learning is the font and foundation of all action." Its curriculum included lectures in political and economic theory, international social movement history, and the principles of trade unionism. A year after it opened in September 1924, the school boasted fifty-six students.[5]

As someone trained in education and in the process of developing a personal understanding of the workers' movement and her own place in it, Tatewaki was undoubtedly impressed by what she saw at the settlement house.[6] But perhaps just as important in influencing the development of the Workers' School for Women was the opening in January 1928 of the Kyōai Jojuku (Mutual Friendship School for Women) in Gunma Prefecture. The Kyōai Jojuku's founding resulted from a joint effort on the part of the All Japan Women's Federation and the Japan Labor-Farmer Party with which the federation was affiliated. Acting in her role as a representative from the Women's Federation, Tatewaki attended the school's opening ceremony on January 5, 1928, about which a notice appeared in the January newsletter of the federation announcing that "Mr. Fuju [Junsaburō] will head the school, which will have as its objective the provision of work-related supplementary education to proletarian women, as well as the imparting of a proletarian class consciousness."[7]

The Kyōai Jojuku was the first facility of its kind dedicated to providing work-related supplementary education (*hoshū kyōiku*) and training for women workers and to developing in female students a proletarian consciousness. Tatewaki's intimate involvement with the beginnings of the Kyōai Jojuku gave her first-hand experience with an educational project that spoke to the class politics she had begun to espouse since first moving to Tokyo.

The Kyōai Jojuku, however, was not the first educational institution in Japan with the objective of imparting a proletarian consciousness, although it was the first established exclusively for women. Japan's first labor school had opened its doors in Tokyo in 1911, under the leadership of Suzuki Bunji. The Japan Labor School (Nihon Rōdō Gakkō) boasted a faculty made up of the leading left and liberal thinkers of the day, including socialist and birth-control advocate Abe Isō, political scientist Yoshino Sakuzō, labor leader Suzuki Bunji, prominent Christian and labor activist Kagawa Toyohiko, and socialist leader Katayama Sen. Its earliest students became the nucleus of one of Japan's earliest labor unions, the Friendly Society (Yūaikai), which Suzuki founded with a speech on "rights and obligations" given at the school.[8]

After the Japan Labor School's founding, the greatest surge in labor school activity occurred in 1924, as proletarian parties prepared for the first general election to be held the following year. In a 1925 report, the Tokyo Social Bureau listed eighteen labor schools in Japan proper and another twenty-two in the annexed colony of Korea. These schools reflected a wide range of political purposes and affiliations. Some, such as the Tokyo City Labor Training Association sponsored by the Social Bureau (whose students included two Tōyō Muslin employees out of forty-five in 1924) focused on social policy–style adult education, including courses in social ethics and Japanese literature. Others, such as the Kyoto Labor School (Kyōto Rōdō Gakkō) founded by the proletarian writer and communist activist Taniguchi Zentarō, sought to impart knowledge relevant to the labor movement and thus to train future union leaders. The curriculum of the Kyoto Labor School included courses in capitalist economics, sociology, law, labor movement history, the Japanese constitution, and Esperanto.[9] Enrollment in most of these schools was open to women as long as they were union members or workers in nonunion factories, but the number of female students was relatively low. Since most of these schools experienced a high drop-out rate, it is difficult to tell whether many of the women who joined such schools ever ended up finishing their course of study.[10]

In this context, the founding of the Kyōai Jojuku in 1928 under the auspices of the All-Japan Women's Federation and the Japan Labor-Farmer Party marked an important acknowledgement on the part of organized labor that the disciplining of female factory labor should not be left solely in the hands of company managers and cultivation groups. In fact, the founding of the school had its basis in a struggle with the local Shojokai, eighty-three of whose members were reported to have defected from the organization en masse to become students in the Kyōai Jojuku as a result of organizing efforts on the part of the Kyōdo branch of the Japan Labor-Farmer Party.[11] This first women's labor school, then, marked the mobilization of the left against the cultivation practices that had become nearly ubiquitous in large textile concerns employing mostly women. The opening of Tatewaki's Workers' School for Women the following year was even more remarkable for having been inspired, funded, staffed, and run completely by women living and working in Kameido and for the pivotal role it would play in the unfolding of the strike at Tōyō Muslin.

Operating without even a blackboard or proper desks, the Workers' School for Women got its start in a modest building rented as Tatewaki and her husband's living quarters in the part of Tokyo's Kameido area known as Muslin Alley (Mosurin Yokochō), home to many of Tōyō Muslin's workers as well as workers from Tokyo Muslin, which also had factories in Kameido. With Tatewaki as its director and an all-female cooperative board consisting of a secretary, a treasurer, and eight founding members, the school offered a "regular course" where students read political-economy and social-science tracts as well as courses in sewing Western and Japanese-style clothing, embroidery, and cooking that were intended to help students financially rather than mold them into ideal future housewives. According to Tatewaki's later recollections, the idea for opening the Workers' School for Women began when Kobayashi Tane, a Tōyō Muslin factory worker with whom Tatewaki sat on the Educational Publishing Committee of the Japan Spinning and Weaving Labor Union (Nihon Bōshoku Rōdō Kumiai), suggested that the older woman open a *juku* (school), since Kobayashi was interested in "studying society" and felt that Tatewaki could offer such teaching.[12] Kobayashi and Tatewaki gathered female workers from Tōyō Muslin and nearby Tokyo Muslin to be the first students at the school.

The school was part of what Dean Kinzley has identified as the "push for social education" during the early years of Shōwa—a movement to "awaken" the masses to reformist goals, "whether those goals were the implementation of true democracy or the launching of revolution."[13] Tatewaki hoped to provide factory workers with a socialist education, and training in practical domestic skills. The attention to domestic training came from the desires of the workers themselves, who, according to Tatewaki, "said they just wanted to do things that people do [*ningen no suru koto o yaritaitte*]."[14] That is, female workers wanted the skills that would make them good wives and mothers in the future and that would help them economically in the present. Young women workers and their families continued to be enticed by company-sponsored educational amenities like those offered by Kanebō in the 1920s, believing such education offered opportunities for gaining the cultural capital not always available in their rural environments. Tatewaki recognized that education in the domestic arts was a significant element in female workers' understanding of their own status—that is, their "individual moral worth"—the recognition of which T. C. Smith has noted was a major factor in labor agitation during this period.[15]

Still, the official announcement of the school's opening made clear that feminist working-class politics, and not visions of domesticity or morality based on the principle of obedience to patriarch and nation, motivated the school's founders: "The time has come for our founding of this Workers' School for Women to compensate for the lack of educational opportunities available to working women. It is born with the sole mission of cultivating women fighters [fujin tōshi]."[16]

A comparison of the curricula of the company-sponsored cultivation groups and Tatewaki's Workers' School for Women shows how the rhetoric of self-improvement and of a particularly feminine morality were bent to different purposes in each case. Where corporate programs stressed shūyō, or "cultivation," Tatewaki offered to her students keimō, or "enlightenment"—a term invested with both the Buddhist meaning of an acquisition of spiritual truth and the more Western notion of rigorous scientific study leading to the acquisition of knowledge-truth from which socialist thought had been born. Originally a slogan of Meiji intellectuals and statesmen such as Fukuzawa Yūkichi, Mori Arinori, and Nishi Amane, by the Taishō and early Shōwa years individuals and groups with a variety of political inclinations had come to invoke keimō as a sign of collective progress.[17] By 1919 Hiratsuka Raichō, the founder of the Meiji women's literary journal Seitō (Bluestockings) could call for a woman leader from the intellectual class to lead Japan's "oppressed" female factory workers in an "enlightenment movement" (keimō undō) that would form the basis for a women's labor movement.[18] Tatewaki's version of enlightenment sought truth in Marxist and women's rights principles, rather than ideologies of family and nation. Where the cultivation groups offered reading lessons using texts with stories of filial piety, Tatewaki assigned readings from Puroretaria keizaigaku (Proletarian Economics), a book edited by Japan Communist Party founder Yamakawa Hitoshi, and other socialist texts with titles such as Fujin to rōdō kumiai (Women and Labor Unions), Fujin undō tōmen no shōmondai (Urgent Problems Facing the Women's Movement), and her own small book, Rōdō fujin mondai (The Working Woman Problem).[19]

No other workers' school had so linked a proletarian and a feminist consciousness and dedicated itself to the production of women fighters. Information regarding the curriculum of the Kyōai Jojuku that got its start a year before Tatewaki founded the Workers' School for Women is not available. However, given that the leadership of the Kyōai Jojuku was dominated by communist men with a class agenda that viewed gender issues as strategically important but secondary to the cause of proletarian revolution, it is probably safe to surmise that Tatewaki's was the first labor school to offer a curriculum that spoke directly to the needs of working women, rather than the needs of a working class that happened to include women.[20] Further, where cultivation groups and company schools had offered sewing and cooking classes in order to turn their workers (eventually) into good wives and wise mothers, the Workers' School for Women included sewing, knitting, and handicrafts as a matter of practical economics. Tatewaki's pedagogy tied the real needs of the school's students for extra income and to be able to save money by, for example, sewing their own clothes, to Marxist theories of capitalist exploitation and feminist readings on the conditions of working-class women. By 1930 the school had indeed succeeded in cultivating women fighters and shifting the focus of *shūyō* from the state and companies to individual and class interests, providing the leadership for the September strike at Tōyō Muslin that year.

NAKAMOTO TAKAKO AND MUSLIN ALLEY

In her work as a labor activist and intellectual in Kameido, Tatewaki was joined by the proletarian writer Nakamoto Takako (1903–91), who documented the Tōyō Muslin strike in a number of short stories and novels published in magazines during the 1930s and in book form after the war. Even in her earliest days of writing about proletarian issues, Nakamoto emphasized the necessity of developing among female factory workers a class-consciousness that could be mobilized against the forces of capital through strikes and worker actions. Just as Tatewaki in her Workers' School for Women hoped to provide *keimō,* or "enlightenment," through an educational curriculum combining practical training and political theory, Nakamoto sought to reveal a process of enlightenment among women workers in her fiction, which would in turn contribute to the development of political consciousness among her readership. Nakamoto was a financial supporter and a frequent visitor to the Workers' School for Women and considered its founder an important friend and ally in the struggle for the rights of women workers. She observed the events of the February 1930 Tōyō Muslin strike firsthand and made them the subject of her longest work of fiction, *Mosurin Yokochō* (Muslin Alley) which she published in 1950.

Like Tatewaki, Nakamoto came to Tokyo to work and study after graduating from a girls' higher school and working for a time as a teacher in her home prefecture of Yamaguchi. She came from a family she herself described as "petit bourgeois": her father taught physical education at a middle school before being wounded in the Russo-Japanese War of 1904–1905. By early 1929 she had begun publishing her stories in the literary journal *Nyonin geijutsu* (Women's Arts), gaining early recognition for "Suzumushi no mesu" (The Female Bell Cricket), which shocked many for its frank sexual nature.[21] That story, which explored some of the harsher realities of sexual desire as manifest through the poverty of capitalism, established themes that would persist in her writings throughout her career.

"The Female Bell Cricket" marked Nakamoto as a follower of the Shinkankaku (New Sensationalist) school of writers, who drew on modernist forms and rejected more conventional expressions of realist representation. But even as "The Female Bell Cricket" provided her first taste of critical success, Nakamoto abandoned what she would later refer to as "the style of the petit bourgeois Shinkankaku school," in order to follow the proletarian movement. Work by the well-known proletarian authors Tokunaga Sunao, whose *Taiyō no nai machi* (Sunless Streets) documented a Tokyo printing press strike, and Kobayashi Takiji, whose novel *Kani kōsen* (The Factory Ship) is generally considered one of the most important pieces of literature to emerge from the short-lived proletarian literature movement, profoundly influenced Nakamoto's conception of the form and purpose of literature.[22] In addition to an insistence on taking the valor of the working classes under the degradation of the capitalist system as the central theme for all proletarian literature, the literary method Kobayashi espoused included forgoing the individual heroes or leading characters and the descriptions of psychology and character central to most fictional writing of the day, and instead focusing on a group of laborers who themselves formed a "collective hero."[23] Nakamoto's concerns with class analysis led her to adopt the part of this method that eschewed focus on a central protagonist, while her insistence on reading the gendered meanings of capitalist dynamics and the experiences of working-class women led to a greater attentiveness to character development than Kobayashi's method would permit. In other words, even after dedicating herself to proletarian literature, Nakamoto never entirely abandoned the individualism so central to Shinkankaku School writing.

After her first published piece appeared in the journal *Nyonin geijutsu* in 1929, Nakamoto increasingly felt compelled to write realistic fiction that would both reflect and inspire the working women whom she took as both object, and increasingly, as her intended audience. Her writings, she hoped, would point the way toward a worker consciousness that social commentators such as Hosoi Wakizō found hopelessly lacking in the young, mostly illiterate women who worked in the textile mills. The depiction of the lives of women in the textile mills presented in Hosoi's *Jokō aishi* (The Sorrowful History of Female Factory Workers), which Nakamoto read soon after its publication in 1925, prompted her to move to Kameido in October 1929 to live among the workers whose sufferings and struggles she hoped to depict in her writing.[24] Hosoi was more concerned with improving working conditions for women so that they might successfully complete their factory service and return home to fulfill their obligations as good wives and wise mothers.[25] Nakamoto saw no such radical distinction between a woman's present (as a worker) and her future (not necessarily preordained as wife and mother), but rather viewed working women's and working-class women's lives as bound together by their common struggles for survival within an oppressive capitalist system. It was these common struggles she hoped to experience firsthand by moving to Kameido.

In the way Nakamoto attributed the potential for class consciousness and radicalism to women workers, she differed not only from Hosoi and his attempt to educate the general reading public (rather than the workers themselves), but also from the approach of many of her male contemporaries in the proletarian literature movement. As Miriam Silverberg has argued, men such as the poet Nakano Shigeharu—also highly influenced by Hosoi's 1925 book—often failed to attribute any potential for class consciousness to the female textile workers about whom they wrote. For Nakano, "factory girls remain a theoretical abstraction used to illustrate a concept . . . of the process of reproduction of a preconscious class."[26] But Nakamoto sought to re-create recognizable characters and situations drawn from the experiences she observed among female factory workers that could serve as models for what she saw as the burgeoning class consciousness of the workers of Kameido.

The passion with which such a large number of workers—most of them young women who had never before belonged to a union or participated in a labor action—fought during the first Tōyō Muslin strike of 1930 that took place in February inaugurated an intense period of union organizing in which Nakamoto took part. For her efforts, she was arrested in February of 1930 along with several women workers also active in organizing for the Japan Communist Party–affiliated union known as Zenkyō (Nihon Rōdō Kumiai Zenkoku Kyōgikai, or the National Conference of Japanese Labor Unions) and held for thirty-one days at the Kameido jail.[27] Shortly after her release, Nakamoto became a "housekeeper" for party central-committee member Iwao Katei on orders from the Japan Communist Party (JCP) leadership.

The housekeeper system put into place by the JCP involved women

with political ties to the party who were recruited to live with and provide sexual as well as domestic services to party men.[28] JCP agitprop director Yamashita Heiji explained the housekeeper system in a 1934 document (written after he had "converted," or renounced communism), in
which he described the need for a communist woman to live with active
communist party members in order to give the appearance of an ordinary
married couple, so as not to arouse suspicion among neighbors. House-
keepers were to stay at home to protect important party-related documents and materials while the male party member went out to work or
to engage in party business or activities. A crucial function of the housekeeper was to be able to determine when a party member had been arrested (by his failure to return home by a certain hour) and to then re-
move all party-related materials to a secure location.[29]

After living with Iwao for about forty days in the summer of 1930,
Nakamoto became JCP chairman Tanaka Seigen's housekeeper until her
second arrest on July 14. First brought to the Fuchū police station,
Nakamoto was then transferred to the Ueno/Takinaka station, where she
was subject to brutal torture that ultimately led to her release on bail
after a prison physician's diagnosis of a nervous disorder (seishinbyō).
She continued her union activities underground, but was finally arrested
yet again for an infraction of the Peace Preservation Law and sentenced
to four years hard labor. She finished a reduced term and was set free,
but did not become involved in leftist writing or politics again until after
the war.[30]

Nakamoto's rendering of the February 1930 Tōyō Muslin strike—
the precursor to the longer and more violent strike that began seven
months later in September—in her novel *Muslin Alley* offers a depiction of the tumultuous events consonant with the many other historical and journalistic records of the strike. Employing a style part fictional, part autobiographical, and part documentary, she sometimes
barely changed the names of her characters from those of the real-life
people they depicted. For example, in the novel the name of Japan Justice League (Nippon Seigidan) leader Sakai Eizō, who mediated the
strike settlement, becomes "Sakai Teizō," while Kobayashi Tane, the
real-life Tōyō Muslin worker who prompted Tatewaki to start up a
school for female workers, becomes "Kobayashi Ine." Uchiyama Chi-
tose, a women's college graduate and dormitory supervisor at the factory who led a communist cell and organized the Tōyō Muslin branch
of Zenkyō, becomes "Komiyama Chigako." And while the novel has
no clear protagonist—in keeping with one of the premises of

Kobayashi Takiji's vision of proletarian literature—one of the central characters is a proletarian writer named Takagi Tamie, based on Nakamoto herself.

Nakamoto used third-person narration throughout *Muslin Alley* as part of this strategy to deemphasize individual in favor of collective actions and identifications. But the use of third person also served to indicate her own ambivalent position as an intellectual, a Marxist, a supporter of the Kameido workers, but not one who could claim a proletarian identity. Never a worker herself, she had tried but failed to get herself hired at the factory in an effort to truly experience the factory worker's life that she attempted to represent in her fiction. In *Muslin Alley* the character Takagi Tamie, a writer who has come to Kameido to live and work with women workers, speaks of knowing that "intellectuals have the work of the intelligentsia" (*interi ni wa interi no shigoto wa aru*), but more than anything she really wants to "know" the female factory workers and their world.[31] Tamie seems bent on finding some kind of authenticity to lend power and legitimacy to her work as an activist writer. Similarly, Nakamoto sought to experience first-hand the life of the female factory worker. As she put it in her autobiography:

> I would go to the worker enclave, and if possible, I would get a job at the factory. By simply watching from the side without getting a job, I would not be able to adequately grasp the true nature of the workers' environment and its social and class connections. The factory is where the working class and the capitalist class are daily locked in struggle. How do exploitation and oppression play out here? I wanted to see with my own eyes, hear with my ears, and experience this directly through my skin and through my muscles.[32]

Only then, she believed, through what Sherry Ortner has described as an "embodied ethnographic stance," could she hope to succeed as an artist and a revolutionary. Such an ethnographic stance required the use of the self as an "instrument of knowing" that was at once intellectual, moral, and spatial.[33] As a writer and a communist—an intellectual and an activist—Nakamato believed that only by living among the women workers of Muslin Alley, and trying to become one of them as much as possible, could she truly understand their sufferings and their world.

Nakamoto's text includes a reading of bodies employing the rhetoric of the generalized social fear of sexual depravity that associated factory workers with prostitution. Her text works to resituate the causes of that fear and to offer an alternative to the disciplinary strategy posited by company educational policies. Early on in the novel, a former factory worker named Kimura Fuyu, whose whereabouts had become unknown, is discovered working in a brothel by one of the male workers who frequents the place. Word of Fuyu's fate spreads among her former coworkers, one of whom—named Kiyo—finds herself disheartened thinking about her "fallen" friend. As Kiyo goes back to her home in Yokochō, near the Kameido branch office of the Labor Union League and across the street from a house sporting an announcement board for the Renters' League (Nakamoto's work is full of the daily-life reminders of the power of worker solidarity), she reflects that even though Fuyu had been one of the hardest workers in the factory, she could only make about thirty yen a month—barely enough to get by on.[34] Nakamoto thus reverses the logic whereby factory workers are seen as inherently susceptible to sexual depravity and instead offers an alternative to the company's conclusion that only constant supervision and surveillance would keep them from prostitution. She argues implicitly that higher wages will do more to keep female factory workers from prostitution than the rigors of company-sponsored discipline.

Nakamoto's analysis provides a contrast to that of Hosoi Wakizō, her literary hero, who tried to rescue the female factory workers from accusations of inherent corruptibility without ever addressing the economic issues involved in prostitution. In *Jokō aishi,* Hosoi claims that factory women fall into prostitution not because they are depraved (as their employers argue), but because the men around them are depraved. As he puts it, "Girls are kidnapped by recruiters and led astray by rakish male operatives."[35] Nakamoto's perhaps less heroic if equally tragic depiction of young women leaving the factories to go into prostitution suggests more agency on the part of the women themselves, but sees that agency circumscribed by economic and social conditions outside their control.

Bodily discipline for Nakamoto meant the dedication of intellectual and physical resources to the local labor union, the woman's movement, and the Communist Party, rather than strict adherence to industrial time and allegiance to company and nation. Her novel abounds with descriptions of the physical battles between workers on the one hand, and the police and the Justice League gangs set upon them by the company, offering a vision of bodies engaged in protest that provides a counterpoint to the regimented calisthenics programs mandated by the company.

During the course of the novel, the character Kiyo gradually grows from a shy, unsure young working woman to a confident leader of the workers' movement. In several key scenes, Kiyo forces herself to speak, locating her strength in her body. Her body, as she puts it, is not her own, but belongs to all workers: "At the meeting on the twenty-fifth, Kiyo had said what she had wanted to say for a long time. Her chest felt as though it had been washed clean, and her heart was at ease. She had gained freedom and courage as though she had just peeled away an outer skin in which she had been wrapped. And the body that shone radiantly after that outer skin had been peeled away did not belong solely to her, she thought, but to all female factory workers—to all workers."[36] The progression Nakamoto posits whereby Kiyo first comes into her own as an individual, then moves to a state of collective consciousness within her immediate environment, and finally sees her part in the collectivity—defined as an (international) movement of workers—performs the inverse operation from company rationalization policies that sought to individuate bodies in order to control their labor. In her fiction, Nakamoto used Kiyo to represent those experiences specific to factory workers as women, while ultimately identifying Kiyo as a worker—and even as the workers' movement itself.[37]

THE TŌYŌ MUSLIN STRIKE OF 1930

The violent actions at Tōyō Muslin in 1930 were part of an era of labor unrest in Japan unprecedented in intensity, breadth, and militancy.[38] The Tōyō Muslin strike was part of a regional and national trend that saw a sudden increase in labor activity during a recessionary period in which companies moved to close plants, lay off workers, cut wages, and implement other policies to improve efficiency and cut costs. This militancy came in large part as a result of rationalization policies and recessionary trends in the textile industry that saw a substantial deterioration in working conditions, including wage cuts and layoffs, throughout the 1920s. Economic historian Shirai Taishirō marks the beginning of this militant trend as 1928.[39] The July 1, 1929, abolition of night work in the textile industry further contributed to the policies of retrenchment and downsizing that played such a prominent role in mobilizing female labor against the companies.

In the case of the cotton textile industry, a process of rationalization began at the turn of the century with mergers and combinations that saw the five largest textile concerns swallow up sixteen smaller companies among them and double their spindlage in a period of less than ten years.[40] By 1928 the country had slipped into a significant recession, prompting textile manufacturers to intensify rationalizing efforts by continuing to move capital and jobs to semicolonial China and by implementing wage cuts and plant closures in Japan.[41] The Great Depression, which began in the United States with the stock market crash of 1929, combined with the Japanese government's decision to return to the gold standard, caused severe deflation in Japan by 1930. The rapid onset of this worldwide economic crisis caused textile companies in Japan to lay off workers and cut wages. With the price of cotton yarn on a downward spiral, Kanebō announced wage cuts of 23 percent, and other cotton-spinning companies followed with cuts of their own.[42] By the time of the onset of the depression, major textile concerns such as Tōyō Muslin, Fuji Gas Spinning in Kawasaki, and Kanegafuchi Spinning in Osaka experienced major labor disturbances as a result of rationalization efforts that had taken as their object first the spheres of capital and technology, and second the individual worker bodies that became the focus of new disciplinary strategies after the abolition of night work in 1929 and that intensified after 1930.

The Nankatsu (an abbreviation for Minami Katsushika) region of Tokyo, where Tōyō Muslin's main factories were located, was a major industrial hub and the site of some of the most important labor activism in the prewar period. In addition to textile concerns, Nankatsu was home to the Ishikawajima Shipyard, Ōshima Steel, Hirofuji Shoemaking, Sakurai Papermaking, Dai'ichi Pharmaceuticals, and the Minami Katsushika Steamship Company, to name only a few of the larger enterprises that experienced labor disputes during this period.[43]

In 1930 Tōyō Muslin operated four factories in the Kameido district of the greater Nankatsu region, with additional factories in neighboring Nerima Ward and in Shizuoka Prefecture. Kameido had only seven years earlier become associated in the public mind with union activity, violence, and state repression in a tragic event known as the Kameido Incident. In the confusion following the Great Kantō Earthquake in September of 1923, police rounded up ten prominent anarchists and union activists and brought them to the Kameido Prison, where they were executed by troops of the Thirteenth Cavalry Regiment. Their initial arrest, claimed authorities, constituted a precautionary effort by the police to prevent social disturbances that these men—all affiliated with either the Nankatsu Labor Association (Nankatsu Rōdō Kyōkai) or the Pure Laborers' Union (Jun Rōdōsha Kumiai)—might have fomented in the chaos that followed the earthquake and resulting fires. Authorities never

adequately explained the rationale for and exact circumstances surrounding the execution of these socialist leaders, and would not admit
to the families of those murdered that they were indeed dead until a
month after the incident.[44]

Not four years after this tragic political event (whose fame has often
overshadowed the story of the thousands of Koreans murdered by police and vigilante groups during the same few days of postearthquake
panic), factories belonging to both of Kameido's major textile companies—Tōyō Muslin and Tokyo Muslin—experienced their first labor disputes. In May 1927, 4,951 out of 5,021 employees in Tōyō Muslin's
Number 1 and Number 2 factories struck for better treatment. This
strike, in which all the workers' demands were met one day after they
were submitted, contributed to a strengthened union presence in the
Kameido textile factories. It also renewed national awareness of the poor
conditions suffered by female textile laborers, and the issue of *gaishutsu
jiyū*—the demand for an end to the virtual imprisonment of workers in
dormitory-factory complexes—a problem that had first entered the public consciousness with the publication of Hosoi Wakizō's book *Jokō aishi*
in 1925 (figure 6).[45]

In February 1930 Tōyō Muslin experienced a more severe labor dispute when workers staged a militant strike that ended two weeks later
in defeat. The February strike, which began in a largely nonunionized
company, resulted in a successful organizing campaign by the Japan
Spinning and Weaving Labor Union, Tōyō Muslin Local Conference
(Nippon Bōshoku Rōdō Kumiai Yō Mosu Shibu Kyōgikai), which managed by the following month to convert worker rage at their defeat and
their continued poor working conditions into a nearly 100 percent
unionized workforce at Tōyō Muslin.[46]

The February strike began with an announcement of Tōyō Muslin's
plans to close its Number 2 Kameido factory, which resulted in layoffs
and transfers affecting 757 employees. Workers quickly organized
protest rallies and mobilized the three unions holding significant con-
stituencies at Tōyō Muslin to begin organizing demonstrations and negotiating a compromise with the company. The company combated the
worker offensive by locking several hundred protesting female workers
in their factory dormitories and calling in members of the right-wing Justice League to counter strike activity through the use of force, often in
conjunction with the police. After continued resistance by workers, the
strike ended in defeat on February 28 when a meeting between company
and union officials mediated by Justice League leader Sakai Eizō resulted

Figure 6. Just after Tōyō Muslin workers struck successfully for greater freedom to go in and out of the factory compound without restrictions in May
1927, approximately three thousand workers at Dai Nippon Spinning went on
strike for more than a month over similar issues. Their banners read "free the
female factory worker caged birds." June 3, 1927. Source: The Mainichi
Newspapers.

in a victory for the company, which made no concessions except the
promise of official union recognition.

The Justice League seems to have gone through a number of incar-
nations from the Meiji era through the postwar period. Scattered references to organizations named Seigidan suggest that there may have
been more than one group so named; however, their similar characteristics point to the likelihood that they were part of a common line-
age. The Justice League(s) were patriotic countergangs, usually es-
pousing highly conservative and nationalistic ideologies and known for
their violence and *yakuza* (underworld) stylings. Documents on the famous Noda strike of 1928–29 indicate that the "Shigeki brothers"
formed a Justice League organization to counter strike activities just
after that dispute began in Chiba Prefecture.[47] Sakai Eizō founded the
Justice League in Osaka—the organization that responded to calls from
Tōyō Muslin to help put down strikes in which Sakai himself played a
pivotal role.[48] Sakai's notoriety among the factory workers of Kameido

was such that he appeared as a central (and evil) character in Nakamoto Takako's novel depicting the labor struggles at Tōyō Muslin.

The incidents that took place at Tōyō Muslin's Kameido factories in 1927 and February 1930 are usually regarded as a prelude to what has come to be known as the "Tōyō Muslin Strike of 1930," which began in Kameido in September of that year, lasted nearly two full months, and threatened to engulf the entire Nankatsu industrial region in a general strike.[49] This second, and larger, Tōyō Muslin strike of the year 1930 began on September 20, when the company announced yet another shutdown. This time management had decided to close the spinning division of its Number 3 factory in Kameido, a plan that would reduce the workforce by an additional five hundred employees. Union leaders believed they had reached an acceptable settlement several days later when the company agreed to retract a nominal number of the layoffs and granted one hundred days severance pay to those who would lose their jobs due to the closure. But contrary to the expectations of male labor leaders, this arrangement did not appease the lower ranks of mostly women workers, who demanded that there be no plant closures and no layoffs.

Scrambling to match the militancy of its members, the union leadership withdrew the agreement and ordered "sabotage" actions beginning on September 25. Workers' initial confrontations with the company and its representatives gave strikers confidence that they would prevail. On September 27, twenty-five hundred female factory workers donned white *hachimaki* headbands as if going off to war and went out to face off with two hundred Justice League strikebreakers sent by the company to intimidate them. The Kameido police arrived before bodily harm befell the Justice League men. On September 29 at 6:00 P.M. about two thousand dormitory-resident female factory workers gathered near the Number 1 factory cafeteria beating drums and chanting May Day slogans. As the police went in to break up the rally, female workers lifted the officers up on their shoulders and carried them around.[50]

By September 30 the strike group had set up a variety of divisions, including control, security, propaganda, information, support relations, meetings, communications, provisions, and personnel. The company responded by setting up its own planning, action, and security divisions. Before the first week of the strike had passed, both sides had begun engaging in a propaganda war, with the union blanketing the neighborhood in posters and leaflets and the company writing letters to strikers, families of strikers, and the shopkeepers and residents of Kameido.[51] After demonstrations by the workers met with continued violence from the Justice League members and police squads called in by the company to counter them, Kameido finally erupted in a street brawl on October 24. Hundreds of male unionists from the region, female workers from Tōyō Muslin, and residents of the local working-class Kameido community lined the streets of Kameido's seventh district from Muslin Alley all the way to the offices of the Kantō Spinning and Weaving Labor Union. As the throng marched toward the Tōyō Muslin factory compound singing the communist workers' anthem "The Internationale," they were confronted by forces assembled by the company. About eighty Justice League members and one hundred police officers blocked off every entrance to the factory dormitories and intercepted the strike group that had gathered just outside the walls of the factory. The street fight broke out as the demonstrators began scaling the walls and company forces doused them with high-pressure hoses.[52]

Two participants in the *shigaisen,* or "street battle," of October 24 described the events in an interview with historians Watanabe Etsuji and Suzuki Yūko published in 1980. Tatewaki Sadayo ran a school for female factory workers in Kameido. Kumagai Kikuko began working at Tōyō Muslin's Number 1 factory in 1926 at the age of fifteen. She joined the union in 1929 and became a member of the strike group's Information Bureau in 1930:

> *Tatewaki:* The street fight began in the evening. The workers came in a line over the bridge from the direction of Komatsugawa. They came over the bridge and from Kameido and other directions and assembled. Before that, the police had come in trucks like black mountains and were all over the place, assembled and waiting at Mizugamimori. Around the union [offices], posters were hung that said: "Faced with sabers, we take the fight to the streets! Don't just stand around and watch the murder of 3,000 female factory workers!" So the police knew what was coming. The arrests began right away, but people struggled against it. At that time, all the electric lights in Kameido had been turned off.
>
> *Kumagai:* Kōtō Densha [a local train company] was also having a strike, but scabs (*uragiri-mono*) were driving the trains in from Komatsugawa. While we were watching them from the Information Bureau, a crowd began to throw stones at a train and burned it out completely. . . .
>
> *Tatewaki:* Then at some point everyone began to scatter. Maybe the strikers knew whose houses they were, but they would enter a

house and then run out the back door to try and escape. After
a while the commotion died down and everything became
quiet in the pitch black. I also returned home to rest. . . .

Interviewer: I have heard that the Tōyō Muslin female factory workers all
went up to the second floor of the dormitory to defend it.

Kumagai: The *boryokudan* ["thug group," referring to the Justice
League] came up to the second floor!

Tatewaki: I could see from outside that [the *boryokudan*] was trying to
rout the female factory workers who had all gathered tight in
a scrimmage formation to defend their position. . . .

Kumagai: When the Justice League came up to the second floor, I said to
everyone, "These guys are called the Justice League, but
they're really just a bunch of thugs. Don't be beaten by
them!"

Tatewaki: The resistance of the female factory workers was fierce, and
the Justice League ended up removing themselves from the
strike and going home. Then the company brought in Sumitomo miners from the Iriyama Coal Mine.[53]

Despite the fierce resistance of the striking workers at Tōyō Muslin
during the October street fight, the union could not sustain the energy
and will among its members to adequately defend its positions within
and outside the factory compound. By the time Justice League members
left the scene, many demonstrators had scattered as well, with nearly two
hundred of them arrested by the end of the street battle. The physical violence promised and delivered by the police, the Justice League, and finally by the Sumitomo miners, together with the rhetorical violence of a
letter-writing campaign initiated by the company that sought to degrade
and demoralize the strikers, ultimately led to total defeat for the workers. On November 19 the strike ended with discouraged union members
pulling out of the strike group. None of the strike objectives had been accomplished, and the company was left to restructure at will and to fire
anyone it determined to have been a "rule breaker." Despite the failure
of the strike, however, the action against Tōyō Muslin created a space
from which female operatives fashioned themselves as *workers,* just as
much as management consistently constructed them as *women.*

EPISTOLARY RHETORIC AND WORKING WOMEN'S BODIES

The political chronology of events that overwhelms most histories of
labor imposes a failure narrative that overlooks the successes of the Tōyō
Muslin strike in challenging the disciplinary regime aimed at female fac-

tory workers that held sway throughout Japan's textile industry. That
the strike ended in defeat seems to have mattered less to the cause of factory women than the process by which the struggle played out, the national attention it drew, and the revolutionary power the event had for
many of its participants. To this day the Tōyō Muslin Strike of 1930 is
known as "the women's strike" and is remembered for the militancy of
female factory workers who took their fight to the streets.[54] Female factory workers fashioned themselves as women fighters (*fujin tōshi*), posi-
tioning themselves squarely alongside male unionists and labor activists
for whom the term *tōshi*, signifying a brave champion and fighter for just
causes, was often used. This militancy represented a vision of womanhood that stood in contrast to the housewife-mother ideal promoted by
the company and to its opposite, the fallen-woman image against which
the company promised to protect all workers under its charge.

Along with the violence of the Justice League thugs and the hoses
brought in by the local police, Tōyō Muslin managers also engaged in a
major letter-writing campaign as a central component of their strategy
to end the strike. As an examination of several of these letters makes
clear, the disciplinary strategies of the textile industry depended on the
projection of the feminine ideal of the housewife, a notion of sexual
morality commensurate with such an ideal, and simultaneously the prevention of any successful labor unionization in the factories.

On October 6, 1930, eleven days after the strike began, company
management made a direct appeal to workers' families in an attempt to
contain the strike. A letter addressed to the male relatives of the striking
female workers requested that they come to Tokyo as soon as possible
to retrieve their daughters and sisters in order to take them back to the
countryside, away from the corrupting influences of the capital. The brief
letter deftly played on rural families' worst fears of what might befall
young girls away from home and ended with a desperate plea for relatives to come and take their "cherished daughters" home as soon as possible: "The Kameido Factory strike . . . has meant that young male and
female workers mingle freely both day and night, resulting over a period
of days in an increase in the number of people whose public morals (*fūki*)
are compromised. This trend has led the company to receive several well-
intentioned warnings from the neighborhood that after the strike has
ended, we should expect at least three hundred female factory workers
to have become pregnant. Such counsel has made us extremely anxious
[about the situation]."[55] Women's labor historian Suzuki Yūko has
claimed that the concern manifest in the letter over the mingling of the

sexes and possible pregnancy of female factory workers is evidence of the extent to which patriarchy had infested capitalism.[56] While Suzuki does not elaborate on her observation, certainly the system of paternalism so central to labor management in the textile industry offered a critical node in a political system grounded in an emperor-centered ideology that took the notion of a family-state as one of its central tropes. The rhetoric of sexual morality in this and other letters drafted by the company during this period pointed to the contradictions of a capitalist system dedicated to intensifying female wage labor while simultaneously policing female sexuality and gender in the service of an ideology of womanhood promoted by cultivation associations and state-sponsored groups such as the Shojokai.

An appeal such as the one in this letter addressed to fathers and elder brothers depended on the rhetorical force of the fear of sexual decadence to which female factory workers were supposed to have been predisposed. Further, it could only be made with its authors' awareness of the balancing act the company must perform: maintaining on the one hand its reputation and authority (both moral and managerial) as provider of parental care and supervision to young, vulnerable women, and simultaneously instilling sufficient concern among workers' families so that they would understand the severity of the crisis—a crisis, the company suggested, directed by outside forces (i.e., the unions) that had led their daughters astray and severely compromised the company's ability to make good on its promises of in loco parentis supervision.

Most of Tōyō Muslin's employees came from farming families from nearby Nagano Prefecture or from the impoverished northern Tōhoku region—families who could scarcely do without the extra income their daughters sent home every month from the factories, much less spare the time and expense of coming down to Tokyo in order to bring home an extra mouth to feed. But the managers of Tōyō Muslin had more than economic matters in mind when they addressed the families at precisely a moment when the already violent dispute seemed poised to escalate.

Tōyō Muslin's letter to families during the height of the strike linked the "compromise of public morals" to the "mingling of young male and female workers" in an urban, industrial setting and offered as the most logical response to this problem the removal of these young girls by their families back to the safety and order of the countryside. In fact, the company's appeal to rural families' fears of the modern city and the sexual decadence it produced proved such a successful strategy that Tōyō Muslin was forced to set up a special office to receive relatives who had

traveled to Tokyo in order to retrieve their daughters. Only days after the
letter had gone out, over one hundred female strikers had been pulled out
of work by their families.[57]

This letter was one of twenty-one such missives dictated by company
managers and addressed variously to male family heads of female employees, dormitory residents, and local Kameido residents.[58] Sent at a
rate of about one every two or three days over the duration of the strike,
these letters employed different rhetorical strategies according to the an-
ticipated response and desired reaction of each targeted audience. In letters to the parents of female factory workers, management used a fear of
the moral corruption of their daughters to persuade families to call striking workers back home. In letters to the local residents of Kameido, the
company faulted the unions and upstart workers for disrupting the community's daily business and promised a return to normalcy once the
strike had been put down.

A letter addressed simply "To Families," but clearly intended to be
read by the wives of striking male workers, belied a certain desperation
in its frenetic jumps between sometimes conflicting arguments. It began:
"Your striking husbands are taking off from work, but are still never
home because of demonstrations, meetings, and speeches. . . . Your children miss their father, and you must have plenty to worry about. What
could your husband be thinking?"[59] The salutation "To Families" con-
flated "family" with the "wife" to whom the letter's arguments were sin-
gularly addressed. In so doing, the letter spelled out a hierarchy of acceptable female social roles, each invested with its own functions and
powers, marking a tension inherent in the status of the women factory
workers here conspicuously absented from the family economy.
"Women" should be "wives" of workers, rather than workers themselves.

The question "What could your husband be thinking?" was meant to
be rhetorical, and the answer obvious: "He puts all his faith in the union
and believes the company will back down. But he is sadly mistaken." The
letter appealed to working-class women's discomfort with the kind of
economic instability that a reliance on factory work caused their families to experience regularly. "If everyone persists in not coming to
work," it continued, "we will hire new workers. Part of the factory is already back up and running." Then, shifting in tone from confident to
threatening, it continued the economic argument: "The company will
not pay wages to striking workers. If the factory does not run, the company does not make any money, and if the company does not make any
money, it cannot pay wages."

This lesson in the operations of capitalist economics with which working-class families were already quite familiar gave way in the next paragraph to a pointed reminder of the repercussions the strike could have in the daily lives of those families: "New Year's is coming. What will you do about the sick? The babies who need milk? The elderly? For the sake of your children, your husband, your entire family, and finally for yourself, use your reason, follow your heart and please, please take back your good husbands from the demon's clutches!" The "demon's clutches" (akuma no te) here refers to the union, depicted frequently in company propaganda as an evil outside force bent on destroying social (and familial) order and harmony.

The next letter, dated October 9, 1930, was one of the very few addressed to the striking female factory workers themselves. Like the letter addressed "To Families," it employed a number of different strategies, including appeals to filial piety and to the rhythms of rural life that would have been familiar to virtually all the female factory workers Tōyō Muslin employed:

It has been over ten days since the strike began. Autumn is setting in, and soon we will all remember what winter nights are like.

All of you also at this time must have much work and many things to do. But with the strike, none of them can get done. Indeed, it seems safe to say that in many ways it is a tremendous waste. Surely your parents and siblings back home, upon reading the exaggerations in the daily newspapers and magazines, will be concerned about you who are separated from them by such a distance, and will worry so much that they will not be able to sleep at night.

All of you, are your actions truly right? How would it be, in the dead of these nights when the moon is full, to clasp your hands to your breast and quietly reflect on the events of these past ten days?

Certainly the union is involved, and various threats and incitements have occurred. But all of you, isn't it now the time, calmly and deliberately, in accordance with your beliefs, your true feelings, to move forward bravely?

The company is waiting for all of you to even one day sooner, go back to the way you were before the strike and return to the bosom of the company. Your original selves! For that, the company will greet you joyously with arms outstretched.

Then, if together with smiling faces we get the factories running again and you return to how you were, what a happy thing will it be for the fathers and mothers of your birthplace!

In the countryside the rice is already ripening, your younger sisters are getting tanned from the sun, and everywhere it is no doubt busy. All of you, at least for your families back home, will you not with a bright heart work diligently for a fruitful harvest this year?[60]

In this letter the union no longer appears as a demon, but nonetheless retains its menacing and coercive character through the references to "threats" and "incitements." The company, it suggests, knows the "true" nature of its "daughters." The purposeful slippage between factory work and agricultural work invites the reader to imagine herself back home, working together with the very family her wages are intended to help support.

While the company letter campaign targeted families, townspeople, and female factory workers themselves, Tōyō Muslin concentrated most of its energy trying to contain the young women whose militancy threatened to undo not only the cotton-spinning company, but to ignite a wave of discontent among wage laborers throughout Nankatsu. Out of the twenty-one letters sent out by the company in their efforts to contain the strike during the fall of 1930, twelve of them were addressed (like the October 6 letter cited above) to the male relatives ("fathers and elder brothers") of female workers, urging them to come to Tokyo to rescue their daughters from the urban corruption and sexual decadence from which the company—given the unpredictable circumstances engendered by the strike—could no longer promise protection.

Tōyō Muslin's letters to families, however, did something more than recognize and use public concerns about sex and the media's linking of sexual and social disorder. It also outlined management's understanding of the multiple dangers involved in the possibility of female labor activism and, by implication, in the existence of female wage labor in general; that is, women workers' opposition to company authority represented a rejection not only of the terms of employment to which they were subject (that is, a system of low wages, poor living and working conditions, and a highly monitored and restrictive environment), but also the rejection of a system of company paternalism modeled on the patriarchal family system, and metonymically linked to the imperial family-state (*kazoku kokka*).

In the context of this letter-writing campaign by the company, the many recountings by labor activists and social critics of what they sometimes described as the slavelike working and living conditions endured by so many young female textile employees—including virtual imprisonment in locked and monitored company dormitories—must be seen in light of industry's complicity with a developing social narrative of working-class women's sexual depravity. This narrative was not simply deployed by the companies as a scare tactic directed toward the parents of workers they wished to manipulate, but constituted a basic premise guiding personnel policy in the textile mills.

While many female factory workers did return home with the relatives who had come from the countryside at the behest of the company to retrieve them, still more hid from their would-be protectors throughout the Kameido neighborhood or simply refused to comply with their parents' wishes, staying to continue working on picket lines and facing down the police. In some cases parents reading the company's letters about the strike became alarmed and came to Tokyo without having a clear understanding of what was going on. Kumagai Kikuko, the union Information Bureau officer mentioned earlier, described in the same 1980 interview how her mother in Fukushima had received one of the company's letters addressed to the families of striking workers and came to Tokyo to retrieve her daughter. Arriving in Kameido, she stumbled across a demonstration taking place in front of Tōyō Muslin's Number 1 factory and, having never seen a labor action or big political demonstration before, thought it was a festival. Remembered Kumagai, "I ended up not going home with her, and I hear she never said a word about it."[61]

Instead of going home with their families, dozens of female mill hands took over the factory dormitories in which many of them lived, turning them into a staging ground for strike actions and successfully fending off attacks by company-hired thugs sent to roust them from their strategic positions. And before the strike ended, hundreds of women workers did battle with the police and antiunion toughs on the streets of Kameido, exposing their bodies to beatings, high-pressure hosings and arrest in order to oppose company rationalization efforts.

The Tōyō Muslin strike stands out among the many instances of labor unrest that took place in 1930 because of its duration, its violence, and the mutually destructive involvement of left-, moderate- and right-wing union factions that tried unsuccessfully to mobilize a united front.[62] It ended in failure for the striking workers, with hundreds of them having lost their jobs permanently and hundreds more sent back home to the countryside. However, the strike has also become noteworthy for the radicalizing effect it had on the female factory workers who participated in the actions of 1930, most of whom—like female worker and strike Information Bureau leader Kumagai Kikuko—had never belonged to a union or taken part in a strike before. Most of all, it offers evidence of the kinds of counterdiscourses women workers created in order to resist the disciplinary mechanisms (such as company-mandated Shūyōdan membership and classes in the domestic arts) employed by factory management. Where management consistently spoke about and to their female employees using a rhetoric of domestic femininity, the female factory workers at Tōyō Muslin characterized themselves as women fighters and clearly articulated their position as workers rather than future housewives.

However, given the heterogeneity of imperial Japan's industrial infrastructure, not all female factory workers would be subject to the same management strategies. Technological and global market changes along with chronic recession resulted in demographic shifts within the textile industry throughout the 1920s, as companies increasingly shifted capital to factories in Japan's colonies and as more and more women from Korea and Okinawa signed on to work in the cotton mills of Osaka and Kobe. As we shall see in the next chapter, non-Japanese women workers were never discussed as future wives and mothers and were more often subject to discourses of ethnicity than discourses of gender.

CHAPTER 5

Colonial Labor

The Disciplinary Power of Ethnicity

By the 1920s an increasing number of nonethnically Japanese women, in particular Koreans and Okinawans, began to take jobs in Japanese factories. Employers, the state, and nonstate entities—including mutual aid and welfare organizations, such as the Sōaikai for Koreans in Japan—developed strategies of ethnic differentiation aimed at preventing labor unrest and maintaining social stability. The use of ethnic difference as a way to manage colonial female labor within the textile factories had as its central purpose the prevention of labor actions against the companies. Even so, it grew out of larger discourses of national belonging that framed the possibilities of defining Korean and Okinawan workers as constitutionally distinct from their Japanese counterparts. Labor unions similarly organized on the basis of ethnic difference. While mainstream Japanese union organizations created women's sections as a way to acknowledge that the needs of working women did not coincide precisely with those of working men, separate Korean unions within Japan made ethnicity rather than gender the salient category of organization for male and female Korean workers.

   Where ethnic Japanese women and girls found that management strategies sought to mold them as women and refused for them other identifying practices that might define them primarily as workers, female laborers from the Japanese colony of Korea and from the newly incorporated prefecture of Okinawa were subject to management and disciplinary strategies by the state and employers that hardly recognized them as women at all. Where Japanese female factory workers experienced various forms of gender management in which company programs and cultivation-group activities taught them the proper modes of feminine virtue, Korean and Okinawan workers were subject to forms of management that emphasized ethnic traits such as tenacity, an easygoing nature, or a follower mentality. The rhetoric of womanhood that permeated textile factories was specifically Japanese in nature. While Japanese female factory workers were seen as future wives and mothers, by the 1920s female Korean and Okinawan workers employed in Japanese factories were constructed as strikemakers and strikebreakers, respectively.

In small acts of resistance involving work and song, as well as in large organized strikes, Okinawan and Korean women used ethnic difference for their own purposes. They subverted and reworked the meanings of difference to achieve momentary shifts in the balance of power between themselves (as workers, women, immigrants, and colonials) and the Japanese state, their employers, and male representatives of the ethnic and labor organizations in which they held membership. At some moments, such as the 1930 strike at Kishiwada Cotton Spinning, Japanese and Korean women cast off the weight of discourses presuming their respective qualities of femininity and ethnic otherness in favor of self-definitions as workers. This refashioning allowed them to form female worker coalitions—tentative and temporary, but effective nonetheless—to challenge employer and Sōaikai control over their living and working conditions. This is not to suggest that either the Japanese or the Korean strikers adhered firmly to a Marxist narrative in which gender and racial oppressions would cease to exist once capital had been defeated and the proletariat could control its own destiny. Rather, they found that strategically defining themselves as workers, and using the resources of the union movement to make their demands, offered an effective method to combat the disciplinary strategies of feminizing and ethnicizing that had been mobilized to control them.

NATIONALITY, CITIZENSHIP, SUBJECTHOOD: DEFINING PEOPLE OF THE "INNER" AND "OUTER" LANDS

The agriculture-based economies of both Okinawa and Korea suffered dramatically during the 1920s, leading first hundreds and then thousands of impoverished young men and women to enter the factories of the Japanese metropole in search of steady work and livable wages. Programs of state

building, the practices of empire, and the ideologies they espoused subjected immigrant/migrant workers to evolving Japanese categorizations of
ethnicity, class, and gender, while the increasing numbers of such workers
contributed to the shape and direction these discourses would take.[1]

A number of scholars have recently noted the significance of an en-
larging discursive as well as physical presence of colonial others in the
creation of a Japanese ethno-national identity.[2] As Japan's colonial empire expanded to include an overall population with a greater diversity
of peoples—many of them moving back and forth between the metropolitan archipelago and the colonies, or between different colonial
spheres—discourse on ethnicity and on national and imperial citizenship
likewise increased.[3] Discussions about Japanese and other ethnicities and
the boundaries of the nation-state took place in the public press, in government and business circles, and in the communities where Japanese
working-class men and women lived and worked alongside laborers
from the colonies. This diversity and the rhetoric surrounding it had profound implications for understandings of what constituted ethnic Japaneseness (*minzoku*) and led to the creation of taxonomies of imperial subjecthood based on ethnicity and place of origin.

The consolidation of the Japanese state began with the Meiji Restoration of 1868 and included incorporation of the Kingdom of the Ryūkyūs—
an island chain to the south of Japan's main islands—as the new prefecture of Okinawa in 1879. The expansion of empire, beginning with the
acquisition of Formosa and the Pescadores in 1895, continued until the
end of the Pacific War, with Korea (annexed in 1910) counted as the most
significant among Japan's colonial possessions. The broadest categories of
exclusion and inclusion used throughout Japan's colonial period to differ-
entiate among the geographical as well as ethno-racial components of the
empire were those of *naichi* and *gaichi*. The Japanese state during its most
frenetic period of colonial acquisition had simultaneously to contend with
defining its own parameters. The *naichi*, or "inner lands," made up those
areas including Okinawa that constituted the Japanese nation-state, while
the *gaichi*, or "outer lands," consisted of those regions, especially colonies
like Korea and Taiwan, that were part of the larger Japanese empire.

Throughout the empire, a complicated series of identifications brought
into play in a still nascent nation-state and simultaneously expanding imperium resulted in a vast and sometimes contradictory taxonomy of referents to describe the various relationships inhering in the colonial condition. In the case of Korea those referents usually comprised some

combination of Naichijin (Japanese), Senjin (Korean—pejorative) and/or Chōsenjin (Korean—neutral). When it came to Okinawa the vocabulary reflected a different set of national and colonial relationships. Since Okinawa had been designated a Japanese prefecture, it was politically part of the *naichi*, the inner lands of Japan proper. And yet the ambiguous status of a people who had a distinct linguistic and cultural heritage precluded Okinawan inclusion in the Japanese ethnos. Thus, Okinawans themselves used the term "Yamatojin" (people of Yamato, the ancient name for Japan) to refer to members of the Japanese ethnos, and *hondo* (mainland) to designate Japan's four main islands, avoiding the assumptions of ethnic homogeneity that underlay use of the terms *naichi* and Naichijin.[4] They preferred, as we shall see, to be referred to by their Yamatojin compatriots as Okinawajin (people from the prefecture of Okinawa), but more often than not, Japanese called them by the old name of Ryūkyūjin, thus undermining claims of inclusion, and therefore privilege, in the nation-state.

Despite theories of a common ancestry and the presumed sameness of Japanese and Koreans that gained some popularity after the annexation, Koreans living and working in the Japanese inner lands rarely experienced sameness in their relations with fellow workers, in their treatment by the companies and labor unions, or in the kinds of cultural, social, and economic support groups available to them.[5] This also was true for women from Okinawa Prefecture. For Okinawan women as for Korean, differences in language and custom proved much more salient to employers and coworkers than did the various discourses of assimilation and inclusion or some universal ideal of womanhood.

After the 1919 pro-independence uprising in Korea, Korean workers in Japan came to represent Japanese citizens' worst fears of potential social disruption, just as they troubled the notion of a coherent national identity within Japan. Meanwhile, Okinawan sameness with the Japanese—a fictive presumption based on the political act of incorporating the island chain into the Japanese imperial polity as a prefecture—allowed industrialists and factory managers to view Okinawan female factory workers collectively as a docile workforce, easily assimilable into the family-state and its paternalistic system of labor relations. These characterizations of Korean and Okinawan female factory workers saw them more as different, sometimes feared, and often uncontainable ethnics rather than as feminine good wives and wise mothers. Korean and Okinawan ethnicity in the factory context erased gender altogether.

OKINAWAN WOMEN WORKERS
AND THE "DISPOSITION OF THE RYŪKYŪS"

The Kingdom of the Ryūkyūs had a long history as an independent country with its own language, culture, and political system before its incorporation into the Japanese nation-state in 1879 as the new prefecture of
Okinawa. Located offshore from two powerful neighbors, the kingdom
had maintained its nominal autonomy first by paying tribute to the
rulers of China's Qing Dynasty, and later by pacifying Japanese leaders
with similar symbolic prostrations made to Japan's erstwhile representatives from the Satsuma clan on the island of Kyūshū. After the restoration, the new Meiji state sought to solidify its control over the southern
island chain. The so-called *Ryūkyū shobun,* or "the disposition of the
Ryūkyūs," added not only a new administrative region that enlarged the
geographic boundaries of the nation-state, but also a population of
newly invented Japanese imperial subjects who in most cases did not
speak Japanese, who had different customs, and whose relationship with
the main islands and their people over the next several decades would be
based on economic necessities more than cultural congruity. The integration of the Ryūkyūs into the Japanese state, then, expanded the possibilities of national identification in a way that would trouble emergent
definitions of Japaneseness.[6]

Emigration from the small island chain began with the exodus to China
of Ryūkyūans protesting the *Ryūkyū shobun* and continued after Okinawa
became a prefecture with labor migration to Hawai'i, South America, the
Philippines, and the Japanese main islands.[7] The worldwide drop in sugar
prices that began in 1920 engendered the most profound of the economic
crises that brought Okinawan youth to work in the factories of Japan's
main island. The small agricultural villages throughout the former kingdom that depended on the sale of sugar cane found that they could not sustain their populations once their primary crop became largely worthless.[8]

Textile industry recruiters made their way to Okinawa to bring young
women to the silk and cotton mills of Japan's main island of Honshū, offering large cash advances just as they did for Japanese women of the
provinces. In the case of Okinawans who had to travel long distances to
reach the factories, the cash advance given to the family was often used
to purchase a new kimono for the trip, boat fare, and train fare needed
to make the last leg of the journey to the mill.[9] The family counted on
earnings sent home to make the sacrifice of their daughter worthwhile.

Company recruiters in Okinawa used many of the same methods used to lure young Japanese girls from their homes in the countryside to the factories in metropolitan areas. Occasionally they promised higher wages than those actually paid or brought the unsuspecting girl to a factory in a more remote area than promised.[10] The following counting song transcribed by an Okinawan researcher develops some of the same themes of difficult work, long hours, and a longing for home depicted in the counting songs of Japanese female factory workers. But the distance of seven islands meant that Okinawans could not travel from home to factory seasonally, as did many Japanese. Okinawan factory workers who fell seriously ill while working at a factory in the *naichi* often died there, not having the resources or strength to get home or the family who could come retrieve them.[11]

As with the counting song transcribed in chapter 3, I have indicated the first line of every verse in the original Okinawan language, each of which begins with a word or word part that is homophonous with the words for the numbers one through five (*hitotsu, futatsu, mitsu, yotsu, itsutsu* in Japanese). Italicized words in the translation indicate the English meanings of the Okinawan number homophones. The bracketed text represents the standard Japanese translation of the Okinawan (or in some cases is explanatory text). The first line is repeated again in English translation, followed by an English translation of the rest of the verse:

1.
Hito-bito chichimisori [Hito-bito kiite kudasai]
People, listen!
I was tricked [by the recruiter]
And went to a cotton-spinning factory in Yamato

2.
Futaoya chichimisori [Futaoya kiite kudasai]
Mother and Father, listen!
I awaken at three o'clock in the morning
From morning till night, I stand at my work

3.
Mibushan aibishi ga [Aitai to omoimasu ga]
I would love to *see* you
But I cannot freely get back to my distant Okinawa
So I will write a letter [instead].

4.
Yuruhiru suru shigoto [Yoruhiru suru shigoto]
Night and day
I suffer through the hardship of work
Living with the sounds of the machinery

5.
Ichi made oyabiran [Itsu made orimasen]
How long must I stay here?
If only I could make some money
And return someday to Okinawa.[12]

Once they arrived at the textile mills of Osaka, Kobe, and other industrializing cities, Okinawan women suffered abuse not only from managers accustomed to overworking their factory employees, but also from Japanese female factory workers for whom the integration of Okinawa into the Japanese state had not effected enough of a consolidation to make their new neighbors at the spinning machines recognizably Japanese. In fact, referring to these new migrants not as Okinawans but as Ryūkyūans became one of the principal means by which Japanese women workers taunted the newcomers.[13] Even when they managed to convince Japanese to refer to them as Okinawan, often the word "pig" did not follow far behind. Because of the higher proportion of pork in the Okinawan diet, many Japanese associated Okinawans with the *eta,* or outcaste class, who historically had engaged in the "unclean" work of butchers and tanners.[14] As one female Okinawan former factory worker recalled in a 1984 interview: "It seems there were a lot of people who hated that the *abura miso* [a kind of soup base] that our parents always sent us for New Year's had pork in it. They used to go after us saying that the pigs were raised on human excrement. We often got teased and bullied so much that it would start fights. Also, when we Okinawans were together we would always speak in dialect. Because the Yamatojin female workers couldn't understand us, they would get mad and start making fun of us."[15]

But use of the Okinawan language within work situations where its speakers found themselves outside the dominant culture could offer opportunities for solidarity as well as for abuse. A former worker from Wakayama Cotton Spinning reported one such case in an oral history collected by Okinawan women's historian Higa Michiko:

It's strange to remember this. The machines had stopped. . . . Spontaneously all the people from Okinawa gathered together. Then we started speaking in the language of the islands, in dialect. We spoke Wachinaaguchi (Okinawan dialect). Then we wanted to sing. Folksongs. At first [we sang] very quietly, but gradually we became impassioned. We kept time, beating on the machines, and gradually our voices got louder and some people even started to dance. Other female factory workers gathered around. It was great! Then the supervisor rushed over. This supervisor was particularly domineering, and a lewd guy. He would offer to do favors for you if you let him touch your breasts, and he was the kind of guy who spread bad rumors. This guy got totally red in the face and came running: "Shut up! What are you singing?" he said, and started stomping his feet on the ground. Then I said, "Hey, Mr. Supervisor! Don't you know this song? This is the Okinawan *Kimi ga yo* [the Japanese national anthem]," and we just ignored him and kept on singing. Boy that was funny, seeing that supervisor's face! He couldn't say anything, just stood there looking stupid. And the song we were singing? It was actually a common festival song.[16]

Tomiyama Ichirō persuasively argues that this episode demonstrates not only the formation of a collective Okinawan identity among migrant workers in the *naichi*—based in this instance on language, song, and dance—but that it does so while also relating that collective subjectivity to the national values embedded in the *Kimi ga yo*, at the time Japan's de facto national anthem whose lyrics extol the glory of the Japanese emperor.[17]

In addition, these women expressed the troubled nature of Okinawans' relationship to the *naichi* through naming the song "the Okinawan *Kimi ga yo*"—part of a strategy to maintain collective identity *and* part of an opposition to the forces of proletarianization at work within the factory system. Invoking the very ambivalence that marked a necessary condition for the political commensuration of Okinawa with the rest of the Japanese body politic, this group of Okinawan women workers used language, song, and dance as vehicles of cultural expression that redefined—if only momentarily—their position within the hierarchical relations of the textile factory. "Keeping time, beating on the machines," they reappropriated both their own productive bodies and the spinning machines—the tools and symbols of discipline and capital. By identifying a folk song as the *Kimi ga yo*, an anthem that symbolized the unity of the imperial state, they manipulated contrasting frames (the local and the national) in order to subvert the disciplinary strategies used within the company.

Factory owners and managers had a clear interest in integrating Okinawan workers into the majority Japanese workforce so that they were considered (and actively constructed) as a more docile labor demographic than Japanese or Korean. The bottoming out of the international sugar market in 1920 that devastated the rural Okinawan economy coincided precisely with Japanese companies' turn away from a Korean labor force increasingly perceived as politically suspect. The failed 1919 pro-independence revolt took colonial administrators on the Korean peninsula by surprise and increased suspicions about the loyalty of Koreans living in Japan to the Japanese imperial state. Factory managers in the textile industry took advantage of the increase in desperate migrant labor from Okinawa just as the Japanese government put into place a series of restrictions that made legal migration from Korea nearly impossible, and as the militancy of Korean women in Japan (initially hired in part to mitigate the militancy of *Japanese* workers) became increasingly evident.[18]

In this process of switching from a Korean to a largely Okinawan pool of colonial labor in the *naichi*, textile-factory managers played on the politics of sameness that was integral to incorporating a heterogeneous Okinawa into the *naichi*. Thus, educating operations and dormitory supervisors not to use the term "Ryūkyū" became part of a style of effective management promoted by the journal *Jokō kenkyū* (Research on Female Factory Workers). In an article published in that journal in 1925, a personnel manager from the Sakai factory of Fukushima Spinning claimed that workers from Okinawa disliked being called Ryūkyūan, the name of the island chain and former kingdom before its integration into the Japanese polity, and insisted on referring to themselves as Okinawan. "They also hate to be treated any differently from female workers from the *naichi*," he explained, "and our factory does not engage in any kind of discriminatory treatment. This is probably the major reason why we have so successfully hired so many Okinawan female factory workers, because we do not treat them differently."[19] But such an admonishment to factory management colleagues to treat workers from Okinawa "the same as female workers from the *naichi*" suggests that in many companies such equitable treatment was not regularly practiced. It also points to a very different relationship to the process of assimilation for Okinawans than for Koreans.

KOREAN FEMALE FACTORY WORKERS AND THE SŌAIKAI

Korean worker migration to the industrial cities of Japan's main islands gained official encouragement after the Korean annexation in 1910 and grew to significant proportions during the labor shortages that accompanied World War I. Colonial landholding policies implemented throughout the Korean peninsula in the years after annexation had the effect of displacing large numbers of smallholding farmers from the lands they had once owned and cultivated, creating an economic crisis that forced families to send their youngest and most able-bodied to find work in other parts of the empire—first in the *naichi* and later in Manchuria.[20] By 1925, 143,000 Koreans had come to live and work in Japan, and by

1930 that number had nearly doubled to 290,000. Most of this population settled in six major cities and their vicinities in the prefectures of Osaka, Tokyo, Aichi, Kyoto, Hyōgō, Kanagawa, and Fukuoka. Osaka in particular became a favorite destination for Korean immigrants, both because of its proximity to the Korean peninsula and because the concentration of industrial factories in the region—pressed by the high demands created by the war—moved to recruit low-paid Korean labor in order to compensate for labor shortages at home.[21] In 1930, over 89,000 Koreans resided in Osaka Prefecture, out of which 77,129 lived in the city of Osaka.[22]

The rhetoric and imagery associated with Koreans in Japan revolved around two central issues: the supposed laziness of Korean workers and the fear of social disruption. Characterizations of Korean workers as lazy, inefficient, unhygienic, and disloyal began even before annexation. By the turn of the century, travel accounts and guidebooks on Korea related the inadequacies of Korean civilization to a Japanese reading public and suggested that only Japanese tutelage might save such a backward culture and bring it into the modern world.[23] After larger numbers of Korean workers began migrating to Japan, Japanese authorities surveyed scores of the new residents and found them "inferior" in constitution and in physical stature, in dedication to their work, and in respect for their fellow human beings.[24]

Labor-management consultant Ishigami Kinji argued in the journal *Jokō kenkyū* that Japanese factory supervisors needed to employ special methods to manage Korean female factory workers. While most of the journal's articles focused either implicitly or explicitly on gender difference in the disciplining of Japanese workers, Ishigami's "Chōsen jokō o tsukau kokoroe" (Methods for Using Korean Female Factory Workers, 1933) emphasized cultural difference as the salient issue in managing Korean workers. In making his argument, Ishigami pointed to the difficulties of assimilationist policy that sought to turn Korean workers into Japanese imperial subjects:

> Recently with the continued increase in the use of Korean female factory workers, we have all become more aware of the so-called Korean female factory worker problem. That is, Koreans are equal [*hitoshiku*] to Japanese, but there are special circumstances that make it impossible to manage *naichi* female factory workers and Korean workers in the same way. This is not a reason to discriminate against them, but these special circumstances that include different histories and climate [*fūdo*] means that they will of course feel differently about things and have different spiritual attitudes and different attitudes toward daily life. Therefore, sometimes assimilation is difficult.[25]

"Equality" for Ishigami did not assume assimilation or even its possibility. Pointing out the "special circumstances" of Korean history and climate, he emphasized cultural difference and the importance of recognizing it in the management of Korean workers. His suggestion that climate determined the attitudes of a people was similar to arguments made at around the same time by the philosopher Watsuji Tetsurō, whose book *Fūdo* (Climate) applied Heidegger's analysis of time to problems of space. Watsuji drew connections between a nation's climate and its culture, arguing that among the countries of Asia, Japan's diverse climate accounted for its more advanced civilization compared to its neighbors.[26] Because of the different "attitudes" the Korean climate produced, the management of Korean workers required different techniques than the management of Japanese.

Ishigami's concern lay not in turning Koreans into Japanese (which at any rate would be "difficult"), but in the practical matters of management and control. Among his "special methods" (*kokoroe hōhō*) for dealing with female Korean workers were admonitions to factory managers to beware of their strong "follower mentality" and collective power and to "skillfully guide to your advantage their strong sense of tenacity." He also urged industrialists to "firmly reject discriminatory attitudes," even though "we Japanese" might not be used to their "slow and easygoing" (he barely resisted saying "lazy") nature.[27]

The perceived need on the part of Japanese industry for docile and low-paid labor initiated the first large migrations of Koreans to Japan and, once established, Korean communities in major industrial cities proved a welcoming environment for those fleeing the poverty of tenantry and landlessness. While Koreans in most industries earned lower wages than Japanese employed in the same jobs, even that low wage in the *naichi* represented nearly double the average daily wage paid in Korea.[28]

Korean migration to Japan began with men, who took on the most dangerous and difficult work in Japan's coal mines and who found other opportunities in the chemical, rubber, and other factories of Osaka, Kyoto, and Hyōgo prefectures.[29] But the labor shortages of the post–World War I years struck the female-dominated textile industry hard. During that period large numbers of young Korean women began arriving in Osaka and Wakayama Prefecture, escorted by recruiters who ferried them across the strait that separates the Korean Peninsula from the island of Kyūshū, and then on to Osaka Bay and the cotton- and silk-spinning factories that awaited them.[30] Korean workers came to the Japanese main islands for many of the same reasons Okinawans ended up in Osaka: poverty at home and the promise of steady work at decent wages in Japanese factories and coal mines. Like Okinawans too, many Koreans came believing they would eventually return home after making money for their families, but often ended up settling in ghettoized communities in urban industrial slums.[31]

Popular mistrust of Koreans within Japan coincided with the earliest migrations, and drew much of its force from the ideology of empire. In an imperial system that privileged the Japanese ethnos within a familial hierarchy of "races," Koreans—and Korea itself—occupied the position of younger brother, at once lacking in the elements of civilization and yet teachable at the hands of the superior Japanese race. By 1932, after the invasion of Manchuria, popularization of the term *gozoku kyōwa,* or "harmony of the five races" of Japanese, Korean, Chinese, Manchurian, and Mongolian, offered a focus for this ideology.[32] "Harmony" indicated not equality, but a functional hierarchy in which each element willingly took its place, here defined both by geographical proximity and the degree of integration into the greater Japanese empire.[33]

The most compelling evidence of Koreans as potential agents of social disruption came on March 1, 1919, when an uprising against Japanese colonial forces in Korea forcefully thrust Koreans into the Japanese public eye as purveyors of "dangerous thoughts." The idea of Korean independence from Japan gained momentum from 1910 to 1919 as the effects of Japanese agricultural and economic policy decimated local economies and as Korean students and intellectuals saw the Russian Revolution and Woodrow Wilson's call for the self-determination of peoples as potential models. Sparked by a pro-independence manifesto issued by a group of radical Korean university students in Tokyo, the March 1 Incident started in Seoul and quickly spread throughout the peninsula, with colonial authorities unable to completely quell the protests for nearly a year. Official and popular discourses of *futei Senjin,* or "Korean malcontents," who menaced the peace and prosperity Japan's colonial government promised to restore to the peninsula, proliferated in the wake of the uprising and constituted the focal point of what became known in Japan during the 1920s as the "Korean problem."[34]

By 1923 fear and distrust of Koreans had escalated to such a level that rumors about anti-Japanese acts sparked a mass vigilante movement against Korean residents of Japan. In the wake of the Great Kantō Earthquake that struck the Tokyo area on the morning of September 3, 1923, such rumors proliferated. As the fires ignited during the earthquake jumped from rooftop to rooftop with frightening speed, finally engulfing the entire city in a destructive blaze, likewise did stories of Koreans poisoning wells and plotting to murder Japanese spread from neighborhood to neighborhood, mobilizing unthinking mobs in murderous vigilante squads. Such unfounded rumors met with little skepticism from the police, who did nothing to stop their circulation until several thousand Korean residents had been murdered.[35]

A number of the victims of the earthquake's initial destruction were female factory workers who were caught under falling brick, trapped between machines, or were burnt alive as the factories they worked in blazed out of control. At least three large factories in the Tokyo metropolitan area—one owned by Fuji Cotton Spinning, one owned by Dai Nippon Cotton Spinning, and one owned by Kurihara Cotton Spinning and Weaving—were reduced to ashes in the hours following the earthquake.[36] One Okinawan spinning operative who worked at Fuji Gas Cotton Spinning in Kawasaki City, Kanagawa Prefecture, and who survived the earthquake reported, "The people who were working in the factory were all wiped out. Those who died were all crushed by the building. The only way they could be identified later was by what they were wearing and what they were carrying on them."[37]

Two years after the earthquake and massacre, the media reported widely on an incident at a school in Hokkaidō that indicated the continuing hostility and mistrust felt toward Koreans in Japan. In 1925 students at the Otaru Higher Commercial School protested the implementation of a new law making military training in higher schools compulsory. The school had set up a military drill for students in which the setting was Japan after an earthquake, and students were to quell an uprising of anarchists and Koreans who were designated "the enemy." Such exercises make it clear that after the massacre of Koreans and the murder of a number of prominent anarchists following the Tokyo earthquake, officials throughout Japan still believed those murders to have been justified and domestic uprisings likely to occur. The new higher-school military exercises, at least in Otaru, identified the biggest threat to Japan's security as a domestic rather than foreign one.[38]

After crushing the 1919 Korean independence movement, the Japanese state moved to institutionally contain Korean migrant laborers, realizing finally that the "temporary sojourners" had indeed become a sizable population of permanent and semipermanent residents.[39] The Sōaikai (Mutual Care Society) offered the perfect vehicle by which the state and private enterprise could mobilize Korean labor in a controlled and expedient fashion. The largest of the prewar Korean reconciliation

(*Naisen yūwa*) and assimilationist (*dōka*) organizations that proliferated during the 1920s and early 1930s, the Sōaikai eventually controlled almost every aspect of Korean female factory workers' work and personal life, from immigration and recruitment to marriage. The organization sent its own recruiters to Korea to bring back workers for Japanese industry, offering through its connections with the Korean Government General (Japan's colonial administration on the peninsula) and companies in Japan a legal (or often illegal) and expedited means of escaping the poverty afflicting rural Korea.[40] The Sōaikai acted as go-between for the hiring of all Korean workers at Kishiwada Spinning, and the organization continued to be involved in labor recruitment from Korea even in the mid-1930s after the practice had become illegal.[41] Similarly, the *Minshū jihō* (People's News) a resident-Korean newspaper, reported in 1935 on the illegal recruitment by Sōaikai representatives of women from Korea to work in the cotton-spinning mills of Wakayama Prefecture, and their arrest upon having been discovered by the Japanese coastal police while escorting their charges on a ship entering Osaka harbor.[42]

Established in 1921 as a Korean immigrant support group and welfare organization by Koreans Pak Chungum and Yi Kidong, the Sōaikai aimed, according to its mission statement, to "eliminate ethnic prejudice [*minzoku-teki sabetsu*]," to "effect Japan-Korea reconciliation [*yūwa*]," and to "provide spiritual education [*kyōka*] and economic welfare to Korean workers" by attending to the principles of "coexistence and co-prosperity."[43] In fact, the organization was in one sense (as historian Sally Hastings has put it) "the instrument of cooperation between Japanese officials and upper-class Koreans to control lower-class Koreans and incorporate them into the Japanese empire."[44] But the organization served a number of sometimes competing purposes: for the state, for the educated upper-class resident Koreans who ran it, and for the large numbers of working-class Korean migrants who joined the Sōaikai out of practical need for the assistance it could provide in such crucial areas as employment, housing, and mediating legal and domestic issues. In addition to its mutual-aid function, the Sōaikai also acted in a strike-breaking capacity, allying itself with the Japanese state and private enterprise in a bid to demonstrate that Koreans resident in Japan had the capacity and the will to police themselves in a way that would correspond to the ideology of empire and the demands of international capital. And in the textile factories, as we shall see, the Sōaikai also became a means for Korean men to exert patriarchal authority over Korean women.

The Sōaikai's main activities included job placement, worker education, and housing referrals for the laborers (both male and female) who made up the majority of the Korean population in Japan. The head office of the organization, located in Tokyo by 1922, operated four free housing facilities where Koreans newly arrived from the peninsula could stay until they found work, while the Osaka office opened a similar facility the following year. Between four hundred and five hundred newly arrived Korean male and female migrant workers—as well as a smaller number of destitute Japanese to whom the doors were also open—took advantage of these facilities each month throughout the 1920s.[45] Free job-placement offices operated in branch locations throughout the country, helping workers navigate the job market in a foreign land while simultaneously providing a valuable service to local employers by negotiating the cultural and language differences that might otherwise prevent access to this low-wage labor pool.

The Sōaikai also mediated disputes among Koreans and between Koreans and Japanese. The main Tokyo office of the Sōaikai and many of its branch offices included a Counseling Section (Sōdanbu) to resolve disputes. In one instance the Sōaikai settled a dispute that stemmed from a fight that broke out in Chiba Prefecture between thirty Seinendan youth organization members and twenty Koreans.[46] While disputes such as this one involving interethnic conflict between rival groups of young men were not uncommon, much conflict revolved around employment-related issues such as employers' failure to pay wages, wage discrimination resulting in lower pay for Korean workers, and discriminatory treatment by Japanese supervisors.[47] One intraethnic conflict reported by the Sōaikai involved a separation case between a Korean man and a Korean woman residing in Japan. The woman had come to Japan to find work after divorcing her husband in Korea, leaving her seven-year-old child behind. Not knowing the language well, "and being a woman," she found herself "enticed" by men who, it was claimed, were skillful at getting what they wanted from her. Distraught, she appealed to the Sōaikai and on April 3, 1923, a certain Mr. Kim—a construction worker with whom she was living—was called into the Sōaikai offices. After both the woman and Mr. Kim were interviewed, Mr. Kim was told that it had been wrong for him to have insisted on their cohabitation. In the end the matter was resolved when both of them "voluntarily" decided they would no longer live together.[48] Individual Koreans could benefit from Sōaikai interventions such as these, while the organization fulfilled its goal of maintaining discipline and order among this potentially volatile poor immigrant community by engaging in such mediations.

To address the issue of Korean cultivation (*kyōka*), the Sōaikai established night schools, which often operated out of their free lodging houses. These schools offered courses in the three subjects Sōaikai leaders believed would best equip the new immigrants to find and keep work and to acculturate themselves to Japanese society. Ethics classes taught a version of imperial subjecthood appropriate for colonials, Japanese language classes served the crucial purpose of giving students the linguistic skills to assimilate, while Korean writing classes for the largely illiterate migrant population allowed workers to send and receive letters from their families back home. This three-course curriculum was so popular among Korean immigrants that in its first year of operation in 1922, the Sōaikai's night school in the Minami Senju district of Tokyo taught on average two thousand students each month.[49]

The growth of Sōaikai membership throughout the 1920s suggested that Koreans in Japan found the organization's services useful. But many observers at the time suggested that coercion and desperation accounted for the membership of most Korean workers, who would be shut out of housing and work had they not agreed to pay dues to the Sōaikai. The *Minshū jihō* newspaper described the organization in quite unflattering terms:

> Those who put on the appearance of being a so-called Japan-Korea reconciliation group are actually engaged in mysterious activities too numerous to count, including food service, building management, factory worker job placement, loan sharking, facilitating temporary returns to Korea, securing the release of those who have been arrested, and trafficking in human beings. There is not one of them who does not take part in sucking the sweat and blood from the ignorant and powerless working proletariat. To put it another way, the Japan-Korea reconciliation people are comrades whose sole purpose is to use cunning to exploit the proletarian worker.[50]

Such accusations were given weight by the numerous reports of Sōaikai abuses of power among the working-class population, some of whom saw the group more as an organized (and sanctioned) crime syndicate than as a Korean welfare organization.

Although founded as a private organization, the Sōaikai had strong ties to important figures in the Japanese government. Only months before Pak (who in 1932 became the first Korean to hold an elected seat to Japan's Lower House) and Yi announced the creation of the Sōaikai in Tokyo, they met with Maruyama Tsurukichi, then part of the Korean

Government General police force, and with Saitō Makoto, governor-
general of Korea, who would soon become a major patron of the
Sōaikai.[51] After the 1923 Kantō Earthquake, the Tokyo police ap-
proached the Sōaikai, which responded by mobilizing between three
hundred and four hundred Koreans a day for over half a year in Tokyo
to aid first in the disposal of dead bodies and later in the removal of de-
bris caused by the fires and in the building of temporary barracks at an
army facility for the Koreans being "protected" by the authorities. For
the police and for the Sōaikai, such cooperation produced positive pub-
licity and created an image of helpful, nonthreatening Koreans after the
tragedy of the postearthquake massacre—an image in direct opposition
to the popularly held views of Koreans as shifty and untrustworthy that
contributed to the massacre in the first place. In all likelihood, however,
the Koreans "hired" by the police department to undertake this work responded to pressure tactics brought to bear by the Sōaikai rather than
any sense of service to the imperial state.[52]

In 1928 the Sōaikai received approval to become a legally incorporated entity, and Maruyama Tsurukichi, former director of Police Affairs
of the Korean Government General, became its first director-general.[53]
The Korean Government General offered an initial grant of forty thousand yen to the organization for the construction of buildings and gave
five thousand yen yearly thereafter. By this time the organization included among the ranks of its leadership a number of prominent figures
from the political and business worlds, including governor-general of
Korea Saitō Makoto, entrepreneur Shibusawa Eiichi, army generals Yamanashi Hanzō and Inoue Kitarō, officials from the Home Ministry Social Bureau, the governor of Tokyo Prefecture, and members of the journalistic elite.[54]

One key function of the Sōaikai was to prevent the "deterioration of
thought" (shisō akka) among Korean workers. According to cofounder
Pak Chungum's 1930 book, Wareware no kokka shin Nihon (Our Nation, the New Japan), the basic ideology of the organization was profoundly influenced by two Japanese ultrarightists and military expan-
sionists, Tōyama Mitsuru of the Genyōsha (Dark Ocean Society) and
Uchida Ryōhei of the Kokuryūkai (Black Dragon Society), both of
whom promoted Japanese expansionism and the suppression of democratic and Marxist-influenced movements in Japan. Such ideological un-
derpinnings lent themselves to the strikebreaking and antiunion efforts
that composed a large part of Sōaikai activities in the 1920s and early
1930s.[55]

Soon after the Sōaikai's founding in Tokyo, branches of the organization quickly sprang up all over the country. Regional Sōaikai head offices administered the activities of branch offices throughout an entire prefecture or within a large industrial belt. By the end of 1923 the organization claimed 2,438 members in Aichi Prefecture alone, or 75 percent of the total Korean population in that prefecture. The Izumi office, established in August 1926 and located in the city of Kishiwada, was the best organized branch in the greater Osaka region and the one that worked with the largest numbers of female textile employees. Further, Osaka Prefecture was a focal point of activity related to Koreans in Japan, since by 1921 it had overtaken Fukuoka Prefecture to become the administrative unit with the largest number of Koreans in Japan.[56] Japanese officials of the Izumi office included the mayor of Kishiwada, the Kishiwada chief of police, the Documents and Statistics bureau chief of Osaka Prefecture, the head of the Kishiwada City Social Bureau, and assemblymen representing Osaka Prefecture and Kishiwada City.[57]

With powerful state interests represented on its board, the Izumi Sōaikai could manage the Korean labor needs of the surrounding community, which had cotton-spinning factories as its primary economic base. And since those factories depended on a large supply of low-wage female labor, the Izumi branch's job-placement office came to handle thousands of cases involving newly arrived Korean women seeking employment in the Osaka area. From September 1923 through September 1927, the Sōaikai Izumi office successfully placed 4,009 out of 4,532 female job seekers, compared to 1,040 out of 1,594 men who had applied for work through the organization. Korean men successfully found work in factories, construction, and odd jobs, while nearly all of the successfully employed women found work in one of the several large cotton-spinning and -weaving factories in the region.[58] The Izumi office had from its inception worked to place female Korean workers in jobs at Kishiwada Spinning. The company ran four large factory operations at different locations throughout the greater Osaka region. It was the largest employer in the area and the largest recruiter of Korean female labor among all the major cotton concerns.

KISHIWADA SPINNING AND COLONIAL LABOR

Originally chartered in 1892, Kishiwada Spinning (known as Kishibō) started its operations with a main factory located in the northern part of the city of Kishiwada, a suburb of Osaka. By 1923 it ranked among the second tier of large textile concerns in Japan, outdone only by the likes of such huge companies as Kanegafuchi, Dai Nippon (with which it would later merge), and Tōyō Spinning. Kishibō began operations with start-up capital of 250,000 yen and 10,368 spindles, and by 1923 the company had expanded its operations to include four factories in the greater Osaka metropolitan area, capital of nearly 10 million yen, 40,748 spindles, 1,164 weaving machines, and 6,210 employees.[59] Like several other large textile companies of its day, Kishibō employed Korean and Okinawan women in addition to the majority ethnic Japanese the company recruited from the greater Osaka region. The original paperwork signed by the prefectural governor of Osaka approving the establishment of Kishibō stipulated that the company recruit workers locally and obtain materials from the surrounding area. But these conditions proved too constricting, and by 1897 the company began recruiting labor from nearby Shiga Prefecture. The labor shortages endemic to the industry during the early years of industrialization only grew worse as demand increased during World War I and as the labor supply recruited from the countryside began to dry up by the early 1920s.[60]

By the time Kishibō began recruiting Korean workers, the practice already had a thirteen-year history. Settsu Spinning in Osaka had been the first factory to recruit women from Korea in 1911, and a variety of textile, chemical, steel, and shipbuilding companies hired small numbers of Koreans over the next decade. But the lack of an established network among Koreans working in Japan who could report back home and reassure their friends, neighbors, and relatives about conditions there made these early recruitment efforts difficult. Not until Japanese companies felt the pressure of the labor shortage during World War I did factory recruitment efforts expand in a concerted way beyond Japanese shores, leading to increases in the numbers of Koreans coming to Japan.[61]

Textile companies had the support of the colonial administration in their efforts to bring workers from Korea to the factories of the main islands.[62] The Government General of Korea facilitated "shipments" of Korean workers to the *naichi* and compiled reports on the successes of various companies in hiring Korean labor. The Government General detailed Kishibō's efforts to recruit Korean factory workers in a 1924 report that extolled the benefits of hiring Korean labor. Kishibō, it reported, had sent company officials to recruit workers from Korea in 1918 as a result of the post–World War I labor shortages. The company returned with fifty Korean girls whose efficiency, the report claimed, was somewhat lower than that of Japanese workers, but who also had lower expectations in terms of housing, food, and wages. Given the lower expense associated with hiring Korean workers, then, the company decided to recruit one hundred more girls who were placed at each of the company's four factories. The following year the company decided to hire several male Korean workers, and one was placed in each factory as a supervisor (*kantoku*).[63]

The use of male Korean workers to supervise the majority female workforce became common by the early 1920s among companies employing Koreans. The vast majority of female Korean workers spoke no Japanese and were unfamiliar with Japanese culture and customs. Having attended only a year or two of elementary school (if any at all), most were illiterate not only in Japanese but in Korean as well. Japanese textile-factory operators found it expedient to hire Korean supervisors to manage the Korean workforce directly, thus facilitating communication between colonial labor and metropolitan management. The Korean men hired for these supervisory positions could speak at least enough Japanese to act as intermediaries between the company and the group of female Korean workers to which they had been assigned.

Japan's textile industry had long employed a system of clustering women and girls from the same regions together, having them live as a unit in the dormitories and work together in the factory. This system of segregation became even more attractive to employers managing a distinct colonial population. Unlike the Okinawan workers who were threatened with punishment if caught speaking or singing in their native language, Korean women and girls usually did not know enough Japanese for such rules to be practical.[64] Language thus served as another marker of proximity to the imperial center. The earlier incorporation of Okinawa into the imperial state and its integration as a prefecture rather than a colony meant that Okinawan migrants were more apt to have had an education in Japanese language skills.

By 1924, according to a Korean Government General report, Kishibō had hired Koreans in its four factories totaling 787 employees, 726 of them women and girls (table 2). In 1920 women made up only 11.5 percent of all Koreans residing in Japan. In 1925 women constituted 17.2 percent of the Korean population; in 1930, 27.7 percent; and by 1940, 37.7 percent.[65] By 1927, out of the 2,308 Koreans living in the city of Kishiwada, 1,389 of them were employed as textile workers. Out of those, 1,248 were women.[66] Indeed, the employment of a large number of female workers from the peninsula at Kishibō's main factory in the city of Kishiwada explains why records show Kishiwada City as home to a

TABLE 2. KOREANS EMPLOYED AT KISHIWADA
SPINNING FACTORIES, 1924

Factory	Male Factory Hands	Female Factory Hands
Honsha	11	199
Nomura	8	212
Haruki	40	219
Sakai	2	96
TOTAL	61	726

SOURCE: Report of the Korean Government General, in Matsushita Matsutsugu, *Shiryō Kishiwada Bōseki no sōgi* (Osaka: Yuniusu, 1980), 20.

TABLE 3. THE OSAKA KOREAN
POPULATION, 1928

City	Men	Women	Total
Osaka (all wards)	28,375	6,642	35,017
Kishiwada	225	1,253	1,478
Sakai	895	755	1,650

SOURCE: "Honshi ni okeru Chōsenjin no seikatsu gaikyō" [The General Situation of Life for Koreans in Osaka], originally published by Ōsaka-shi shakaibu chōsa-ka in 1929, reproduced in *Kindai shomin seikatsushi*, vol. 2, *Sakariba, uramachi*, ed. Minami Hiroshi (Tokyo: San'ichi shobō, 1984), 172.

much larger number of Korean women than men, while the nearby city of Osaka claimed over four times more Korean men than women. The population statistics for Osaka were much more representative of the ratio of male to female Koreans living in Japan on the whole (table 3).

GENDER, ETHNICITY, AND THE LABOR MOVEMENT

To combat ethnic discrimination and to contest unsatisfactory working conditions, Korean female factory workers had to find discursive spaces outside of the Japanese narratives that cast Koreans as rebellious and unproductive. One of the ways they did this was to privilege a worker identity over an ethnic identity in their dealings with managers and the company. In this, their interests dovetailed with those of Japanese women workers who similarly borrowed from the language of the labor movement to cast themselves as oppressed workers rather than idealized women. The image of "good wife, wise mother" that sat so uneasily with

Japanese workers was even less useful to Koreans who had no access to the ethnic Japaneseness upon which such visions of femininity were predicated. Instead, Korean women protested by borrowing selectively from the language of the labor movement, by working together with Japanese women workers, and simultaneously by identifying the discriminatory treatment they suffered as an ethnic minority.

To say, however, that companies did not discipline their female Korean workforce *as* women, and that the Korean workers similarly did not adopt a highly gendered discourse in their dealings with management, is not to say that gender played no role in the management of Korean female labor. On the contrary, company practices of hiring male Korean managers to oversee the mostly female Korean workers indicates a strategy of simulating the patriarchal structures of authority with which the workers would have been abundantly familiar. Further, the demographics of Korean labor in factories throughout Senshū are striking. Located just south of the city of Osaka within Osaka Prefecture, the Senshū region included over a dozen cities. Among them, Sakai, Kishiwada, Kaizuka, and Izumi all boasted factories run by some of the area's major textile companies. As we have seen with the case of Kishiwada City, the vast majority of Koreans living and working in these cities were, in fact, female. This makes it particularly notable that managers chose to deal with Korean workers as ethnics, rather than as women.

As the largest industrial employer in the Senshū region, Kishibō easily became the target of labor actions. The first recorded strike at Kishibō took place at the company's Nomura factory on August 12, 1919, when nineteen (Japanese) male workers unsuccessfully demanded a 30 percent wage hike. In 1921 about 150 women employed in the company's main factory participated in a one-day walkout.[67] In July 1922, Korean workers struck at the company's Haruki factory, protesting discriminatory treatment that left Koreans with lower wages and fewer bonuses than their Japanese counterparts. By this time the Kishibō Haruki plant had the largest concentration of Korean female factory workers in Osaka Prefecture. About 10 percent of the Haruki plant's workers were Korean, and 80 percent of the Korean workforce (a total of 219) were women. Despite the protests of the male Korean supervisors who initiated the strike, the company argued that the lower wages were justified because of low Korean worker productivity and frequent absenteeism. The strikers were forced back to work after three days.[68] This Korean workers' strike reflected a pattern repeated in similar actions during this period: negative views of Korean workers as inefficient and unproductive contributed to discrimination, which led to a labor action to combat discrimination, which in turn reinforced negative stereotypes of Koreans as rebellious and strike-prone.

Similarly, because of its size and prominence in the region, Kishibō became the focal point of organizing by a nascent labor movement beginning in the 1920s. The union movement, however, much like management itself, split workers into ethnic categories. Mainstream labor unions focused on ethnic Japanese workers, while specifically Korean unions emerged to organize the migrant population. Japan's largest union, Sōdōmei (Japan Federation of Labor), got its start organizing (Japanese) men in the electrical and manufacturing industries, and many of its early members were skilled workers and foremen.[69] In 1922 labor leader Nishio Suehiro began a several-year campaign by Sōdōmei to organize the textile companies of western Japan. By 1925, 758 men and 225 women workers at six of the area's largest companies had been organized, more than half of them employees at three different Kishibō factories.[70] The rate of unionization within the textile industry at this time was a mere 1.2 percent; and even within this small number of organized workers, women were significantly underrepresented.[71] The proportion of unionized women to men in textile factories was nearly in inverse proportion to the total number of women to men employed in the industry. Union efforts to organize women remained lukewarm due to perceptions that the female labor force—young and considered largely transient—was "ignorant and lacking in consciousness" (muchi mujikaku).[72] Still, by 1916 the Yūaikai, predecessor organization to the Sōdōmei, had established a women's section, and the Hyōgikai (the far left wing of the Sōdōmei that broke away to form its own union in 1925) created a women's section in 1927.[73]

While the mainstream Japanese unions made efforts—albeit sometimes less than strenuous ones—to organize textile workers around the "special needs" of women, Korean women workers found themselves subject to ethnicizing projects rather than incorporation into a category of women workers. Around the same time the Sōdōmei began its concerted effort to organize the textile industry, the first Korean labor unions formed in Osaka and in Tokyo. Up until the early 1920s, Korean workers had expressed little interest in a Japanese labor movement that believed them to be backward and unorganizable and that held of them the same negative stereotypes as did the rest of Japanese society. Thus, the earliest Korean organizations had focused, like the early Sōaikai, principally on relief work and mutual aid.[74] But by the mid-1920s the

Osaka Korean Labor League (Ōsaka Chōsen Rōdō Dōmeikai) had begun organizing workers in the industrial belt of western Japan, forging an alliance with the Sōdōmei.[75]

While organizing efforts among Korean female workers did not meet with great success throughout the 1920s, the unions' activities in the area strengthened a worker consciousness among female textile workers. Sōdōmei helped mobilize worker discontent in 1929 when Korean and Japanese workers at Kishibō staged a walkout to protest layoffs at the company's Nomura factory and to demand better working conditions.[76] The September 1929 issue of *Rōdō fujin* (Working Woman), the organ of the women's section of Sōdōmei, related the compromise settlement of that strike without mentioning the significant involvement of Koreans. The article began by characterizing Terada Jinyomo, the president of Kishibō, as a "notorious miser" who had "ignored both the Factory Law and the prohibition on night work, compelling hard labor and lowering wages." The worker response to these conditions was to organize a labor union, the leaders of which Terada promptly fired. Not to be cowed by the company's actions, the workers struck:

> On July 18, [the workers] declared war on the Great Terada Clan, beginning the struggle and the shift to a war of waiting. All five thousand participants continued to hold down the fort, but by August 1, the strike was resolved with the [acceptance of] the following favorable terms:
>
> 1. Reinstatement of the thirty dismissed workers.
> 2. The reinstated female factory workers are to be treated as cordially as possible.
> 3. Strike expenses and daily wages [for the period of the strike] will not be paid.[77]

Legends regarding the miserliness of company president Terada abounded throughout this period. A 1928 newspaper article tells of Terada insisting that the fare for a train ride was not twelve sen, but six, and forcing the driver to stop and let him off because he refused to pay the greater amount. Terada was infamous for beating down the price on anything he had to purchase, whether for himself personally or for any of the many businesses he founded. Terada refused to buy insurance for his factories, even after the Haruki factory of Kishibō burned down just before going into production, and believed workers would become lazy if paid too much.[78] Striking workers often pointed to Terada specifically (and to his brothers Motokichi and Rikichi, who ran different companies within the family's commercial empire) as representative of Japan's early industrial capitalist system that they believed cared only about capital accumulation and nothing about human labor and human suffering. Point three from the September 1929 *Rōdō fujin* article clearly suggests that not all the terms of the settlement were decided in favor of the workers; nonetheless, as with the Tōyō Muslin strike discussed in the previous chapter, this 1929 strike set the stage for a larger confrontation in 1930—one in which Koreans would play an even more prominent role.

On March 15, 1930, Kishiwada Bōseki announced a wage cut. Within days, indirect employees (odd jobbers and cafeteria help) managed to get back 5 percent of that cut through negotiations with the company. But the firm refused to negotiate with its regular factory employees, and workers at Kishibō's Sakai factory quickly mobilized in opposition.[79] By May 4 the *Osaka Asahi* newspaper morning edition featured the headline: "One hundred female factory workers escape Kishibō, Koreans at the Sakai factory protest wage cut." The newspaper noted that Kishibō had cut wages three times within two months, totaling a 12 percent reduction. When combined with the company's cutback in operations, the article claimed, this had resulted in a nearly 40 percent real wage decrease for both male and female workers. In response, workers staged a protest rally on May 3, which the company quickly squelched. The article described what transpired next:

> One worker opened the back gate, and out of 539 [workers], about 100 (mostly Korean [Senjin] women workers) fled out like an avalanche, taking refuge with the Labor-Farmer Party Sakai office and the Korean Labor Union, and finally withdrawing to the head office of the Senshū Joint Labor Union. The escaped women workers still in their work uniforms went up to the second floor of the main office and improvised by cooking themselves a meal with donations that had been made to the union saying, "we will fight to the end." According to Mr. Yamamoto, the factory's personnel manager: "Things have been quiet within the factory, and we have been operating as usual until 11 P.M. each day since the third [of May]. We estimate the escapees to number about sixty, and expect them to have returned by the fourth. If they return, we are ready to take them back any time."[80]

But instead of returning to the factory on May 4 as personnel manager Yamamoto had predicted, workers instead presented the company on that date with a list of demands, including the reversal of all pay cuts that had been announced since the beginning of the year and promises of no further layoffs, improvements in the quality of food and level of sanitation in company cafeterias, improvements in bathroom facilities, company-paid education classes, freedom of movement within and outside the factory compound, and the ability to freely send and receive mail.[81] The rejection of these demands set off a strike of unusual length (nearly six full weeks) that gained immediate fame as an example of successful cooperation among Japanese and Korean workers in an industrial labor action.[82] Despite company attempts to divide the workers along ethnic lines, Japanese and Korean workers based their cooperation on shared experiences as workers and on a set of shared demands.

Wages figured as a prominent issue in the disturbances at Kishibō and, indeed, Korean workers throughout Japan generally received lower wages than their Japanese counterparts. A 1924 report titled *Chōsenjin rōdōsha ni kan suru jōkyō* (The Condition of Korean Workers), published by the Home Ministry Social Bureau, shows that Korean cotton-spinning factory workers in Osaka that year received approximately 8 percent less in wages than their Japanese counterparts and approximately 10 percent less in the city of Kobe, while wage differentials between Koreans and Japanese in other occupations such as ceramics and papermaking could be as much as 40 or 50 percent.[83] Fees charged by the Sōaikai constituted part of the reason for lower wages among Korean female workers. As a Japanese former manager at Kishibō remembered some years later: "It was a system in which the Sōaikai was contracted to manage the workers. I was a manager, but even so I never managed the Korean workers. . . . For this reason, when the company calculated wages it took out a Sōaikai fee from the Korean women workers. This was compulsory."[84] The *Osaka Asahi* newspaper reported in 1925 on a survey conducted by the Korean Female Factory Worker Protection League (Chōsen Jokō Hogo Renmei), which had looked into factory conditions in the cities of Kishiwada, Haruki, and Sakai, all places in which Kishibō had operations. The survey found that a newly hired Korean female worker making approximately fifty sen as a daily wage paid twenty sen per month for Sōaikai membership dues, which was collected by her (Korean) supervisor at the company.[85] In other words, instead of allowing the regularly employed Japanese company managers to directly manage Korean workers, the company contracted with the Sōaikai to provide Korean managers who would be directly responsible for Korean female workers. Korean managers, it was believed, were better able to facilitate the linguistic and cultural differences between the Korean workers and their Japanese employers. But just as important was the Sōaikai's role in containing union activities and the possibility of labor disruptions among a group of workers increasingly viewed as militant, independence-minded, and strike-prone.

Indeed, by the time of the six-week-long strike in May and June of 1930, the union presence at Kishibō had grown significantly. The strike committee formed in early May included the Osaka Korean Labor Union (Ōsaka Chōsen Rōdō Kumiai), the Senshū Joint Labor Union (Senshū Gōdō Rōdō Kumiai), and union leaders from the National Council of Japanese Labor Unions (Nihon Rōdō Kumiai Zenkoku Kyō-gikai, or Zenkyō), which mobilized Korean day laborers to help protect against strikebreakers and the inevitability of company thugs being brought in to break up the strike.[86]

Where Tōyō Muslin had employed right-wing members of the Japan Justice League as violent strikebreakers in Tokyo (as discussed in the preceding chapter), Kishibō relied on the Sōaikai for the same purpose. Most of the female Korean workers employed at Kishibō had been recruited by the Sōaikai, whose control over the conditions of their employment and immigration convinced many of them not to participate in the work stoppages.[87] But the Sōaikai already had a history of violent interventions in labor disputes, and its members did not hesitate when called upon by company officials at Kishibō to break up a workers' rally held within the factory on May 7.[88] The violence continued over the course of the next several weeks, with one Korean participant in the strike recounting the events some years later:

> On May 15 in the evening, we held a demonstration march. The Korean day laborers and women of Sakai were joined by Japanese and marched to the factory. There we met with a corps of police. The police yelled at us, "Get back, or we'll beat you to death," and other things to menace us. Things grew violent and people began to riot, throwing sticks and stones and anything else they could get their hands on. The factory windows were all broken out, and the solid brick factory gates were smashed. Men and women were covered with blood from the broken shards of glass and the police beatings. Over seventy people were arrested. After that nearly everyday there was a confrontation. On the 18th four Japanese were caught. On the 24th, other factories were called in. On the 26th, more people were arrested. On the 27th, over thirty Koreans and Japanese were arrested.[89]

Finally on June 13, acknowledging their depleted ranks and the hopelessness of the situation, the strike committee withdrew all of its demands and accepted defeat. Ten key union leaders and members of the strike committee were fired and the remaining female workers returned to work.[90]

STRIKEMAKERS AND STRIKEBREAKERS

By the time of the Kishibō strike, factory owners had come to see Korean workers above all others as strike-prone and difficult to control. A Home Ministry Social Bureau report of 1929 warned that "when one or two Koreans get laid off, one hundred go on strike."[91] And one year after the Kishibō strike, the *Nihon rōdō nenkan* (Japan Labor Yearbook) issued the following report: "Using the excuse that most of the strikers at Kishi-wada Spinning were Korean workers, many companies in the Senshū area have begun to lay off Koreans [Senjin]. The Izumi headquarters of the Sōaikai has called an emergency meeting of its officials to formulate a response and are simultaneously mounting a campaign to elicit the understanding of the capitalists and other influential people in the Senshū region."[92] Koreans by this time marked a site of social disruption in a way that Okinawans did not. In fact, throughout the 1920s Okinawan female factory workers were increasingly favored over Korean workers by textile employers. In 1922 seven hundred Okinawan female factory workers were hired to replace 596 Koreans at the Fuji Gas Spinning's Ōita factory.[93] By the time the effects of the Great Depression were being felt in 1930, companies engaged in downsizing often targeted Korean workers first, and in several strike situations involving Korean and Japanese workers Okinawans were hired as strikebreakers. The group power (*danketsuryoku*) possessed by Korean female workers identified by labor consultant Ishigami Kinji as central to an understanding of their management would have been quickly understood by his colleagues as an allusion to their tendency to strike.[94]

The differences in the treatment and expectations of Korean and Okinawan female factory workers cannot be attributed solely to economic expediency, especially since Okinawan workers did not receive lower wages than ethnic Japanese employees as was often the case with Korean workers. Rather, this differential approach reflected a strategy to combat organized labor. And there was no immediate reason why assimilation for Okinawans should be more attainable than for Koreans. Both Okinawans and Koreans came to cities like Osaka as nonnative speakers of Japanese, with different customs of dress and food, and as migrants from areas seen as poor and backward. The structure and leadership of support organizations led by and for Okinawans and Koreans living in the main islands, combined with Japanese discourses on racial difference that hierarchized different groups within the imperial polity, largely determined assumptions about degrees of national belonging.

Where the Prefectural Association (Kenjinkai) that dominated Okinawan public life in Osaka increasingly moved toward a policy of
"lifestyle reform," Korean organizations and their memberships had less
clear relationships to the policy and practices of assimilation.[95]

On the one hand, the Sōaikai, which called itself an assimilationist
group, concerned itself as much with maintaining control and discipline
over poor immigrant workers as with providing them with practical forms
of welfare. The lack of resources and cultural facility of such workers made
them the targets of suspicion and discriminatory treatment from mainstream Japanese, which in turn made them especially in need of mutual aid
and support and simultaneously vulnerable to Sōaikai coercion and abuse.
At times, as when they went on strike at Kishibō, Korean female factory
workers viewed the Sōaikai as representative of the repressive powers of
capitalism and resisted assimilation attempts that failed to offer them any
tangible benefits. Meanwhile, Korean labor unions maintained a radical
agenda based on ideas of class and racial equality that persisted into the
1930s. The dictates of international communism that demanded that each
country could have only one communist party, however, led to the dissolution of the Korean Communist Office in Japan (Chōsen Kyōsan Nihon
Sōkyoku) in favor of an ethnic section (*minzokubu*) that was established
within the Japan Communist Party structure and given the mandate to lead
the Korean movement in Japan. Despite the Comintern's stand against the
kind of capitalist imperialism that had led to the influx of Korean workers
into Japan, international communism operated squarely within a nation-
state framework that disallowed contending national (ethnic) agendas
within a single state system. Shortly after the 1930 strike at the Sakai factory of Kishibō, orders came from the Profintern (the "Red International
of Labor Unions") to dissolve the communist-affiliated Korean labor
unions operating within the *naichi* into the Japanese communist-affiliated
Zenkyō.[96] This absorption of Korean unions has been celebrated by some
historians as a positive move demonstrating the ability of Japanese and
Korean unionists to work together effectively, the breaking down of the
"hedge" between them (as shown in the Kishibō strike), and the recognition of this fact by the Profintern. The dissolution of specifically Korean
unions within Japan, however, meant that Korean workers had to defer to
the goals of the dominant Japanese ethnic labor movement.[97] The merg-
ing of a union organized specifically to address the needs of Koreans into
a broader Japanese institution that did not prioritize the circumstances and
demands of its minority members may have precluded the possibility of
full Korean participation in future labor actions.

To integrate female Korean workers into the metropolitan industrial workplace, companies used mediated forms of control rather than direct appeals to the workers themselves. In part because of linguistic and cultural differences, the Sōaikai and male Korean supervisors were enlisted to recruit and retain female workers and to make sure they performed their jobs efficiently with the least amount of disturbance. The Sōaikai recruited workers from Korea and within Japan, arranged for their legal immigration and placement at a work site, and sought to manage most aspects of their lives. But unlike the cultivation groups that mobilized female Japanese workers through appeals to moral and cultural values, the Sōaikai used the language of assimilation in which docility and diligence were promoted under the rhetoric of performing Japaneseness more than performing any particular notion of womanly virtue. In fact, the Sōaikai's ability to promote assimilation was actually quite weak, as evidenced by the segregation of Korean workers within the physical space of the factory and its dormitories, by the use of Korean managers to oversee them, and by the very need companies had for the interventions of the Sōaikai in virtually all aspects of Korean worker management, from recruitment to strikebreaking. That employers and management specialists such as Ishigami Kinji treated Koreans as an ethnic rather than a gendered labor group suggests that assimilationist rhetoric used by Japan-Korea reconciliation groups did not translate into actual assimilation among workers. Instead, social harmony was promoted both by textile companies and the Sōaikai, even at the cost of Korean women's individual dignity and the equality the Sōaikai purported to espouse.

Epilogue

Managing Women in Wartime and Beyond

The period between World War I and the Manchurian Incident of 1931 that marked the outbreak of hostilities between Japan and China was the most crucial in the formation of industrial discourses about class, race, gender, and the nation. The 1920s saw attempts to rationalize industry in which managers sought to cultivate an efficient and docile workforce by promoting a strong consciousness of womanhood in its female workers. Many of the elements of the paternalist policies adopted to this end emphasized women's role as future wives and mothers; offered educational opportunities in the domestic arts, home economics, and etiquette; and promised to protect young women's chastity through careful monitoring of their whereabouts and behavior. Once put into place, many of these practices persisted throughout wartime and well into the postwar period.

Developments in labor-management strategies in Japan's wartime and postwar textile industry took place in the context of several conditions: the dissolution of unions and the consolidation of labor during the late 1930s and early 1940s under a regime that Andrew Gordon has dubbed "imperial fascism"; the American occupation–authored constitutional and legislative changes that gave significant rights to women and to workers in the immediate postwar period; new popular conceptions of democracy and human rights that emerged during the occupation; the decline of light industry (textiles) as a major force within the Japanese economy; attempts to revitalize that industry as part of the postwar economic recovery; and the renewed sense of national pride that coincided with the 1964 Tokyo Olympic Games and the beginning of the era of high economic growth.

WARTIME MOBILIZATION AND WOMEN'S INDUSTRIAL LABOR

The years 1930 and 1931 marked the high point for strikes throughout Japan.[1] In 1930 several of the largest cotton-spinning concerns experienced strikes, including those at Tōyō Muslin and Kishiwada Spinning discussed in chapters 4 and 5, as well as strikes at Kanegafuchi Spinning and Fuji Gas Spinning. But after the Manchurian Incident in September 1931 and the beginning of wartime mobilization on a national level, the discourse prevalent during the Meiji period linking women workers to national interests (which had been downplayed in the intervening years in favor of an emphasis on corporate interests), began to be reasserted. Counterdiscourses and images of womanhood that competed with the ideal produced through factory discipline ceased to be viable as the country headed toward war and as the labor movement succumbed to state control. In 1933 an article in *Ie no hikari* (Light of the Home), a widely circulating magazine for rural women, featured ten female factory workers who had just returned from a special visit to Manchuria: "The grand undertaking of Japanese migration to the continent will not succeed by the bravery of men alone. Surely the reassuring partnership of women will be necessary. At Nisshin Cotton Spinning, many of whose employees come from the countryside, model female factory workers were chosen from among their factories all over the country. On May 23, those chosen set off to make comfort visits [*imon*] to the Imperial Army units throughout Manchuria. They stayed in Japanese immigrant villages and have recently returned."[2] The representation in this article of model female factory workers via a photographic portrait of the group of smiling girls sporting sashes with the words "Greater Japan National Defense Ladies' Association" written on them echoed the style and sentiment of Uno Riemon's *Kōjo risshindan* (Stories of Factory Girls Getting Ahead), a didactic work for female factory workers that appeared over two decades earlier. Just as Uno had emphasized filial piety and the benefits the success of a factory girl would bring to her family and village, for the editors of *Ie no hikari* these model workers represented the purest feminine element of the Japanese countryside—a population the state was encouraging to move to Manchuria as farmer-settlers.[3] The countryside from which these ten female factory workers had come—and the values of cooperativism, physical and spiritual purity, and patriotism associated with it—had triumphed, at least momentarily, over the materialism and individualism of modern urban life.

The years after the beginning of outright hostilities with China in 1937 brought great changes to Japan's economy and industrial structure, but remarkable continuities in terms of the management of female labor.[4] These continuities, however, were not always recognized as such by representatives of the state, whose rhetoric often suggested that the very concept of female labor was new. Although for decades the textile industry had focused in its labor-management strategies on the cultivation of female workers as future good wives and wise mothers, wartime discussions of women's wage work began with the premise that few if any women had worked in factories before the current crisis. Now with the state taking the lead in managing the recruitment of labor for wartime mobilization, wage work was discussed explicitly as undesirable for women. Further, it was argued that moves toward integrating women into the labor force should be taken as a last resort, with a consciousness of women's special characteristics (i.e., their biological function as mothers) always in mind. Such an elision of the history of the disciplining of female industrial labor could take place because of the rapidly changing nature of the Japanese economy and its workforce

Throughout the war years, agriculture remained the largest sector employing women (see table 4), with textiles the largest industrial employer of female labor. In 1940, for example, 56.6 percent of gainfully employed women worked in agriculture and 15.3 percent worked in manufacturing. Most of those in manufacturing worked in the textile mills.[5] But this continuity masked the very different labor market and industrial landscape that developed out of the exigencies of war. In fact, the very nature of the textile industry began to change radically in 1940 with announcements of Prime Minister Konoe's plans for a "New Order" in Japan to complement the New Order the imperial state envisioned for all of Asia. Some of the most well-known elements of this domestic New Order occurred in the political arena, notably the dissolution of political parties and the founding of the state-authorized Imperial Rule Assistance Association (Taisei Yokusankai) to replace them in 1940. But implementing the economic New Order began earlier, with the passage in 1938 of the National General Mobilization Law (Kokka Sōdōin Hō) and the state founding of the Patriotic Industrial Service Federation (Sangyō Hōkoku Renmei, or Sanpō) that same year. Economic rationalization ef-

TABLE 4. NUMBER OF INDIVIDUALS EMPLOYED
IN AGRICULTURE, 1920–1940

Year	Female	Male	Total
1920	6,346,098	7,593,048	13,939,146
1930	6,365,100	7,578,857	13,943,957
1940	7,183,839	6,365,311	13,549,150

SOURCE: Adapted from Umemura Mataji et al., *Rōdōryoku* (Tokyo: Tōyō keizai shinpōsha, 1988), 202–203.
Note: Workers include Japanese nationals and individuals from the colonies.

forts that had been initiated by industries during the recessions of the 1920s, and taken up with renewed energy after the worldwide depression of the early 1930s, were now orchestrated by the government.

Sensing that voluntary efforts might blunt the force of changes ordered by the state, the Japan Spinners Association quickly moved to rationalize on their own terms. As a result of meetings held in November 1940, the seventy-seven companies represented within the association agreed to consolidate their operations. Within three months only fourteen cotton-spinning companies remained, each of them boasting over five hundred thousand spindles.[6] By August 1941 the representatives of the remaining fourteen cotton-spinning companies devised a grading system for the various factories held among them. A-class factories would remain operational, B-class factories would go off-line and be considered reserve factories, and C-class factories would be shut down. Those factories in the last category would have their machinery scrapped and their buildings turned over for munitions production and use by other heavy industries.[7] Soon after the outbreak of the Pacific War, government pressure increased, with representatives of the Ministry of Commerce and Industry's Cotton and Staple Fiber Control Association (Men Sufu Tōseikai) demanding further rationalization and consolidation. Hostilities with the United States and other Western nations had resulted in Japan's loss of access to raw cotton, as well as a substantial portion of its export market for spun cotton and textiles.[8] In 1943 government pressure to restructure resulted in the reduction of the number of cotton-spinning companies from fourteen to ten (the "Big Ten"), each with over one million spindles.[9]

But even within these large remaining companies, many individual factories were converted from textile production to war production. While many of the factories thus converted remained nominally part of the textile concern, they were largely used for aircraft and chemical production as ordered by the state. The example of Tōyō Spinning by 1943 is illustrative:

> The Toyo Cotton Spinning Company had 53 plants, 38 for cotton, 4 for rayon and staple fiber, 9 for wool, and one each for silk spinning and wood pulp production. Only 22 were in operation producing textiles. Ten had been fitted for aircraft parts and accessories in collaboration with Nippon Aircraft Company, Chuo Industries, Kawasaki Aircraft. Two had been turned over to Toyo Steel Company, one had been leased to Sumitomo Metal Industries Company for the manufacture of butanol. Two had been turned over to Toa Chemical Industry Development Company, one to Kodo Alcohol Company, and the remainder were used for the expansion of affiliated companies such as Toyo Synthetic Chemical Industry, Toyo Heavy Industries, Toyo Rubber-Chemical Industry, etc.[10]

The consolidation of cotton-spinning companies and the conversion of many of the remaining textile factories for war production resulted in a significant decrease in labor requirements for the industry. Between 1940 and 1944 the number of workers employed in the textile industry decreased by more than half (table 5).

It is difficult to say what happened to the many women previously employed in the textile industry whose jobs were cut through these mergers and the downsizing of the industry as a whole. It seems likely that some of them returned to their villages and became part of the growing number of women involved in paid agricultural work. Others may have taken jobs in the service industries in the cities, working in restaurants and inns. This was most likely the case for most of the Korean women formerly employed in now-defunct companies like Kishiwada Spinning. Still others would have made the shift—along with the factories they worked in—from textile production to the production of chemicals and airplanes and other war materiel.

The wartime disintegration of the textile industry, long a major employer of women, meant that the forms and meaning of women's wage work shifted during the 1940s—but the emphasis on women's primary function as mothers and managers of the domestic sphere only heightened as the need for labor grew. The state, now more involved than ever in directing industry and the labor market, continued even in the face of major labor shortages to promote pronatalist policies that supported what many considered to be Japan's unique family system. In January 1941, nearly a year before the attack on Pear Harbor, the government issued a formal population policy that aimed to increase

TABLE 5. NUMBER OF INDIVIDUALS
EMPLOYED IN TEXTILES, 1940–1947

Year	Female	Male	Total	Percent Female
1940 (Oct. 1)	1,043,625	582,684	1,626,309	64.2
1944 (Feb. 22)	569,527	239,225	808,752	70.4
1947 (Oct. 1)	640,922	409,090	1,050,012	61.0

SOURCE: Adapted from Umemura Mataji et al., *Rōdōryoku* (Tokyo: Tōyō keizai shinpōsha, 1988), 260–261.

Japan's population in both the short and long term as part of the over-all development of the Greater East Asian Coprosperity Sphere (Daitōa Kyōeiken). The Coprosperity Sphere, announced by Foreign Minister Matsuoka several months earlier, envisioned a cooperative political and economic block consisting of the countries and colonies of East and Southeast Asia, all under varying degrees of Japanese control. Increasing the country's population, many government officials believed, was crucial to the maintenance of Japan's leadership position within the Coprosperity Sphere. In addition, it would help alleviate Japan's labor shortage. The cabinet thus set forth a population policy in early 1941 designed to increase the country's ethnic Japanese population to one hundred million by 1960.[11] In order to achieve this goal, the state sought to lower the average age of marriage by three years and to promote families of at least five children for each married couple.[12] Birth control had already been proscribed by the National Eugenics Law of 1940, and it was believed that keeping women away from wage work outside the home would further the goals of this population policy.

Japan's wartime labor policy discouraged women from entering into wage work except under certain circumstances where such work was deemed to have the least potential to interfere with the obligations of motherhood. This resulted in a slight decline in the overall percentage of women in the industrial workforce between 1930 and 1944 despite the great need for labor to replace men conscripted into the military. In fact, women seem to have disproportionately replaced men in the agricultural sector rather than in factory work. The percentage of women engaged in manufacturing and construction in 1930 was 24.6 percent, compared to 23.7 percent in 1944. Women engaged in agriculture and forestry in 1930 accounted for 45.3 percent of all women in the civilian labor force, while by 1944 the percentage had risen to 58.4 percent.[13]

Most official discussions related to the possible conscription of women's labor included concerns not only about the protection of motherhood, but also about the preservation of public morals. In November 1941 the Citizens' Labor Patriotic Cooperation Order mandated thirty days per year of labor service from unmarried women between the ages of fourteen and twenty-five. But this part of the order related to women's labor was scarcely enforced. Instead, officials worried about the establishment of proper facilities for women within workplaces. Vice Minister of Health and Welfare Takei Gunji complained in 1943: "The state of affairs today is such that even in factories that have experience managing large numbers of women, there is often not even a separate women's dressing room (*keshōjō*), to say nothing of the fact that there is no one to oversee the management of women workers. What will happen to young unmarried women put into such a place? If women are put in the midst of men, something strange [*hen*] that is neither man nor woman will emerge, and I worry for Japan's future."[14] In Takei's assessment, textile factories with a great deal of experience managing women seem to have been overlooked. He does, however, echo concerns raised nearly two decades earlier by Hosoi Wakizō in his book *Jokō aishi* (The Sorrowful History of Female Factory Workers), in which Hosoi expressed a similar fear that women working alongside men in factories might result in some abnormal form of sexless women (see chapter 2).

A plan developed by the central office of the Patriotic Industrial Service Federation (Sanpō Chūō Honbu) expressed similar anxieties about the susceptibility of womanhood to degradation when exposed to a wage-labor environment. In "Sagyō ni josei no tokusei o hakki joshi kinrō kanri yōkōan naru" (A Plan for Women's Labor Management and the Utilization of Women's Special Characteristics in Manufacturing, 1943), the authors cite as one of their central guidelines for female labor "the protection of women's special character." The plan warns, "Up to now, women with jobs have lost their fundamental character. We must prevent the so-called neutering [*chūseika*] and masculinization [*danseika*] trend that occurs in such cases."[15]

This "Plan for Women's Labor Management" summed up many of the concerns voiced by national and local officials about female labor during the war, most of which resonated with the understandings of womanhood that drove labor-management policies in the textile mills of the 1920s and 1930s. While this document's title indicated an intent to make suggestions about labor management, very little of the actual document spoke to the problems of production or the process of work itself.

Instead, it focused on how women engaged in factory work could retain their "special characteristics" as women and future mothers—or how, in the words of the introduction, wage work could be organized in such a way as to "not get in the way of women's motherly sacrifices [*boseiteki gisei*]."[16] To this end, the "plan" called for special facilities for women workers. It recommended the establishment of educational programs; cultivation training in subjects such as sewing, etiquette, handicrafts, and cooking; "guidance in sentiment," which consisted of training in the tea ceremony, flower arranging, music, and traditional Japanese poetry; proper recreational activities; and training in emergency medicine and nursing. It also called for special facilities for women nursing babies and for women with children. The recommendations for personnel and marriage counseling facilities were especially explicit. The personnel and marriage counselors should be women "in order to properly understand the inner feelings of women workers"; counselors should be of sufficient age and education; and the supervisor of the female counselors should be men.[17] To prevent the deterioration of morals, the plan recommended counselors for delinquent girls and facilities to monitor their mores, such as the hiring and training of factory personnel whose job it would be to keep track of public morals (*fūki chōsa kakari*).[18]

The brief discussion of the kinds of work appropriate for women suggests that not only should women be protected from work, but work should be protected from women. Women, the document claimed, are less efficient workers because they have typically been in the workforce for a short time, and because of this they have inferior technical skills. They possess poor judgment regarding work and lack initiative. Women lack a will to work, and they are "emotional and talkative." Because of these essential qualities, the plan argued, there are many types of work that men do that are not suitable for women. Women, the authors suggested, are most suited to "light" or "easy" work such as secretarial and office jobs that require skills in accounting or typing. Factory work was not listed among the various jobs appropriate for females.[19]

After the attack on Pearl Harbor, Japan's labor needs reached crisis levels. Even so, pronatalist policies consistent with prewar ideologies of womanhood meant that women were not encouraged to work outside the home, especially not married women. Women, it was believed, could best serve the country by raising the birth rate. Long-term strategies for increasing Japan's population and *future* labor force took precedence over immediate needs for both skilled and unskilled labor. With no system of compulsory labor service for women, the country had to rely on other sources to fill the need for production in essential industries. Students, older men who had not been drafted into the army, and later Korean men forcibly brought to Japan from the colony joined younger women already in the workforce, many of whom shifted to jobs in different industries. Women were organized into the National Defense Ladies' Association (Kokubō Fujinkai), which not only encouraged factory work among Japanese women, but sent a number of its prominent members to Korea to extol the virtues of wartime cooperation to women there.[20] Despite the massive mobilization of people and resources throughout Japan and its colonies, however, the war effort ended in disaster with the atomic bombings of Hiroshima and Nagasaki.

THE ŌMI KENSHI SPINNING STRIKE OF 1954

Defeat at the hands of the U.S. military in 1945 signaled radical changes in labor legislation and women's status under the law. The largely American-authored postwar constitution that went into effect in 1947 included an article that banned discrimination on the basis of sex and that made men's and women's rights equal within the institution of marriage. The following year the Labor Standards Law provided various protections for pregnant and nursing workers and spelled out certain parameters for the running of company dormitories. Dormitories, for example, should be administered in a manner that protected "the autonomy of dormitory life" and allowed for self-governance by the residents. Further, Article 94 of the law stipulated that "an employer shall not infringe upon the freedom of the personal lives of workers living in dormitories attached to the enterprise."[21]

Despite these radical changes of law, the systems of management and control of female workers developed in the textile industry during the prewar period persisted postwar. Two events—the Ōmi Kenshi Spinning strike of 1954 and the Tokyo Olympics of 1964—help us better understand the continued salience of prewar systems of female labor management, even in the face of a declining textile industry. The Ōmi Kenshi strike has regularly been cited as the "last gasp" of a dying style of management that had characterized the prewar period. By the 1950s, tactics such as censoring workers' mail, restricting freedom of movement within and outside the factory compound, and other methods of worker control and surveillance were not only illegal under the Labor Standards Law, but were broadly seen as antithetical to the principles of democracy popularized during the period of U.S. occupation.[22] This postwar environment created a habitus for female workers within the textile industry in which they could oppose unfair treatment in the name of democracy and human rights.

For 106 days in 1954, the Japanese public witnessed through daily news coverage the spectacle of a textile industry strike led by female factory workers. The most significant postwar textile labor disturbance, the Ōmi Kenshi Spinning strike marked not only the end of some of the most egregious forms of paternalistic prewar labor management, but also coincided with the end of the textile industry as the most significant wage-labor opportunity for Japanese women.[23] Light industries such as silk and cotton textile production had been promoted by the occupying authorities as a way to reground Japan's devastated postwar economy, with cotton singled out for special attention by American authorities recognizing the potential market in Japan for U.S. stocks of raw cotton.[24] But the wartime dismantling of cotton-spinning machinery made the rehabilitation of the industry difficult and expensive. The number of operating spindles owned by Japanese companies had shrunk from a peak of 9 million in 1937, down to a low of 300,000 by the end of 1945. By 1948 the number had risen to 2.2 million—still less than 25 percent of the prewar peak operating capacity.[25]

By the mid-1950s the Japanese government had begun to shift its economic policy to emphasize heavy industries such as iron, steel, coal, and chemicals, as newly industrializing countries in the region began to challenge Japan in the production and trade of textile goods.[26] Beginning at this same time, leaders in Japan's nascent electronics and transistor industry began employing women in large numbers for precisely the same reasons they had earlier been employed in textiles: they could be paid lower wages than men and they were believed to possess quick and nimble fingers most suitable for such demanding and detail-oriented factory work.[27] For a while in the 1950s, employers in these two industries—textiles and transistors—competed for young, low-wage female labor. But by the end of the decade, shifting government priorities that deemphasized textiles as a crucial motor for the Japanese economy, an increase in jobs in the new high-tech industries, and an increase in jobs for women that did not involve factory work all led to the decline of textiles as a major wage-labor opportunity for women. It was precisely during this transitional period marking the decline of textiles as a key Japanese industry that the female workers of Ōmi Kenshi Spinning made their demands.

The Ōmi Kenshi Spinning strike has been characterized as unusual not only for its length, but in that workers framed their demands using the postwar rhetoric of human rights. The Ōmi Kenshi strike was precipitated not by wage cuts or layoffs, as was the case for many Depression-era strikes such as the 1930 Kishiwada Spinning strike, but by the formation of a union and management's efforts to block the union by refusing to recognize it and firing several of its leaders. In this sense, the Ōmi Kenshi strike was a test of the power of a nascent labor movement.

Ōmi Kenshi factories produced parachutes and aircraft during the war.[28] After the war, it was one of many smaller textile companies to benefit from occupation decisions to promote the rebuilding of the cotton industry by limiting the growth of the Big Ten cotton-spinning companies. Authorities considered the Big Ten tainted by their connection to wartime financial cliques and thought the companies could potentially monopolize the industry if left to grow unchecked. The government thus allowed only smaller, independent companies to have access to badly needed new spinning machinery after the war.[29] By the early 1950s, Ōmi Kenshi had emerged as one of the more successful of these companies, with new American-made machinery, seven factories in five prefectures, and business offices in Osaka, Tokyo, and Nagoya. By far the main work of the company involved the spinning of cotton and staple fibers, with smaller divisions in silk spinning and various weaving operations.[30]

Even though wages for both male and female workers at Ōmi Kenshi were approximately one-third those paid to employees of the Big Ten at the time of the strike, wages were not central to worker demands.[31] In fact, the company's wages were likely quite similar to those at a number of other smaller textile companies that had been able to expand their operations thanks to occupation-era policies.[32] Instead, the majority female striking workforce focused on what they considered to be unfair practices and intolerable working conditions.

Still, the basic causes of the strike as well as the demands of workers were consistent with prewar precedents. The twenty-two demands presented to management—the majority of which were eventually accepted as part of the strike settlement—reflected the same kinds of concerns that had been articulated in the 1920s and 1930s. The first group of demands concerned the company's recognition of the union and the dissolution of company-sponsored worker-representative groups. The second category included demands related to working conditions and payment, such as the guarantee that working hours be limited to eight hours per day, a guarantee of paid holidays and a monthly one-day "menstruation leave" for women workers, and the institution of extra pay for overtime and night-shift work. Notably, all of the demands in this category were legal requirements under the 1947 Labor Standards Law, a law that Ōmi Kenshi had been found in violation of hundreds of times at each of its seven factories by the time of the strike.[33] A third category can be classified as those demands related to living conditions at Ōmi Kenshi factories. These included demands for the improvement of cafeteria and living spaces and the employment of security and cleaning personnel for these areas.

But it was a final group of demands—those that the workers and the general public saw as demands for human rights—that constituted the largest number of the twenty-two points put to the company and that mobilized popular opinion in favor of the strikers. Human rights issues included demands that workers be allowed to attend night schools and pursue educational opportunities; the recognition of the right of workers to marry and to not be separated from their spouses; the freedom to engage in cultural activities such as moviegoing and hiking; the cessation of company violations of privacy in the form of searching private property and reading personal letters; the right to leave the factory grounds; and stopping the practice of forcing workers to spy on one another.[34]

The kinds of paternalistic policies in place at Ōmi Kenshi could only exist in a company structured largely along the lines of interwar textile concerns. Ōmi Kenshi employed a majority female workforce out of a total of approximately thirteen thousand workers in 1953. The vast majority of those female operatives lived in company dormitories on the grounds of one of the company's seven factories. Like their predecessors in interwar factories, most of them were quite young, lacking in education, and came from poor rural areas—mostly in the northeast, or Tōhoku region, or from the western island of Kyushu.[35] But also like their predecessors, the women striking at Ōmi Kenshi's factories strategically employed and reshaped a variety of contemporary discourses to make their case to the company, the state, and perhaps most importantly to the public. One of these was the older, but still quite familiar, discourse of jokō aishi, or the "sorrowful history of female factory workers."

Originally the title of Hosoi Wakizō's best-selling 1925 book on the horrible working and living conditions of factory women, the term jokō aishi became part of popular parlance immediately upon publication of this work as shorthand for talking about the evils of capitalism and especially about women's suffering under early capitalist development. We have seen in chapter 2 how Hosoi equated the plight of female factory workers with the condition of the nation, and in chapter 4 how his book influenced activists and writers such as Nakamoto Takako to dedicate their lives to the cause of female factory workers. But writers after Hosoi (most of them writing in a social-science vein, as had he) continued to author influential works that emphasized the persistence of so-called feudal forms of labor and family relations and that manifest themselves most clearly in the case of female factory work. The historian Miyake Yoshiko has termed this narrative "*jokō aishi* discourse," which she defines as social scientists' narratives of Japanese female factory work that examine the partnership between patriarchy and early capitalist development and that tend to view patriarchy as a feudal remnant, and thus sex discrimination as secondary to the problem of socio-economic class. Miyake identifies this discourse with the works of Hosoi; with the Marxist theoretician Yamada Moritarō, whose influential *Nihon shihonshigi bunseki* (Analysis of Japanese Capitalism, 1934) discussed the "slave-like" condition of female factory workers but only counted male workers as part of the proletariat; and with Yamamoto Shigemi, who continued the discourse in the postwar period with his widely selling book *Aa Nomugi tōge* (Ah, Nomugi Pass), which was followed by a sequel and a movie version of the original book.[36]

While Yamamoto's work would not be published until 1977, there was enough popular recognition of *jokō aishi* discourse by 1954 that striking female workers at Ōmi Kenshi could play upon its power to great effect. Toward the middle of the strike, groups of female workers took turns riding in a bus decked out with signs designed to elicit support from local residents as well as from the broader public who would see images of the bus in national newspapers. Along with the large characters reading "On strike!" that adorned the side of the vehicle, the front of the bus sported a sign that read "*jokō aishi*" in big lettering (figure 7). The purpose of this invocation was no doubt to connect in the minds of the public an image of prewar and wartime industrial relations, and all its attendant abuse of workers, with the persistence of such abuses in a postwar, postoccupation Japan. This postwar Japan boasted a progressive constitution replete with civil rights for all citizens, labor laws designed to protect the rights and dignity of both male and female workers, and a vigorous worker and union movement. As one scholar put it as recently as 1999, Ōmi Kenshi labor-management practices "were so backward that the Natsukawas [the family that owned and ran the company] were outcasts even in industrial circles."[37] Women workers effectively used this older narrative of *jokō aishi*, positing the continued existence of the back-

Figure 7. A bus used by striking workers at Ōmi Kenshi Spinning to garner public support for their cause sported banners demanding an end to the "sorrowful history of female factory workers" as it drove down the streets of Osaka. June 9, 1954. Source: The Yomiuri Newspapers.

ward structures of prewar Japanese society that had led to defeat, in conjunction with the new language of democracy and human rights, to mobilize broad opposition to the feudal labor relations practiced by the Natsukawa clan.

In fact, the Natsukawas did employ a management style that was quite similar to that practiced by most cotton-spinning concerns during the interwar period. The company engaged in a propaganda war with the union and striking workers that played to some of the same popular fears about women's sexual purity as had Tōyō Muslin letters to workers' families during the 1930 strike at Kameido. A flyer authored by company officials and dropped by plane over different neighborhoods of Tokyo caught the attention of the novelist Mishima Yukio, who described the scene in his 1964 book *Silk and Insight (Kinu to meisatsu)*:

> Suddenly there was the noise of an engine over Twin Hill, and then a single-engined plane emerged into view as it circled low. When it came above Narutaki, it dropped something, which in no time turned into innumerable

pieces of paper spreading like a cast net, some, blown by the east wind, scattering down towards Fusae and Hiroko. . . . The flyers fluttered down to the leafy cherry trees in the hospital garden, stopping as if magnetized. By then, arms were out of many windows, vying to catch them, amid young screams and coughs.[38]

Mishima's novel used fictional characters, such as the spinning-factory worker Hiroko in the passage above, to tell the story of the Ōmi Kenshi strike that had so gripped the nation. While the novelist changed the name of the company, its owner, and some minor details of the actual events, his rendering of the strike and the conditions of factory workers borrowed heavily from the historical record.

Mishima went on to reproduce the language of the actual flyer dropped on Tokyo residents. The flyer began by calling the strike and the union that sponsored it "cowardly," "evil," "shameless," and a challenge to both the law and the authority of the police. It listed examples of violence and property damage caused by the striking workers and ended with what its authors undoubtedly believed would be the most incendiary accusation: the strike "has allowed groups of picketing hoodlums to force themselves into women workers' bedrooms and has incited young men and women in some places to violate social customs under the pretext of 'Freedom of Marriage.' "[39]

For a spinning company with paternalist policies and obligations to protect and defend the chastity of young women who had come from the countryside to work in its factories, accusations that outside elements such as labor unions and their leaders had nefarious designs on these young charges seemed a potentially effective way to sway the general public. But by 1954 the public had turned toward a belief that the methods used by the company to "protect" its workers were nothing more than an extreme form of past oppressive policies, and the company lost not only the dispute with workers but also the propaganda war.

NICHIBŌ SPINNING AND JAPAN'S OLYMPIC WOMEN'S VOLLEYBALL TEAM

The strike at Ōmi Kenshi Spinning marked the end of an era for Japanese workers and the textile industry, but the 1964 Tokyo Olympic Games marked another kind of milestone, one in which women workers propelled the nation pridefully back into the international community after the devastation of war and defeat. On October 23, 1964, with most of the nation watching the live broadcast on newly purchased

Japanese-made television sets, Japan's Olympic women's volleyball team defeated the Soviet team to capture gold (figure 8).[40] It was one of sixteen gold medals for Japan at the Tokyo Olympics, but the live broadcast of the gold medal match made it one of the most watched, with the national broadcast network NHK recording an 85 percent viewer rating.[41] The fact that the final match was against the Soviet Union made the victory "particularly sweet," as historian Yoshikuni Igarashi has noted, "since the Soviet Union had been one of the most detested countries in postwar Japan for its declaration of war in the final days of the Asia Pacific War and its detention of Japanese POWs in Siberia."[42] Not only did 1964 mark the first time the games had been held in Asia, but it was also the first year volleyball was played as an Olympic sport.

What makes this Olympic team of interest here, however, is that the coach and all but two of the team's players were employees of the Nichibō Cotton Spinning Company.[43] The "Witches of the Orient," as the team had been dubbed by the media leading up to the Tokyo Olympics, were part of a company-sponsored team, and the company was one of postwar Japan's largest textile concerns.[44] Of the two non-Nichibō players, one, Kondō Masako, was from the Kurashiki Cotton Spinning team, and the other, Shibuki Ayano, was from the Yashica (a camera company) team.[45] Japan's Olympic women's volleyball team was, for all intents and purposes, the company team of Nichibō's Kaizuka factory. Just as the 1910 didactic tract *Kōjo kun* (Instructions for Factory Girls) referred to factory girls as "flowers of the people," Japan's women's volleyball team was described as the "flower of the Games."[46]

The Tokyo Olympics marked the emergence of Japan onto the international stage after ignominious defeat in the Pacific War and a lengthy period of recovery from the catastrophic damage that fifteen years of total war mobilization, several years of fire bombings, and two atomic blasts had wrought. The team's hard-driving coach, Daimatsu Hirofumi, represented the perseverance, dedication, and single-minded purpose that the country would need to remake itself and reclaim a sense of national pride in the postwar world. His gold-medal victory proved that it could be done, and with women as the vehicle of this remaking. Daimatsu's unrelenting drive came in large part from his wartime experiences. But in his sometimes brutal insistence on discipline, rigorous training, and selflessness in the face of national need, Daimatsu also resembled the mindset of the factory managers and Shūyodan leaders who had organized female factory workers into rows of five to scrub wooden floors in the "dust-rag dance."

Figure 8. Members of Japan's gold medal–winning Olympic women's volley-ball team—most of them employees at Nichibō Spinning—are received by the emperor and empress at a reception honoring Japan's Olympic athletes. Team captain Kasai Masae is at the far left. November 5, 1964. Source: The Mainichi Newspapers.

Daimatsu had been hired by Nichibō as a regular employee in 1941, after finishing college where he had become an accomplished and dedicated volleyball player. He recalled that the man who interviewed him for the position had sternly warned him, "Daimatsu, you can't play volleyball once you join Nichibō. Nichibō is the place you work. When you were in school you played volleyball, but once you join Nichibō you can't play anymore."[47] Before his first year of employment ended, however, Daimatsu received orders to report for military service. He spent the next six years as a soldier and prisoner of war, barely surviving in the jungles of Burma and enduring two years in a British POW camp in Rangoon.

Daimatsu returned to Nichibō after repatriation to Japan and worked for a year in the General Affairs Section of the company's head office in Osaka. Like most of the larger textile companies, Nichibō had several factory locations in addition to the head office, most of them near the city of Osaka. In 1948 Daimatsu was transferred to the Amagasaki factory, where he began working with the factory's women's volleyball team.

By 1953 company officials decided to try to develop a team that could represent the company nationally and perhaps internationally as well. Because of his work with the Amagasaki team, Daimatsu was chosen to lead the effort. He began his coaching work at Nichibō's Kaizuka factory—where officials had decided to locate the company's flagship team—by recruiting girls just out of higher school to come to work at the factory. These girls, all of whom had been volleyball players in higher school, joined a small number of players already working at Kaizuka who had passed muster with Daimatsu, plus a few more women recruited to Kaizuka from other Nichibō factory teams. By 1958 Daimatsu had molded a team capable of winning Japan's four major volleyball titles, and company officials were ecstatic (figure 9).[48]

The women factory workers who made up Daimatsu's world championship team, and later Japan's Olympic team, hailed mostly from agricultural backgrounds. Kasai Masae, the team captain and oldest member of the Olympic team at age thirty-one, was the fourth child of a farming family in Yamanashi Prefecture. Like many prewar textile factory workers, she traveled far from home to take her first job in 1952 at Nichibō's Ashikaga factory, located in Tochigi Prefecture. A company scout had seen her play on her higher-school volleyball team and recruited her into the company. The following year, Daimatsu spotted her playing on the Ashikaga factory team and had her transferred to Kaizuka, where she eventually became a star player.[49]

In a preface to a 1963 best-selling book by Daimatsu, his wife, and several of the Nichibō Kaizuka team members about their road to victory in the world championship games, the novelist Ishihara Shintarō wrote that the team knew the meaning of "hard training," a form of discipline that youth of his own generation had lived, but one unknown to most Japanese born in the postwar period. By "hard training," Ishihara meant the long hours of practice, the hands swollen and bloodied from the pounding of the ball, and the sometimes brutal psychological treatment at the hands of a coach like Daimatsu. More than the scientific training and the emphasis on technique popular in sports by the 1960s, the spiritual strength gained through hard training, he claimed, made the winning difference.[50]

Volleyball became popular in Japan almost as soon as it was introduced into the country. It was invented in 1895 in Massachusetts by a physical director of the Young Men's Christian Association as an alternative to the more physically demanding sport of basketball. Because it required little specialized equipment and could be played almost anywhere, it spread quickly in both rural and urban areas in Japan, especially among the poor. As Okuno Takeo wrote in the women's journal *Fujin kōron* (Women's Forum) shortly after the 1964 Olympic Games: "[When I think about volleyball], I envision girls suffering from malnu-

Figure 9. The Nichibō Kaizuka factory women's volleyball team defeated the Polish team with a spiked ball in the third set at a tournament in Nagoya on June 7, 1962. This was the team's sixtieth straight win. Source: The Mainichi Newspapers.

trition hard at playing volleyball—the only sport that they could afford—in a corner of a dark, filthy factory. Volleyball was a sport for the poor. It was a sport of factories, a sport for lunchtime and factory rooftops."[51] But from much earlier, volleyball was also seen as a sport particularly suited to girls. In 1924 volleyball figured prominently during the Japan Girls' Olympics held that year. This national event featured girls' higher-school teams from across the country. The Himeji Girls' School team beat the Kobe First Girls' Higher School to emerge as the winner among a field of sixteen teams. Notably, a large proportion of these teams came from towns that had textile factories.[52]

Nichibō, in fact, introduced volleyball as a company team sport in 1923 as a "workplace refresh sport" aimed at encouraging employees to relieve stress through physical exercise with their coworkers.[53] The company attributed the success of its 1964 volleyball team to prewar systems of management that promoted sports as part of a set of practices related to worker cultivation. Nichibō claimed that with the establishment of the prewar dormitory system, the creation of facilities for the cultural and educational development of employees and dorm residents was "more a company social wage, emanating from moral responsibility and principles of a higher order," rather than a labor-management policy.[54] Company sports teams were one of these amenities built into the system of paternalism that had bridged the interwar, wartime, and postwar periods.

The forms of disciplining female factory workers created the particular circumstances leading to the successes of Japan's Olympic women's volleyball team. As Sakuta Keiichi, writing in 1967 on Japan's "cultures of shame," has noted: "The customs of Japanese life, the rules of order and cleanliness governing the factory and the uniformity of action they nurtured, the tight-knit communal life fostered by the dormitory system, the silent support of nameless people, and the particular way that [Nichibō] president Hara Kichibei exerted his power—these were all necessary conditions for the creation of a strong team. It goes without saying this was the patriarchal structure of what can be called the House of Daimatsu Team."[55] Nichibō Kaizuka team member Tanida Kinuko described the life she and fellow employees on the team experienced during its most successful years: As a production factory, Kaizuka operated on three work shifts. All the players, who were office workers, lived in the dorm, and all of them were on the "afternoon" shift, which actually ran from 8:00 A.M. to 4:30 P.M. A typical daily schedule would be to wake at 6:30, clean one's room and have breakfast to be at work by 8:00 A.M. The cafeteria always served the same food, claimed Tanida, so sometimes workers would go out and spend their own money to buy different food. At 4:30 the workday ended and team members would go directly to practice. Practice under Daimatsu would often last until 1:00 A.M. Once the women got back to their dorms, they would still need to bathe and launder their clothes. Bedtime was often not until 2:00 A.M.[56]

Such a daily routine left no time for personal lives, though the players were frequently asked whether they had boyfriends or about their plans for marriage. Player Miyamoto Emiko's stock answer to such questions was that she would wait to find a man to marry who was taller than she, since "men don't like it when their wives are taller than they are."[57] Kasai Masae, already past thirty and the oldest player on the team, stated with resignation that if she had a boyfriend she would want to spend time with him, and that would take time away from practice. More than that, though, she complained that the salary she received from Nichibō was quite low—not enough to buy clothes and other things that she liked. No matter, though: "When we are at practice, we forget we are women."[58] Unlike her prewar female textile employee counterparts for whom womanhood consisted of a set of domestic skills, filial piety, and a spirit of sacrifice for the nation, Kasai and her teammates lived in a postwar Japan marked by high economic growth and ideas about womanhood defined through consumption.

The disciplinary practices that led to the rise of the Nichibō Kaizuka women's Olympic volleyball team were strikingly similar to those that resulted in the 106-day strike at Ōmi Kenshi ten years earlier. Each company featured long working hours, workers with rural backgrounds, and the circumscription of worker movement made possible by the dormitory system. On the surface, Ōmi Kenshi was the story of the defeat of the old order, while the Olympics marked the emergence of the new Japan erected on the successes of rebuilt industries and the sacrifices made during wartime. The strike at Ōmi Kenshi highlights the importance of newly realized civil rights for women and for labor in a Japan still emerging from the devastation of war. In its relentless drive for profits at the expense of worker health, safety, standards of living, and basic human rights, Ōmi Kenshi stood for a part of Japan's past and what American occupying authorities referred to as the feudal traditions that had led the country down the path toward militarization. Ironically, the efforts by interwar managers to promote womanly virtues in their workers were not a significant part of Ōmi Kenshi's management strategy. The company reflected not so much prewar treatment of women workers as pre-*interwar* use of female labor as an expendable commodity. The humanism and compassionism that marked post–World War I management strategies was largely absent at Ōmi Kenshi, allowing workers to protest their treatment based on appeals both to new postwar legal civil rights and to a strain of prewar anxiety about the status of women under capitalism embodied in the *jokō aishi* discourse.

Nichibō, however, did offer the kinds of amenities lacking at Ōmi Kenshi, and the volleyball team that made it to the Olympics was one of these. The gold medal won by the team represented a refighting of the war but with a different, this time positive, outcome. Coach Daimatsu used military techniques to train his volleyball "soldiers" so that they could defeat Japan's archrival, which could no longer be its patron the United States, but the Soviet Union with whom no peace treaty was ever signed. But replaying the war on the volleyball court meant not only creating player-soldiers, it also meant reviving Japan's most important prewar industry—the cotton-spinning factories that helped build the wartime military-industrial economy using female labor. It also meant

female factory workers sacrificing for the nation so that the "flowers of
the people" could become the international "flower of the Games."

In the previous chapters I have outlined the competing discourses within
which female factory women experienced labor relations practices; how
"woman" and "worker" were set up in opposition to one another; and
how managers, social reformers, and female workers themselves variously deployed images of "woman" and "worker" to further their own
objectives. By the time the prohibition on night work for women and
children went into effect in July of 1929, factory managers in the textile
industry had already developed a highly gendered system of labor discipline. The rationalization of capital and technology that had begun in the
1920s reached its zenith with the rationalization of worker bodies that
took place once the law banning night work had finally been implemented. After 1929 the intensity with which company managers sought
to direct the working and nonworking lives of female workers increased
as worker dissatisfaction more and more manifested itself in the form of
strikes and labor actions.

The types of education promoted within the factories for female
workers, including Shūyōdan activities that emphasized national duty
and filial piety, sought to cultivate workers as ideal Japanese *women*
even more than ideal industrial *workers*. Cultivation groups engaged
women and girls in calisthenics and ritual cleaning activities, in addition
to offering instruction in sewing, flower arranging, and the tea ceremony.
Corporate strategies of worker discipline thus sought to mold workers
as women whose time in the mills would be temporary and who would
soon marry and become managers of households and mothers of the next
generation of Japanese citizen-subjects. For managers, invoking an ideal
Japanese womanhood rather than an ideal of industrial laborer offered
a means by which the contradictions of "woman worker" could be, if
not resolved, at least used to greatest advantage by employers intent on
minimizing labor-management conflict.

If industrial managers sought to cultivate female workers as future
wives and mothers, they did so precisely because they knew that as workers (and not simply as women) female employees could organize, union-
ize, and could make demands of employers. Like the workers of Tōyō
Muslin, they could engage in strikes and street battles, and they could
and did use the language of Marxism (learned in such venues as Tatewaki's Workers' School for Women) to locate themselves not as women
working for company and nation, but as "women fighters" acting col-

lectively—sometimes across lines of ethnicity and colonial status—as they struggled against the "tyranny of capitalism." Some labor schools, such as the Kyōai Jojuku and Workers' School for Women, replaced company textbooks on subjects such as etiquette and national language (*kokugo*) with political tracts about proletarian economics and women and the labor movement. Within this counterdiscourse, female factory workers insisted on a (working) classed understanding of womanhood that more fully took into account their needs and aspirations.

But these discourses and counterdiscourses predicated on an ethnically coherent womanhood were of little use to women workers from the colony of Korea and the prefecture of Okinawa, newly (and tenuously) incorporated into the national body. These women often spoke little if any Japanese and were often illiterate even in their native language. For the companies employing them who sought to integrate newly available forms of labor into a system always looking for efficiencies, womanhood figured much less than ethnicity in their management strategies. The efficiencies of hiring colonial labor included the possibility of paying lower wages and the hope that women and girls far from home, unaccustomed to the language and customs of the metropole, and desperate to improve their situation would be less likely than Japanese workers to engage in organized protest. The different statuses and living conditions of Koreans and Okinawans within Japan proper meant that this docility lasted longer in practice among Okinawans hoping to be counted as part of the Japanese ethnos than it did for Koreans, for whom assimilation was more difficult. Koreans struggled not only against their treatment within the factory, but also against the assimilationist organizations that claimed to advocate for the welfare and just treatment of Koreans in Japan while just as often working coercively as recruiters and as strike-breakers for the companies.

Once the war with China intensified in 1937, government-directed rationalization and consolidation of the textile industry eliminated the need for colonial labor, and many Japanese women were also pushed out of the industry to take jobs in agriculture or in service industries. Even as the spinning machines and factories of the textile companies that had once formed the backbone of the economy were being dismantled to make room for war production, the state was redeploying much of the rhetoric about women used by the textile industry in the interwar period to argue against the expansion of women's labor in industry during wartime. Instead of taking positive steps to mobilize women's labor for the war effort, government officials worried about the fate of Japan's family system should women engage in wage work in large numbers. Authorities expressed identical concerns about purity and chastity in the factory environment as industry managers and social commentators had expressed with such immediacy in the wake of the ban on night work in 1929. By the 1940s Japan's ambitious population policy for growth told women that the time to be wives and mothers was now. Those women who found themselves working in wartime factories making cloth, or parachutes, or airplanes—for personal economic reasons or because, it was said, they were willing to sacrifice their own welfare for the good of the state—could expect to find better amenities for childcare and nursing than had ever been available before. Motherhood-protection and labor-protection advocates found their greatest support in a state mobilized for total war.

Attempts to revitalize the textile industry following the war resulted in the reinstatement of many of the same practices of labor paternalism that had been developed during the interwar period. In most cases, female textile labor still came from the countryside. Further, company appeals to families and workers still depended on the construction of employees as future wives and mothers in need of benevolent care, education, and protection. These narratives met with postwar ideologies that in some instances countered their persuasive force and in other instances worked to bolster them. New ideas about democracy and women's rights allowed women workers to argue against the coercive aspects of paternalism that circumscribed their movements and their personal relationships. But by the 1960s a country poised on the edge of economic high growth and ready to rejoin the international community on an equal footing could point to the prewar and wartime qualities of discipline and sacrifice embodied by the women volleyball players of Nichibō as examples of how much paternalism could achieve—for a team, a company, and the nation.

The patterns of labor management in the textile industry developed during the interwar period and persisting into the postwar era are a central part of a larger story about the fraught relation between women and wage work in Japan more generally. The concern of the state and industry with protecting the special characteristics of Japanese womanhood that could be undone by wage labor has been a major feature not only of the management of textile factory workers, but also for the "transistor girls" who followed them in the 1950s and 1960s and for the management of women in white-collar jobs in the late twentieth and early twenty-first century.[59] Until the domestic sphere in which women properly "belong" is no longer seen as antithetical to the public world of work, women will have to contend with management policies that regard them as temporary labor in need of protection and womanly cultivation rather than as workers worthy of long-term investment and recognition of their productive worth.

Notes

INTRODUCTION

1. Kawada Shirō, "Kachōsei kazoku soshiki no hōkai, kazoku seido hōkai no kiun," in *Nihon fujin mondai shiryō shūsei*, vol. 5, *Kazoku seido*, ed. Yūzawa Yasuhiko (Tokyo: Domesu shuppan, 1976), 438.

2. I borrow the term "boundary marker" as applied to women from Anne McClintock, who argues that European men feminized boundaries in imperial narratives in order to contain them. Anne McClintock, *Imperial Leather: Race, Gender and Sexuality in the Colonial Contest* (New York: Routledge, 1995).

3. On feminized Okinawans as a marker of the limits of Japanese identity, especially in Taiwan, see Alan S. Christy, "The Making of Imperial Subjects in Okinawa," in *Formations of Colonial Modernity in East Asia*, ed. Tani E. Barlow (Durham, NC: Duke University Press, 1997).

4. Gordon does gesture toward the importance of gender and includes discussions of women's labor and labor actions, but on the whole his work focuses on male workers. Andrew Gordon, *Labor and Imperial Democracy in Prewar Japan* (Berkeley: University of California Press, 1991).

5. E. P. Thompson, *The Making of the English Working Class* (New York: Vintage 1966).

6. Anna Clark has revisited E. P. Thompson's work using a gender analysis to suggest that a part of English radical political struggles of the nineteenth century was the attempt to "universalize [a] class-bound notion of gender" that placed women in the domestic sphere and "in which individual men joined together as equals to form the public sphere of politics." As in Japan, this ideal of separate spheres was unattainable for many working-class families in which the wages from women's outside work formed a necessary contribution to the family economy. Anna Clark, *The Struggle for the Breeches: Gender and the Making of the British Working Class* (Berkeley: University of California Press, 1995), 2.

7. Janet Hunter, "Factory Legislation and Employer Resistance: The Abolition of Night Work in the Cotton-Spinning Industry," in *Japanese Management in Historical Perspective: The International Conference on Business History 15; Proceedings of the Fuji Conference*, ed. Yui Tsunehiko and Nakagawa Keiichirō (Tokyo: University of Tokyo Press, 1989), 243–245.

1. FROM HOME WORK TO CORPORATE PATERNALISM

1. Tomioka is often referred to as Japan's first textile factory, but in fact the Satsuma clan had begun operations at its own cotton mill as early as 1867. See Naosuke Takamura, "The Cotton Spinning Industry in Japan During the Pre–World War I Period: Its Growth and Essential Conditions," in *Innovation, Know How, Rationalization and Investment in the German and Japanese Economies, 1868/1871–1930/1980,* edited by Hans Pohl (Wiesbaden, Germany: Franz Steiner Verlag GmbH, 1982), 208; W. Miles Fletcher III, "The Japan Spinners Association: Creating Industrial Policy in Meiji Japan," *The Journal of Japanese Studies* 22, no. 1 (Winter 1996): 53. Thomas Smith's classic account of the Meiji state's role in early Japanese industrialization reports that Japan's first mechanized silk-reeling mill was started by Matsudaira Tadayoshi, the former *daimyō* (feudal lord) of the Maebashi domain, in 1870. Thomas C. Smith, *Political Change and Industrial Development in Japan: Government Enterprise, 1868–1880* (Stanford: Stanford University Press, 1965), 57.

2. David Wittner argues that the values suggested by the Meiji slogan "civilization and enlightenment" had a greater influence on decisions concerning equipment, architecture, technology, and training in both the new silk and the burgeoning steel industries than more practical economic considerations. David Wittner, "Iron and Silk: Progress and Ideology in the Technological Transformation of Japan, 1850–1895," (Ph.D. diss., Ohio State University, 1999).

3. Koyama Shizuko, *Ryōsai kenbo to iu kihan* (Tokyo: Keisō shobō, 1991).

4. Jordan Sand, *House and Home in Modern Japan: Architecture, Domestic Space, and Bourgeois Culture, 1880–1930* (Cambridge, MA: Harvard University Asia Center, 2003), 57.

5. Tanino Setsuko, "Bōseki jokō taishokugo no kōkyō ni kan suru chōsa," *Sangyō Fukuri* 12, no. 2 (1937), cited in Ōshima Eiko, "Ryō taisenkan no joshi rōdō: Bōseki, seishi jokō o chūshin ni," in *Nihon joseishi,* ed. Joseishi sōgō kenkyūkai (Tokyo: Tōkyō Daigaku shuppankai, 1982), 38. The survey also notes that about 9 percent returned home due to illness (mostly tuberculosis), and 4 percent of those died.

6. Janet Hunter discusses a number of these surveys in *Women and the Labour Market in Japan's Industrialising Economy: The Textile Industry before the Pacific War* (New York: RoutledgeCurzon, 2003), 287–292.

7. Yoneda Sayoko, "Shufu to shokugyō fujin," in *Nihon tsūshi,* ed. Iwanami kōza (Tokyo: Iwanami shoten, 1994), 183–184.

8. Shizuko Koyama, "The 'Good Wife and Wise Mother' Ideology in Post–World War I Japan," *U.S.-Japan Women's Journal, English Supplement,* no. 7 (1994): 41–42. On the new concept of "home" in the Meiji period, see Jordan Sand, "At Home in the Meiji Period: Inventing Japanese Domesticity," in *Mir-*

ror of Modernity: Invented Traditions of Modern Japan, ed. Stephen Vlastos (Berkeley: University of California Press, 1998), 191–207. These changes in Meiji Japan bear some resemblance to those in nineteenth-century New York City described by Christine Stansell, who argues that the sexual division of labor was not created, but was reinforced, by industrial patterns taking shape at that time. These "outside" (putting-out work; in the Japanese context, *naishoku*) and "inside" (factory work) configurations employed preexisting patterns of familial relations. Sometimes this meant hiring entire families, but mostly it meant utilizing the patriarchally based sexual hierarchies of the family within the workplace. Christine Stansell, *City of Women: Sex and Class in New York, 1789–1860* (Chicago: University of Illinois Press, 1987).

9. Yokoyama Gennosuke, *Nihon no kasō shakai* (1899; Tokyo: Iwanami bunkō, 1995). For an English translation (with an excellent translator's introduction) of Yokoyama's important work, see Eiji Yutani, "*Nihon no kaso shakai* of Gennosuke Yokoyama" (Ph.D. diss., University of California, 1985).

10. Tsūshō sangyōshō, Chōsa tōkeibu, ed. *Kōgyō tōkei gojūnenshi = History of the Census of Manufactures for 1909–1958,* vol. 3 (Tokyo: Ōkurashō insatsukyoku, 1963), 39, 42, and frontispiece. Tables on these pages give the following figures for profits in the textile industry relative to all other industry: 1910, 50.7 percent; 1914, 48.1 percent; 1919, 51.0 percent; 1925, 50.2 percent.

11. E. Patricia Tsurumi, *Factory Girls: Women in the Thread Mills of Meiji Japan* (Princeton: Princeton University Press, 1990).

12. Seishi orimono shinpōsha, "Your Employer Is Your Second Set of Parents," in *Shūshin kunwa: Kōjo no kagami* (Tokyo: Seishi orimono shinpōsha, 1912), 6–7.

13. Takenobu Toshihiko, ed., *Jokō tokuhon* (Tokyo: Jitsugyō kokumin kyōkai, 1911), 1.

14. See for example Takenobu, *Jokō tokuhon;* Seishi orimono shinpōsha, *Shūshin kunwa;* and Sangyō fukuri kyōkai, ed., *Kekkaku yobō dokuhon* (Tokyo: Sangyō fukuri kyōkai, 1930).

15. Katō Tomomasa, *Kōjo kun* (Tokyo: Katō Tomomasa, 1910), 5.

16. Koji Taira, *Economic Development and the Labor Market in Japan* (New York: Columbia University Press, 1970), chapter 5; Hunter, *Women and the Labour Market in Japan's Industrialising Economy,* chapter 5.

17. Andrew Gordon, "The Invention of Japanese-Style Labor Management," in *Mirror of Modernity: Invented Traditons of Modern Japan,* ed. Stephen Vlastos (Berkeley: University of California Press, 1998), 19–36.

18. Quoted in Sheldon M. Garon, *The State and Labor in Modern Japan* (Berkeley: University of California Press, 1987), 30.

19. Runaways from silk- and cotton-spinning mills were common before the 1920s, as girls attempted to escape the physical or sexual abuse they experienced at the hands of male recruiters or factory supervisors. Various examples are scattered throughout Hosoi Wakizō, *Jokō aishi* (1925; Tokyo: Iwanami bunkō, 1993), and Yamamoto Shigemi, *Aa Nomugi tōge* (1979; Tokyo: Kadokawa bunkō, 1994).

20. Tōjō Yukihiko has written extensively on the importance of notions of *jinkaku* for the development of attitudes about work and labor-management

policies among women in Japan's silk industry. Tōjō Yukihiko, *Seishi dōmei no jokō tōroku seidō: Nihon kindai no hen'yō to jokō no 'jinkaku'* (Tokyo: Tōkyō Daigaku shuppansha, 1990). Thomas Smith has documented the importance of new understandings of *jinkaku* among workers, along with their demands for recognition of their humanity and status more generally, after the First World War. Thomas C. Smith, "The Right to Benevolence: Dignity and Japanese Workers, 1890–1920," in *Native Sources of Japanese Industrialization, 1750–1920* (Berkeley: University of California Press, 1988), 236–270.

21. William M. Tsutsui, *Manufacturing Ideology: Scientific Management in Twentieth-Century Japan* (Princeton: Princeton University Press, 1998).

22. Kanebō kabushiki kaisha shashi hensanshitsu, ed., *Kanebō hyakunenshi* (Osaka: Kanebō kabushiki kaisha, 1988), 87–89.

23. Today the company's official name is Kanebo Ltd. Since the 1960s it has moved increasingly away from textile production and into the areas of foods, cosmetics, pharmaceuticals, and personal-hygiene products. While Kanebo Ltd. now includes a fashion division, its textile materials operations were spun off to subsidiaries in 1996. Mutō's tenure corresponded to some high-level administrative restructuring within the company. He began his leadership of Kanebō as its managing director. He was given the new title of company president in 1921, which he held until retirement. Kanebō kabushiki kaisha shashi hensanshitsu, *Kanebō hyakunenshi*, 1005.

24. Nakagawa Keiichirō and Yui Tsunehiko, eds., *Keiei tetsugaku keiei rinen*, vol. 1 (Tokyo: Daiyamondosha, 1969–70), 392–398. In Japan, where linguistically differentiated forms of address are used to indicate hierarchical social relations, such a gesture makes more of an impression than it might in an English-speaking milieu. Stories of Mutō's humanism abound in official Kanebō histories and are usually tied to discussions of the success of his labor-management policies. See for example Kanebō kabushiki kaisha shashi hensanshitsu, *Kanebō hyakunenshi*, 61.

25. Sugihara Kaoru, "Nihon ni okeru kindaiteki rōdō = seikatsu kateizō no seiritsu: Uno Riemon to Kōgyō Kyōikukai no shisō," in *Taishō Ōsaka suramu: Mō hitotsu no Nihon kindaishi*, ed. Sugihara Kaoru and Tamai Kingō (Tokyo: Shin hyōron, 1996), 34.

26. Uno Riemon, *Kōjo risshindan* (Tokyo: Kōgyō Kyōikukai, 1910).

27. Uno Riemon, *Teikoku seima Ōsaka seihin kōjō* (Osaka: Kōgyō Kyōikukai, 1922).

28. Earl H. Kinmonth, *The Self-Made Man in Meiji Japanese Thought: From Samurai to Salary Man* (Berkeley: University of California Press, 1981), 54–59.

29. Taira, *Economic Development and the Labor Market in Japan*, 99. See also Gordon, "The Invention of Japanese-Style Labor Management."

30. Hazama Hiroshi's important work on Japanese labor-management relations is one of the most influential to make the argument for a connection between prewar policies of compassionism and the postwar system of Japanese-style labor management. Hazama Hiroshi, *Nihon rōmu kanri shi kenkyū* (Tokyo: Daiyamondosha, 1964), a portion of which has been translated as Hiroshi Hazama, *The History of Labour Management in Japan*, trans. Mari Sako and Eri Sako (New York: St. Martin's Press, 1997).

31. This translation is from R. P. Dore, "The Modernizer as a Special Case: Japanese Factory Legislation, 1882–1911," *Comparative Studies in Society and History* 11, no. 4 (October, 1969): 439. For more on Soeda and his role during debates within the bureaucracy about the factory bill, see Sheldon M. Garon, *Molding Japanese Minds: The State in Everyday Life* (Princeton: Princeton University Press, 1997), 26.

32. Nōshōmushō Shōkōkyoku, ed., *Shokkō jijō,* with an introduction by Okouchi Kazuo (Tokyo: Kōseikan, 1971); Yokoyama, *Nihon no kasō shakai.* Yokoyama came to the attention of government officials after publication of *Nihon no kasō shakai* and was in fact hired in 1900 by the Ministry of Agriculture and Commerce to work on factory surveys that became part of *Shokkō jijō.* Yutani, "*Nihon no kaso shakai* of Gennosuke Yokoyama," 7. Tachibana Yūichi discusses Yokoyama's work in relation to the survey methodology eventually adopted by the ministry for its report. Tachibana Yūichi, *Hyōden—Yokoyama Gennosuke* (Tokyo: Sōkisha, 1979), 169.

33. Ishihara Osamu, *Jokō to kekkaku,* edited and with an introduction by Kagoyama Takashi (Tokyo: Kōseikan, 1970).

34. Garon, *Molding Japanese Minds,* 50.

35. A review of the holdings at the Ōhara Institute for Social Research in Tokyo, which houses possibly the largest number of prewar Social Bureau documents, turns up over five hundred Home Ministry Social Bureau reports and hundreds of similar publications by the Social Bureaus of Tokyo and Osaka. As one might expect, the reports issued by the central government's agency tended toward the level of national policy and also included international surveys of labor and welfare policy in the United States and England for comparative purposes. The metropolitan Social Bureaus, on the other hand, investigated the specificity of local working and living conditions in their cities and often focused on particular industries.

36. See Garon, *The State and Labor in Modern Japan,* chapter 1, for the history of the Factory Law as political history and the history of the prewar Japanese bureaucratic state.

37. Sumiya Mikio, "Kōjōhō taisei to rōshi kankei," in *Nihon rōshi kankeishi ron,* ed. Sumiya Mikio (Tokyo: Tōkyō Daigaku shuppan, 1977), 1. Sheldon Garon agrees that "factory legislation originated in the 1880s as part of the young regime's drive to industrialize" and notes that "officials of the Industrial Bureau (Ministry of Agriculture and Commerce) began studying Western examples of workers' legislation and factory regulations as early as 1882." The bureau's first draft of factory legislation appeared in 1883. Garon, *The State and Labor in Modern Japan,* 18–21. Kagoyama Takashi provides a more detailed chronology of bureaucratic steps leading to the passage of the law in Kagoyama Takashi, introduction to *Jokō to kekkaku,* by Ishihara Osamu (Tokyo: Kōseikan, 1970), 4–8. Most accounts of these events (including all those mentioned here) are based on Oka Minoru's 1,152-page treatise, *Kōjōhō ron.* Oka was a civil servant involved in the entire process of formulating the Factory Law and became chief of the Industrial Bureau starting in 1910, just before the law's passage. His firsthand account of these events is the most detailed available. Oka Minoru, *Kōjōhō ron* (Tokyo: Yuhikaku shobō, 1917).

38. Ishihara Osamu's Industrial Bureau–commissioned studies paint a stark picture of the devastating effects of tuberculosis on the population of female factory workers and its potential spread throughout the country. Ishihara, "Eiseigakujō yori mitaru jokō no genjō," in *Jokō to kekkaku*. For a brief treatment of Ishihara's work and an overview of the problem in English, see Janet Hunter, "Textile Factories, Tuberculosis, and the Quality of Life in Industrializing Japan," in *Japanese Women Working*, ed. Janet Hunter (New York: Routledge, 1993), 69–97. See also William Johnston, *The Modern Epidemic: A History of Tuberculosis in Japan* (Cambridge, MA: Harvard Council on East Asian Studies 1995), for a more detailed study of the history of this disease in Japan.

39. Sumiya, "Kōjōhō taisei to rōshi kankei," 2; Kagoyama, introduction to *Jokō to kekkaku*, 6. See also Hunter, "Factory Legislation and Employer Resistance," 246–248; and Andrew Gordon, *The Evolution of Labor Relations in Japan* (Cambridge, MA: Harvard Council on East Asian Studies), 66–67.

40. Garon, *The State and Labor in Modern Japan*, 43–44.

41. Garon, for example, in *The State and Labor in Modern Japan*, reads the history of the prohibition of night work in this way.

2. KEEPING "IDLE YOUNGSTERS" OUT OF TROUBLE

1. Ōbayashi Munetsugu, *Minshū goraku no jissai kenkyū: Ōsaka-shi no minshū goraku chōsa* (Tokyo: Ōhara shakai mondai kenkyūjo, 1922).

2. Yamanouchi Mina, *Yamanouchi Mina jiden: Jūnisai no bōseki jokō kara no shōgai*, with an introduction by Ichikawa Fusae (Tokyo: Shinjuku shobō, 1975), 21.

3. Tōyō Mosurin kabushiki kaisha, "Tōyō Mosurin kabushiki kaisha ni okeru jokō no shisō chōsa," *Jokō kenkyū* 1 (January 1925): 88. There is a discrepancy between the title as it appears in the table of contents of *Jokō kenkyū* ("Tōkyō Mosurin") and the title on the first page of the article ("Tōyō Mosurin"). There were separate companies with each of these names operating around this time, each with factories in the Tokyo area employing enough female operatives to account for the 1,494 responses recorded as the survey sample.

4. Frederick Winslow Taylor, *The Principles of Scientific Management* (New York: Harper & Brothers, 1911).

5. Henry Ford, *My Life and Work,* in collaboration with Samuel Crowther (Garden City, NY: Doubleday, Page and Company, 1922).

6. On the origins of the term "rationalization," see Robert A. Brady, *The Rationalization Movement in German Industry: A Study in the Evolution of Economic Planning* (Berkeley: University of California Press, 1933), which remains the authoritative work on the German rationalization movement.

7. Sakisaka Itsurō and Iwai Akira, eds., *"Gōrika" to wa nani ka* (Tokyo: Kawade shobō shinsha, 1974), 25.

8. Mary Nolan has written an extensive treatment of the adaptation of American models of efficiency in 1920s German industry. Mary Nolan, *Visions of Modernity: American Business and the Modernization of Germany* (New York: Oxford University Press, 1994).

9. National Industrial Conference Board, *Rationalization of German Industry* (New York: National Industrial Conference Board, Inc., 1931), vi.

10. For an analysis of the work of the Special Bureau on Industrial Rationalization (which William Tsutsui calls the Temporary Industrial Rationalization Bureau) and one of its most important standing committees (the Production Management Committee), see William M. Tsutsui, *Manufacturing Ideology: Scientific Management in Twentieth-Century Japan* (Princeton: Princeton University Press, 1998), 72–84.

11. On the Reich Board for Economic Efficiency, see J. Ronald Shearer, "Talking about Efficiency: Politics and the Industrial Rationalization Movement in the Weimar Republic," *Central European History* 28, no. 4 (1995): 483–506; and Mary Nolan, *Visions of Modernity*.

12. Despite such provisions in the law that appear to privilege state control of cartel arrangements, some scholars have remarked at the dominance of *zaibatsu* (financial clique) power within the Special Bureau on Industrial Rationalization and the government's relative weakness. See Chalmers Johnson, *MITI and the Japanese Miracle: The Growth of Industrial Policy, 1925–1975* (Stanford: Stanford University Press, 1982), 162; and Eleanor Hadley, *Antitrust in Japan* (Princeton: Princeton University Press, 1970), 124.

13. Miles Fletcher has written a series of articles on the Spinners Association, arguing that the organization worked together with politicians and the government to eliminate taxes and tariffs deemed disadvantageous to Japan's cotton industry from the Meiji period on. W. Miles Fletcher III, "The Japan Spinners Association: Creating Industrial Policy in Meiji Japan," *The Journal of Japanese Studies* 22, no. 1 (Winter 1996): 49–75; "Co-operation and Competition in the Rise of the Japanese Cotton Spinning Industry, 1890–1926," *Asia Pacific Business Review* 5, no. 1 (Autumn 1998): 45–70; "Economic Power and Political Influence: The Japan Spinners Association and National Policy, 1900–1930," *Asia Pacific Business Review* 7, no. 2 (Winter 2000): 39–62; and "The Impact of the Great Depression: The Japan Spinners Association, 1927–1936," in *Building a Modern Japan,* ed. Morris Low (New York: Palgrave Macmillan, 2005), 207–232.

14. Naosuke Takamura, "The Cotton Spinning Industry in Japan During the Pre–World War I Period: Its Growth and Essential Conditions," in *Innovation, Know How, Rationalization and Investment in the German and Japanese Economies, 1868/1871–1930/1980,* ed. Hans Pohl (Wiesbaden, Germany: Franz Steiner Verlag GmbH, 1982), 211.

15. For an overview of the process of consolidation in the cotton industry, see Takamura Naosuke, *Nihon bōseki gyōshi josetsu* (Tokyo: Hanawa shobō, 1971). By 1919 another configuration known as the "Big Six" included those companies with more than 150,000 spindles. The six were Dai Nippon Cotton Spinning, Tōyō Cotton Spinning, Fuji Gas Cotton Spinning, Kanegafuchi Cotton Spinning (Kanebō), Osaka Gōdō, and Tokyo Gas Cotton Spinning.

16. Oka Minoru, the pro–Factory Law director of the Industrial Bureau who oversaw much of the preparations to bring the bill to the diet, recalled after its passage into law, "It has taken thirty years for this law to be enacted, during which time there have been twenty-three different ministers overseeing its

progress, fifteen different directors of the Industrial Bureau and of the Commerce and Industry Bureau, and over one hundred revisions of the draft of the bill." Kagoyama Takashi, introduction to *Jokō to kekkaku,* by Ishihara Osamu (Tokyo: Kōseikan, 1970), 4. One year after the Factory Law went into effect, Oka penned a nearly twelve-hundred-page book recounting the history of the factory bill and its passage into law. Oka Minoru, *Kōjōhō ron* (Tokyo: Yuhikaku shobō, 1917). For the most detailed analysis of the long history of the factory bill in English, see Sheldon M. Garon, *The State and Labor in Modern Japan* (Berkeley: University of California Press, 1987).

17. Yokoyama Gennosuke, *Nihon no kasō shakai* (1899; Tokyo: Iwanami bunkō, 1995), 208; Eiji Yutani, "*Nihon no kaso shakai* of Gennosuke Yokoyama" (Ph.D. diss., University of California, 1985), 345.

18. Ōshima Eiko, "Ryō taisenkan no joshi rōdō: Bōseki, seishi jokō o chūshin ni," in *Nihon joseishi,* ed. Joseishi sōgō kenkyūkai (Tokyo: Tōkyō Daigaku shuppankai, 1982), 10.

19. Nishikawa Hiroshi, "1920 nendai no Nihon menshi bōsekigyō no 'gōrika' to dokusen taisei," *Tochi seido shigaku* 62, no. 2 (1974): 20–21. Gary Saxonhouse and Gustav Ranis examine the Japanese cotton industry's early profitability successes in producing an "unprecendentedly shoddy product" in their "Technology Choice and the Quality Dimension in the Japanese Cotton Textile Industry," in *Japan and the Developing Countries: A Comparative Analysis,* ed. Kazushi Ohkawa and Gustav Ranis (New York: Blackwell, 1985), 155–176.

20. On the intensification of labor, see Orimoto Sadayo, "Kōjo rōdō fujin mondai," in *Fujin Daigaku: Fujin mondai hen* (1932), cited in Suzuki Yūko, *Jokō to rōdō sōgi: 1930 nen Yō Mosu sōgi* (Tokyo: Renga shobō shinsha, 1989), 12–13. Orimoto (née Tatewaki) shows the increased ratio of spindles per worker through the 1920s as follows: 1920: 22.2; 1923: 25.5; 1927: 28.4; 1928: 30.8; 1929: 36.3; 1930: 47.0. The large jump between 1929 and 1930 is likely a result of the abolition of night work.

21. Nittōsha, "Shinyagyō haishi ni tomonau yoka zenyō no mondai," *Jokō kenkyū* 5, no. 3 (March 1929): 64–65.

22. Aihara Takeo, "Gojin wa ika ni susumu beki ka," *Jokō kenkyū* 5, no. 7 (July 1929): 13.

23. Ujihara Shōjirō, ed., *Yoka seikatsu no kenkyū* (Tokyo: Kōseikan, 1970), 93. This saying has a rough equivalent in English: "Idle minds are the devil's workshop."

24. The various leisure spaces and opportunities available to American working men in Massachusetts at this time—including saloons, Fourth of July celebrations, and movie theaters—are discussed in Roy Rosenzweig, *Eight Hours for What We Will: Workers and Leisure in an Industrial City, 1870–1920* (New York: Cambridge University Press, 1983).

25. Ishigami Kinji, "Shinyagyō haishi ni sai shite," *Jokō kenkyū* 5, no. 7 (July 1929): 2–3.

26. Ishigami Kinji, "Yoka zenyō to kun'iku gengyō," *Jokō kenkyū,* no. 56 (August 1929): 1, 4.

27. Ishigami Kinji, "Kinshuku setsuyaku to kinrō kyōiku (ge)," *Jokō kenkyū,* no. 62 (October 1929): 13.

28. The infiltration of rationalist ideology into daily life occurred not only among female factory workers, nor only in Japan. Miriam Silverberg notes the ubiquity of admonishments to rationalize daily life directed toward housewives in her study of the women's magazine *Shufu no tomo* in her book, *Erotic Grotesque Nonsense: The Mass Culture of Japanese Modern Times* (Berkeley: University of California Press, 2006). David Harvey discusses Fordism as producing a consumer class in America in *The Condition of Postmodernity: An Enquiry into the Origins of Cultural Change* (Cambridge, MA: Blackwell, 1989), 26. And as early as 1933 the American economist Robert Brady, writing on German economic innovations, remarked that "industrial rationalization . . . elevates the material level of living of the masses of the people as a condition to its continued existence; their interest in its techniques gradually carries its secularizing influence into every nook and cranny of national life." Brady, *The Rationalization Movement in German Industry*, 406.

29. On Taishō-era women's magazines, see Kindai josei bunkashi kenkyūkai, ed., *Taishōki no josei zasshi* (Tokyo: Ōzorasha, 1996), especially the essay by Miki Hiroko, "Taishōki no josei zasshi: Hataraku onna no kikanshi o chūshin ni," 3–53. In English, see Barbara Sato, *The New Japanese Woman: Modernity, Media, and Women in Interwar Japan* (Durham, NC: Duke University Press, 2003); and Sarah Frederick, *Turning Pages: Reading and Writing Women's Magazines in Interwar Japan* (Honolulu: University of Hawai'i Press, 2006). For analyses that focus more closely on the readerships (including female factory workers) of women's magazines, see Maeda Ai, *Maeda Ai chosakushū, dai-2-kan: Kindai dokusha no seiritsu* (Tokyo: Chikuma shobō, 1989), 155–98; and Nagamine Shigetoshi, *Zasshi to dokusha no kindai* (Tokyo: Nihon editaa sukūru shuppan-bu, 1997), chapter 5. For an exhaustive list of Meiji- and Taishō-era women's magazines that includes brief descriptions of each, see Nakajima Kuni, *Nihon no fujin zasshi, kaisetsu hen* (Tokyo: Ōzorasha, 1994). This volume includes as an appendix a valuable timeline compiled by Miki Hiroko titled "Kindai fujin zasshi kankei nenpyō," which lists publication dates for virtually all prewar women's magazines, as well as publisher/editor listings, and a chronological chart of significant related events.

30. Nittōsha, "Rōdō sōgi o chūshin toshite (jō)," *Jokō kenkyū*, no. 101 (November 1930): 14, 19–20.

31. Jazz was part of what Miriam Silverberg has termed the culture of "commodified eroticism" that characterized much of Japan's "modern moment." Miriam Silverberg, *Erotic Grotesque Nonsense*.

32. Miki Hiroko has written in detail about the "women's magazine reform debate" that took place among publishers, editors, contributors, and readers of women's magazines in 1928 and 1929. These debates were prompted by increased censorship by government authorities who pointed to what they considered the large amount of sex-related content in these magazines as particularly problematic. Miki Hiroko, "Taishōki no josei zasshi," 10–11.

33. On the working woman (*shokugyō fujin*) and how she came into the popular consciousness during this period, see Yoneda Sayoko, "Shufu to shokugyō fujin," in *Nihon tsūshi*, ed. Iwanami kōza (Tokyo: Iwanami shoten, 1994); Okuda Akiko, "Shokugyō fujin no tanjō," in *Mainoritei toshite no joseishi*, ed.

Okuda Akiko (Tokyo: San'ichi shobō, 1997), 235–270; and Murakami Nobuhiko, *Taishōki no shokugyō fujin* (Tokyo: Domesu shuppan, 1983).

34. Shakaikyoku rōdōbu, "Shinyagyō haishi no yoka riyō to fukuri shisetsu (ge)," *Jokō kenkyū*, no. 118 (May, 1931): 3–4.

35. Yokoyama, *Nihon no kasō shakai*, 207, translated in Eiji Yutani, *"Nihon no kaso shakai* of Gennosuke Yokoyama," 362.

36. Yokoyama Gennosuke, *Naichi zakkyōgo no Nihon* (1899; Tokyo: Iwanami shoten, 1954), 27, quoted and translated in Eiji Yutani, *"Nihon no kaso shakai* of Gennosuke Yokoyama," 98.

37. Nittōsha, "Jokō no sei ni kan suru mondai," *Jokō kenkyū* 5, no. 7 (July, 1929): 70–72.

38. Jeffrey Weeks, *Sex, Politics, and Society: The Regulation of Sexuality Since 1800* (New York: Longman, 1989), 57; Joan Wallach Scott, *Gender and the Politics of History* (New York: Columbia University Press, 1988), 162.

39. Much Western feminist scholarship has demonstrated the constructed nature of the category of "woman" and the problems associated with assuming a coherent and transcendent identity based on the kinds of biological criteria that have been used to distinguish the sexes. See for example Denise Riley, *Am I That Name? Feminism and the Category of 'Women' in History* (Minneapolis: University of Minnesota Press, 1990). For an example of a historical deconstruction of the political meanings associated with words used to designate "woman" in the Chinese case, see Tani E. Barlow, "Theorizing Woman: *Funü, Guojia, Jiating* (Chinese Woman, Chinese State, Chinese Family)," in *Body, Subject and Power in China,* ed. Angela Zito and Tani E. Barlow (Chicago: University of Chicago Press, 1994), 253–289.

40. Ishigami, "Yoka zenyō to kun'iku gengyō," 14.

41. To a degree, representations of the *shokugyō fujin* overlapped with those of the *moga*, or "modern girl," who was known for "her short hair and long, straight legs." Miriam Silverberg, "The Modern Girl as Militant," in *Recreating Japanese Women, 1600–1945,* ed. Gail Lee Bernstein (Berkeley: University of California Press, 1991), 242. Mariko Tamanoi also notes that "slender" and "delicate" bodies were associated with women of the middle and upper classes. Mariko Asano Tamanoi, *Under the Shadow of Nationalism: Politics and Poetics of Rural Japanese Women* (Honolulu: University of Hawai'i Press, 1998), 93.

42. Nittōsha, "Jokō no sei ni kan suru mondai," 73.

43. Nittōsha, "Jokō no sei ni kan suru mondai," 75.

44. Nittōsha, "Shinyagyō haishi ni tomonau yoka zenyō no mondai," 69.

45. Oka, *Kōjōhō ron,* 248–249.

46. Akamatsu Keisuke has conducted the most extensive historical and ethnographic research on *yobai*. Akamatsu Keisuke, *Yobai no minzokugaku* (Tokyo: Akashi shoten, 1994); and *Yobai no seiairon* (Tokyo: Akashi shoten, 1994).

47. See for example Ishigami Kinji, *Jokō no shitsukekata to kyōiku* (1921; Tokyo: Nihon tosho senta, 1984), 192–194.

48. Hosoi Wakizō, *Hosoi Wakizō zenshū,* vol. 4 (Tokyo: San'ichi shobō, 1956), 192–213.

49. Ishigami, *Jokō no shitsukekata to kyōiku,* 111–116.

50. The Japanese term *dōseiai*, or "same-sex love," was a neologism introduced into medical as well as popular discourse at the turn of the century as a
translation of the word "homosexuality" as it was used by European and American sexologists and practitioners in the newly created field of psychoanalysis.
Gregory Pflugfelder argues against using "homosexuality" to refer to same-sex
sexual relations in Japan because it assumes a conceptual link between male-male
and female-female erotic relations that did not exist prior to the Meiji period.
Gregory M. Pflugfelder, *Cartographies of Desire: Male-Male Sexuality in Japanese Discourse, 1600–1950* (Berkeley: University of California Press, 1999), 4–7,
175–176. The period under discussion here, however, falls well after introduction of the term *dōseiai* in Japan, and while the uses and nuances of that term
were surely not isomorphic with those of the word "homosexuality" in America
and Europe (and its German and French cognates), *dōseiai* retained the clinical
and somewhat pejorative inflection of "homosexuality." Makoto Furukawa has
attributed the early twentieth-century coinage and use of the term *dōseiai* to a
growing awareness (popular or medical, he does not specify) of the prevalence
of female-female sexual relations for which no indigenous Japanese term existed.
Makoto Furukawa, "The Changing Nature of Sexuality: The Three Codes
Framing Homosexuality in Modern Japan," trans. Angus Lockyer, *U.S.-Japan
Women's Journal*, no. 7 (1994): 115–16. Jennifer Robertson likewise follows Furukawa in arguing that early Japanese sexologists used the term *dōseiai* to refer
especially to female-female relations because its linguistic derivation (i.e., the
term *ai*, or "love") captured more of the supposed platonic or spiritual nature of
female homosexuality as opposed to male-male eroticism, which was attributed
a more carnal nature. Jennifer Robertson, *Takarazuka: Sexual Politics and Popular Culture in Modern Japan* (Berkeley: University of California Press, 1998),
68. On the history of same-sex erotic relations among women in prewar Japan,
see for example Jennifer Robertson, "Dying to Tell: Sexuality and Suicide in Imperial Japan," in *Queer Diasporas,* eds. Cindy Patton and Benigno Sanchez-
Eppler (Durham, NC: Duke University Press, 2000), 38–70; and Gregory M.
Pflugfelder, " 'S' Is for Sister: Schoolgirl Intimacy and 'Same-Sex Love' in Early
Twentieth-Century Japan," in *Gendering Modern Japanese History,* ed. Barbara
Molony and Kathleen S. Uno (Cambridge, MA: Harvard University Asia Cen-
ter, 2005), 133–190.

51. Komine Shigeyuki and Minami Takao, *Dōseiai to dōsei shinjū no kenkyū*
(Tokyo: Komine kenkyūjo, 1985).

52. Hosoi Wakizō, *Jokō aishi* (1925; Tokyo: Iwanami bunko, 1993),
369–370. Karel Capek (also known as Karl Chapek) was a Czech playwright
who coined the term "robot," which was first used in his play *R.U.R.: Rossum's
Universal Robots* in 1921, four years before Hosoi's book was published. Jennifer Robertson describes the common understanding of *chūsei* as it developed
in this period as "between sexes/genders." Robertson, *Takarazuka,* 71. However, Hosoi's usage here suggests not that (female) sex/gender was in any way
ambiguous, but rather that sexuality itself had been sublimated.

53. Hosoi, *Jokō aishi,* 370.

54. Kagoyama, introduction to *Jokō to kekkaku,* 15.

55. Statistics indicate a correlation between high out-migration and regional

rates of tuberculosis. Family members engaged in *dekasegi*, or "migrant work" (often in factories and/or in urban areas) seemed to put the family at risk for infection. Janet Hunter, "Textile Factories, Tuberculosis, and the Quality of Life in Industrializing Japan," in *Japanese Women Working*, ed. Janet Hunter (New York: Routledge, 1993), 93.

56. Hiratsuka Raichō, "Haha ni naru jōkō no mondai," in *Rōdō mondai no shinzui*, ed. Segawa Genji (Tokyo: Hakuyūsha, 1919), 91.

57. Sakura Takuji, *Seishi jokō gyakutaishi* (1927; Tokyo: Kaihōsha, 1981), 167–168. Hosoi's *Jokō aishi* (The Sorrowful History of Female Factory Workers) focuses on the cotton industry, while Sakura's book performs a similar analysis of the silk industry. Hosoi intended to write a second volume on the silk industry himself, but barely managed to survive an acute case of tuberculosis long enough to see the first book to completion. He died in 1925. Sakura's book (first published in 1927) is described in the original preface as an attempt to write the second volume that Hosoi had envisioned. Sakura's language reflected the growing influence of Japan's eugenics movement on popular discourse. On the Meiji-era beginnings of Japan's eugenics movement (which culminated in the 1940 passage of the National Eugenics Law) and its consideration of women's bodies, see Sumiko Otsubo, "The Female Body and Eugenic Thought in Meiji Japan," in *Building a Modern Japan: Science, Technology, and Medicine in the Meiji Era and Beyond*, ed. Morris Low (New York: Palgrave Macmillan, 2005), 61–81. Eugenics debates in Japan and the popularization of scientific and medical language they helped engender—particularly among social reformers—took place simultaneously with similar debates in Europe and the United States. See Daniel J. Kevles, *In the Name of Eugenics: Genetics and the Uses of Human Heredity* (Berkeley: University of California Press, 1985).

58. The most thorough treatment of Ishihara's work is the introduction by Kagoyama Takashi to a collection of Ishihara's major research works. Kagoyama, introduction to *Jokō to kekkaku*, 3–46. English-language discussions of Ishihara appear in William Johnston, *The Modern Epidemic: A History of Tuberculosis in Japan* (Cambridge, MA: Harvard Council on East Asian Studies, 1995), 83–88; and Hunter, "Textile Factories, Tuberculosis, and the Quality of Life in Industrializing Japan," 69–97.

59. Nittōsha, "Enjin no chimata o sakete: Kantei ni jinji jikyoku o danzuru danchōro," *Jokō kenkyū*, no. 54 (August 1929): 20.

60. Ishigami, "Yoka zenyō to kun'iku gengyō," 3.

61. On the shift from viewing labor as "unlimited" and "disposable" to a business philosophy that aimed to retain workers through welfare and education programs, see Koji Taira, *Economic Development and the Labor Market in Japan* (New York: Columbia University Press, 1970); and Janet Hunter, *Women and the Labour Market in Japan's Industrialising Economy: The Textile Industry before the Pacific War* (London: RoutledgeCurzon, 2003).

62. Shakaikyoku rōdōbu, "Shinyagyō haishi no yoka riyō to fukuri shisetsu (ge)," 6–7.

63. Ōshima, "Ryō taisenkan no joshi rōdō," 14.

64. Nittōsha, "Shinyagyō haishi ni tomonau yoka zenyō no mondai," 64.

65. Ishigami Kinji, "Jokō no taiiku to hōshō taisō," *Jokō kenkyū*, no. 89 (July 1930): 1.

66. Nittōsha, "Rōdō sōgi o chūshin toshite (ge)," *Jokō kenkyū*, no. 104 (December 1930): 14.

67. Nakamoto Takako, "Shokufu," in *Hikari kuraku* (Tokyo: San'ichi shobō, 1947), 91.

3. CULTIVATION GROUPS AND THE JAPANESE FACTORY

1. On efforts to educate women as good wives and wise mothers, see Koyama Shizuko, *Ryōsai kenbo to iu kihan* (Tokyo: Keisō shobō, 1991). Miyoshi Nobuhiro provides a detailed study of early twentieth-century industrial education for women in *Nihon no josei to sangyō kyōiku: Kindai sangyō shakai ni okeru josei no yakuwari* (Tokyo: Toshindō, 2000). On reform movements that took prostitution as their object, see Yuki Fujime, *Sei no rekishigaku* (Tokyo: Fuji shuppan, 1999) and "The Licensed Prostitution System and the Prostitution Abolition Movement in Modern Japan," *Positions: East Asia Cultures Critique* 5, no. 1 (1997): 135–170. On attempts to combat juvenile delinquency, see David R. Ambaras, *Bad Youth: Juvenile Delinquency and the Politics of Everyday Life in Modern Japan* (Berkeley: University of California Press, 2005).

2. Tsutsui makes a compelling argument against earlier historicizations of the notion of cultivation, which characterized the differences between *shūyō* and *kyōyō* as chronological (with *shūyō* defining Meiji culture and *kyōyō* defining Taishō culture), in favor of a reading that sees the difference more appropriately situated along class axes of elite versus mass culture. Tsutsui Kiyotada, "Kindai Nihon no kyōyōshugi to shūyōshugi," *Shisō*, no. 812 (February 1992): 151–173. Both *shūyō* and *kyōyō* are most aptly translated into English as "cultivation" or "self-cultivation."

3. Translated in Earl H. Kinmonth, *The Self-Made Man in Meiji Japanese Thought: From Samurai to Salary Man* (Berkeley: University of California Press, 1981), 256. While this selection on the one hand seems to promote the massification of *shūyō* ideology by emphasizing moral rectitude over material wealth and privilege, Kyoko Inoue argues persuasively that Nitobe's early configuration of *shūyō* was consistent with hierarchical notions of *jinkaku*, or "moral personality," that was another keyword in the *shūyō* movement. Kyoko Inoue, *Individual Dignity in Modern Japanese Thought: The Evolution of the Concept of Jinkaku in Moral and Educational Discourse* (Ann Arbor: Center for Japanese Studies, University of Michigan, 2001), chapter 1.

4. On the culture of elite male youth of this era, the central debates among them, and the impact those debates had on Meiji politics and culture, see Kenneth B. Pyle, *The New Generation in Meiji Japan: Problems of Cultural Identity, 1885–1895* (Stanford: Stanford University Press, 1969).

5. Kinmonth, *The Self-Made Man in Meiji Japanese Thought*, 58, 256.

6. Tazawa Yoshiharu, "Seinen undō," in *Shakai seisaku taikei,* ed. Hasegawa Yoshinobu (Tokyo: Daitō shuppansha, 1927), 66.

7. On the proliferation of women's journals during the Taishō period, see Miki Hiroko, "Kindai fujin zasshi kankei nenpyō," in *Nihon no fujin zasshi, kaisetsu hen,* edited by Nakajima Kuni (Tokyo: Ōzorasha, 1994), 171–222; Miki Hiroko, "Taishōki no josei zasshi: Hataraku onna no kikanshi o chūshin ni," in

Taishōki no josei zasshi, edited by Kindai josei bunkashi kenkyūkai (Tokyo: Ōzorasha, 1996), 3–53; and Barbara Sato, *The New Japanese Woman: Modernity, Media, and Women in Interwar Japan* (Durham, NC: Duke University Press, 2003). On mass culture during the Taishō period, see Minami Hiroshi, *Taishō bunka* (Tokyo: Keisō shobō, 1965); Miriam Silverberg, *Changing Song: The Marxist Manifestos of Nakano Shigeharu* (Princeton: Princeton University Press, 1990); and Jennifer Robertson, *Takarazuka: Sexual Politics and Popular Culture in Modern Japan* (Berkeley: University of California Press, 1998), 32–37, which analyzes the differences between "mass" and "popular" culture.

8. Sato, *The New Japanese Woman,* 134.

9. Sato, *The New Japanese Woman,* 137.

10. Watanabe Yōko, *Kindai Nihon joshi shakai kyōiku seiritsushi: Shojokai no zenkoku sōshikika to shidō shisō* (Tokyo: Akashi shoten, 1997), 335.

11. On women's roles as producers and reproducers, see Kathleen S. Uno, "Women and Changes in the Household Division of Labor," in *Recreating Japanese Women, 1600–1945,* ed. Gail Lee Bernstein (Berkeley: University of California Press, 1991), 17–41; and Yoshiko Miyake, "Doubling Expectations: Motherhood and Women's Factory Work Under State Management in the 1930s and 1940s," in *Recreating Japanese Women, 1600–1945,* ed. Gail Lee Bernstein (Berkeley: University of California Press, 1991), 267–295.

12. Tazawa, "Seinen undō," 8–9; Torarokuro Shimomura, *Seinendan: Young Men's Leagues of Japan,* trans. Kaizo Matsuda (Tokyo: Dai Nippon Rengo Seinendan, 1937), 24–28.

13. Ambaras, *Bad Youth,* chapter 1.

14. Miyachi Masato, *Nichi-Ro sengo seijishi no kenkyū: Teikoku shugi keiseiki no toshi to nōson* (Tokyo: Tōkyō Daigaku shuppankai, 1973), 46–67; Richard J. Smethurst, *A Social Basis for Prewar Japanese Militarism: The Army and the Rural Community* (Berkeley: University of California Press, 1974), chapter 2.

15. Kenneth B. Pyle, "The Technology of Japanese Nationalism: The Local Improvement Movement, 1900–1918," *Journal of Asian Studies* 33, no. 1 (1973): 58.

16. For an excerpt from the text of the directive to prefectural authorities—one of many regarding the youth associations issued by the state in the years 1910–19—and an analysis of its contents, see Hirayama Kazuhiko, *Seinen shūdanshi kenkyū josetsu,* vol. 1 (Tokyo: Shinsensha, 1978), 21–30.

17. Shimomura, *Seinendan,* 38. The introduction to this official English-language translation of a short monographic overview of Seinendan history and mission also places the Seinendan in the context of other male youth associations of the day, such as the Boy Scouts and the Hitler Youth. In fact, the Japanese youth organizations also influenced other nations' attempts at achieving similar goals of inculcating national values among male youth. By the time of the Russo-Japanese War (1904–5), England's Lord Baden-Powell, founder of the Boy Scouts, looked to Japan's male youth organizations as a model for his "code of scouting." Michael Rosenthal, *The Character Factory: Baden-Powell and the Origins of the Boy Scout Movement* (New York: Pantheon, 1986), 54–55.

18. Hirayama, *Seinen shūdanshi kenkyū josetsu,* vol. 2, 73.

19. Yokusan undōshi kankōkai, ed., *Yokusan kokumin undōshi*, with an introduction by Kitagawa Keiji (Tokyo: Yumani shobō, 1998), 1037.

20. For an analysis of the growing consolidation of indigenous religious practice into an ideological form known as "state Shintō," see Carol Gluck, *Japan's Modern Myths: Ideology in the Late Meiji Period* (Princeton: Princeton University Press, 1985), 138–143.

21. Daikichi Irokawa, *The Culture of the Meiji Period*, ed. and trans. Marius B. Jansen (Princeton: Princeton University Press, 1985), 282–284. Irokawa identifies Meiji ideologues, including Hozumi Yatsuka, Katō Hiroyuki, and Inoue Tetsujirō, as the originators of the term "family-state," used after 1910 as a conceptual pillar to support the emperor system. On "family-state," see also Gluck, *Japan's Modern Myths*, 187–188.

22. My usage here is perhaps closer to the negative view of *kyōdōtai* invoked by Maruyama Masao and Takeuchi Yoshimi, who both saw *kyōdōtai* as enabling the rise of militarism and fascism, than to Irokawa Daikichi's recuperation of the concept as a populist antidote to the emperor system. Daikichi Irokawa, *The Culture of the Meiji Period*, 273–280.

23. The term *shojo* signifies an unmarried girl, or "virginal maiden," which would perhaps have been the closest contemporary translation. The category was used analogously with the term *seinen* (youth), which contained no specific gender designation but generally referred to male youth.

24. This is one of the principal arguments made by Watanabe Yōko in her recent monograph on the Shojokai. Watanabe Yōko, *Kindai Nihon joshi shakai kyōiku seiritsushi*.

25. Amano Fujio, *Nōson shojokai no soshiki oyobi shidō*, with an introduction by Chino Yōichi (Tokyo: Nihon tosho senta, 1984), 100–102.

26. On the culture of elite higher schools for boys and the kinds of disciplinary strategies used in those higher schools, see Donald Roden, *Schooldays in Imperial Japan: A Study in the Culture of a Student Elite* (Berkeley: University of California Press, 1980). On higher education for girls, see Barbara Rose, *Tsuda Umeko and Women's Education in Japan* (New Haven: Yale University Press, 1992). On the parameters of urban reform, see Sheldon M. Garon, *Molding Japanese Minds: The State in Everyday Life* (Princeton: Princeton University Press, 1997); Ambaras, *Bad Youth*.

27. On the scope and purpose of supplemental education—especially for workers—during this period according to the Kyōchōkai, a highly influential labor-relations organization founded by a coalition of government officials and entrepreneurs, see Kyōchōkai, ed., *Saikin no shakai undō: Sōritsu jisshūnen kinen shuppan* (Tokyo: Kyōchōkai, 1929), 951–952.

28. Yokusan undōshi kankōkai, *Yokusan kokumin undōshi*, 1039.

29. Watanabe Yōko, *Kindai Nihon joshi shakai kyōiku seiritsushi*, 65.

30. See Sheldon M. Garon, *The State and Labor in Modern Japan* (Berkeley: University of California Press, 1987), 43–44, 100–102; and Iwao F. Ayusawa, *A History of Labor in Modern Japan* (Honolulu: East-West Center Press, 1946), 121–235.

31. For a discussion of Amano's role in the bureaucratization of the Shojokai, see Watanabe Yōko, *Kindai Nihon joshi shakai kyōiku seiritsushi*, 101–118.

32. A number of the songs sung by female workers in the cotton-spinning factories have been transcribed in Hosoi Wakizō, *Jokō aishi* (1925; Tokyo: Iwanami bunkō, 1993), 404–417, while the songs of silk-spinning and -reeling girls appear in Yamamoto Shigemi, *Aa Nomugi tōge* (1979; Tokyo: Kadokawa bunkō, 1994). Patricia Tsurumi has translated and analyzed a number of these songs in E. Patricia Tsurumi, *Factory Girls: Women in the Thread Mills of Meiji Japan* (Princeton: Princeton University Press, 1990).

33. This song (both lyrics and music) is transcribed in Hosoi, *Jokō aishi*, 413–414. I have transliterated the first line of each verse from Hosoi and provided a translation of each verse from Tsurumi, *Factory Girls*, 159. I have provided the first five of a total of fifteen verses in order to give a sense of the counting structure and the expressive content of the lyrics.

34. For an example of this practice of *kaeuta*, or "changing song," among *komori* (caretakers of children, who were often children themselves), see Mariko Asano Tamanoi, *Under the Shadow of Nationalism: Politics and Poetics of Rural Japanese Women* (Honolulu: University of Hawai'i Press, 1998), 75–76. Miriam Silverberg has discussed how Hosoi Wakizō, the social reformer and socialist writer who collected the songs of female cotton-factory workers (including the one cited above), "treat[ed] the songs as new creations actively constructed by a new class producing new words to express relationships within the factory." Silverberg, *Changing Song*, 106–107.

35. Watanabe Yōko, *Kindai Nihon joshi shakai kyōiku seiritsushi*, 124–125.

36. Amano, "Shojokai to kōjo no renraku," *Shojo no tomo* (August 1919), cited in Watanabe Yōko, *Kindai Nihon joshi shakai kyōiku seiritsushi*, 125.

37. Cited in Watanabe Yōko, *Kindai Nihon joshi shakai kyōiku seiritsushi*, 132. On the significance of the concept of *jichi*, or "self-government," as it was used by statesmen from Meiji onward to signify and produce "a safely apolitical means of national integration," see Gluck, *Japan's Modern Myths*, 190–200. On agricultural cooperatives, youth groups, and other rural organizations as institutional expressions of state-promoted *jichi*, see Kerry Smith, *A Time of Crisis: Japan, The Great Depression, and Rural Revitalization* (Cambridge, MA: Harvard University Asia Center, 2001), 88–93.

38. Yokusan undōshi kankōkai, *Yokusan kokumin undōshi*, 1039–1040.

39. For the most thorough explanation of the structural development of the Seinendan, see Hirayama, *Seinen shūdanshi kenkyū josetsu*, vol. 2.

40. On "racial instinct," see Shimomura, *Seinendan*, 2. The word *minzoku* (race or ethnos) appeared frequently in writings of the Taishō and early Shōwa periods, usually to signify the Japanese as part of a distinct, organic, and homogeneous culture. For examples of scholarship that attempts to untangle the meanings of the word, its uses, and its relationship to nationalism, see Tessa Morris-Suzuki, *Re-Inventing Japan: Time, Space, Nation* (Armonk, NY: M. E. Sharpe, 1998), chapter 5; and Kevin M. Doak, "What Is a Nation and Who Belongs? National Narratives and the Ethnic Imagination in Twentieth-Century Japan," *American Historical Review* 102, no. 2 (April 1997): 283–309.

41. "Hitotsu no kotae," *Rōdō fujin* (June 1933), reprinted in Hōsei Daigaku Ōhara shakai mondai kenkyūjo and Sōdōmei gojūnenshi kankō iinkai, eds., *Rōdō fujin*, vol. 6 (Tokyo: Hōsei Daigaku shuppankyoku, 1978), 186–189. Aka-

matsu Tsuneko held the directorship of Sōdōmei's Women's Bureau, and was instrumental in founding and editing *Rōdō fujin*. For more on Akamatsu and her work with Sōdōmei, see Suzuki Yūko, *Josei to rōdō kumiai (jō): Rōdō kumiai fujinbu no rekishi* (Tokyo: Renga shobō shinsha, 1990), 113–123.

42. Shakaikyoku rōdōbu, "Shinyagyō haishi no yoka riyō to fukuri shisetsu (ge)," *Jokō kenkyū*, no. 118 (May 1931): 4–5.

43. Shūyōdan undō hachijūnenshi hensan iinkai, ed., *Shūyōdan undō hachijūnenshi: Waga kuni shakai kyōiku no genryū*, vol. 4, *Shiryō hen* (Tokyo: Shūyōdan, 1985), 47.

44. Harry Harootunian, *Overcome by Modernity: History, Culture and Community in Interwar Japan* (Princeton: Princeton University Press, 2000), 294.

45. Garon, *Molding Japanese Minds*.

46. Takashi Fujitani has described how the Department of Shintō Affairs, created in April 1868 immediately following the Meiji Restoration, "established uniform guidelines for rites to be performed at all shrines throughout the nation. The government's specialists on Shintō rituals generally modeled these newly prescribed rites for local shrines on rites performed within the imperial household and thereby gave local rites an imperial and a national significance." Takashi Fujitani, *Splendid Monarchy: Power and Pageantry in Modern Japan* (Berkeley: University of California Press, 1996), 11–12.

47. I would agree with Hazama Hiroshi, who emphasizes that what the Shūyōdan practiced was a "cultivation method" and not a religion, while acknowledging the strong spiritual tone and various Buddhist and Shintō forms that were employed as part of that method. Hazama Hiroshi, ed., *Nihon rōmu kanrishi shiryōshū, dai-2-ki, dai-9-kan: Uno Riemon chosakusen; Mohan kōjōshū* (Tokyo: Gozandō shoten, 1989), 17.

48. Shūyōdan henshūbu, ed., *Shūyōdan sanjūnenshi* (Tokyo: Nihon tosho senta, 1991), 238.

49. Shūyōdan undō hachijūnenshi hensan iinkai, *Shūyōdan undō hachijūnenshi*, vol. 3, *Seishin to jigyō*, 175–181.

50. Shūyōdan henshūbu, *Shūyōdan sanjūnenshi*, 136.

51. Nishikawa Yūko, *Kindai kokka to kazoku moderu* (Tokyo: Yoshikawa kōbunkan, 2000).

52. Nishikawa Yūko, "Sumai no henyō to 'katei' no seiritsu," in *Nihon josei seikatsushi*, vol. 4, *Kindai*, ed. Joseishi sōgō kenkyūkai (Tokyo: Tōkyō Daigaku shuppankai, 1990), 1–49. A translated version is Yuko Nishikawa, "The Changing Form of Dwellings and the Establishment of the *Katei* (Home) in Modern Japan," trans. Mariko Muro Yokokawa, *U.S.-Japan Women's Journal, English Supplement* 8 (1995): 3–36. The word *katei*—written with the Chinese characters for "family" or "house" and "garden"—was originally used as a translation of the English word "home." However, as Nishikawa points out, *katei* quickly became incorporated into the Japanese language and developed its own history of use, therefore rendering any direct correspondence between the English "home" and Japanese *katei* untenable. See also Jordan Sand, "At Home in the Meiji Period: Inventing Japanese Domesticity," in *Mirror of Modernity: Invented Traditions of Modern Japan,* ed. Stephen Vlastos (Berkeley: University of California Press, 1998), 191–207.

53. Shūyōdan henshūbu, *Shūyōdan sanjūnenshi,* 136–137.

54. Hitachi has been one of the Shūyōdan's most important corporate clients since 1926.

55. Shūyōdan undō hachijūnenshi hensan iinkai, *Shūyōdan undō hachi-jūnenshi,* vol. 4, *Shiryō hen,* 24–25.

56. Shūyōdan undō hachijūnenshi hensan iinkai, *Shūyōdan undō hachi-jūnenshi,* vol. 1, *Gaishi,* 109–110.

57. On Hiranuma's political life, see Richard Yasko, "Hiranuma Kiichirō and Conservative Politics in Pre-War Japan" (Ph.D. diss., University of Chicago, 1973). Yasko refers to both the Shūyōdan and Kokuhonsha as "conservative pressure groups." Hiranuma resigned his position with the Shūyōdan in 1936 in order to dedicate himself to his political career. He became prime minister for a brief time in 1939, and he held a number of high-level posts in the Konoe cabinets that governed from 1937 to 1939 and again from 1940 to 1941. After the war he was convicted as a Class-A war criminal at the Tokyo War Crimes Tribunal and was sentenced to life imprisonment.

58. Shūyōdan henshūbu, *Shūyōdan sanjūnenshi,* 230.

59. On the history of the Kyōchōkai, see W. Dean Kinzley, *Industrial Harmony in Modern Japan: The Invention of a Tradition* (New York: Routledge, 1991). Hazama Hiroshi has noted that the most powerful *zaibatsu,* or "financial/industrial groups," such as Mitsui, Iwasaki and Yasuda, did not embrace the new movement of "cooperation and harmony" promoted most forcefully by the Kyōchōkai, while their less successful competitors, such as Shibusawa and Wada Tōyōji, did. Hiroshi Hazama, *The History of Labour Management in Japan,* trans. Mari Sako and Eri Sako (New York: St. Martin's Press, 1997), 40–41.

60. Osaka Spinning was founded in 1880 and began operations in 1883; Mie Spinning was founded in 1886 and began operations in 1888. These two companies later merged to create Tōyō Spinning in 1914.

61. Naosuke Takamura, "The Cotton Spinning Industry in Japan During the Pre–World War I Period: Its Growth and Essential Conditions," in *Innovation, Know How, Rationalization and Investment in the German and Japanese Economies, 1868/1871–1930/1980,* ed. Hans Pohl (Wiesbaden, Germany: Franz Steiner Verlag GmbH, 1982), 210–215. The hazards of night work in the textile industries were numerous, but one of the most common and most deadly was the fires that broke out with great frequency when overtired workers accidentally knocked over the gas lamps or lanterns used to light the factories after nightfall.

62. In this, Uno might fruitfully be compared to Hosoi Wakizō, the author of *Jokō aishi* (The Sorrowful History of Female Factory Workers) discussed in chapter 2, who came from a similar background of poverty and also worked as a factory hand in the textile mills. But while Hosoi (who, like Uno's sisters, died of tuberculosis contracted at the mills) aligned himself with the proletarian and workers' movements, the trajectory of Uno's career and the projects he undertook more closely fit the profile of the middle-class social reformers (described by Sheldon Garon) who aligned themselves with state interests during this period. Garon, *Molding Japanese Minds.*

63. Biographical information in these paragraphs is drawn from Hazama Hiroshi, *Nihon ni okeru rōshi kyōchō no teiryū: Uno Riemon to Kōgyō Kyōikukai*

no katsudō (Tokyo: Waseda Daigaku shuppanbu, 1978), 18–28. Hazama paints Uno as having strong leftist leanings, but Uno's role as the ILO labor representative from Japan during the period when the government refused to allow organized labor to select its own delegate further highlights the degree to which government and business leaders favored Uno's politics and approach to labor-management issues. In many ways Uno's philosophy of labor relations complemented the efforts of leading industrialists and statesmen who had come together to form the Kyōchōkai in 1919.

64. Sugihara Kaoru, "Nihon ni okeru kindaiteki rōdō = seikatsu kateizō no seiritsu: Uno Riemon to Kōgyō Kyōikukai no shisō," in *Taishō Ōsaka suramu: Mō hitotsu no Nihon kindaishi,* ed. Sugihara Kaoru and Tamai Kingō (Tokyo: Shin hyōron, 1996), 29–58.

65. Kaoru Sugihara, "The Transformation of Social Values of Young Country Girls: Towards a Reinterpretation of the Japanese Migrant (Dekasegi) Industrial Labour Force," in *Aspects of the Relationship Between Agriculture and Industrialisation in Japan,* ed. Janet Hunter (London: Suntory Toyota International Centre for Economics and Related Disciplines, London School of Economics and Political Science, 1986), 35.

66. Uno Riemon, *Kan'ai no reika ni kagayaku mohan kōjō: Tōyō Bōseki Himeji kōjō* (Osaka: Kōgyō Kyōikukai shuppanbu, 1927), 27; reprinted in Hazama Hiroshi, ed., *Nihon rōmu kanrishi shiryōshū, dai-2-ki, dai-9-kan: Uno Reimon chosakusen; Mohan kōjōshū* (Tokyo: Gozandō shoten, 1989).

67. Shūyōdan undō hachijūnenshi hensan iinkai, *Shūyōdan undō hachijūnenshi,* vol. 2, *Undō no tenkai,* 88.

68. Hazama Hiroshi has referred to Uno as an *atarashiya*—someone who likes "new" things—in the context of his fascination with the technologies of modern society. In addition to the camera he carried to factory observation visits, he also owned an 8 millimeter film camera, which he brought to Geneva when he visited as Japan's labor representative to the ILO. Photography and moving pictures marked only the beginning of his interest in technology. He also had a fondness for tinkering with small motors and at some point converted a small fishing boat into a motorboat for himself. Hazama, *Nihon ni okeru rōshi kyōchō no teiryū,* 26.

69. Uno Riemon, *Kan'ai no reika ni kagayaku mohan kōjō,* 15–17. Radio calisthenics had first been popularized in 1928, when a life/health-insurance executive returned from a visit to the United States where radio calisthenics were being promoted for good health. He quickly secured cooperation from the physical-education chief of the Ministry of Education, from leaders of the Life Insurance Association, and from the new Japan Broadcasting Association to begin radio calisthenics broadcasts throughout Japan. Ishibashi Takehiko and Satō Tomohisa, *Nihon no taisō: Hyakunen no ayumi to jitsugi* (Tokyo: Fumaidō shoten, 1966), 194. These broadcasts quickly became known as "national calisthenics." It seems, however, that the exercises Uno witnessed, as well as many other such exercises performed en masse by female factory workers in cotton-spinning company yards, often did not accompany a radio program, but were instead directed by leaders from within the company. For a useful history of radio calisthenics in Japan, see also Takahashi Hidemine, *Subarashiki rajio taisō*

(Tokyo: Shōgakkan, 1998), especially 21–22 for a brief listing of *rajio taisō* (radio calisthenics) broadcasts from 1928 to the present.

70. Uno Riemon, *Kan'ai no reika ni kagayaku mohan kōjō*, 14–15.

71. Uno Riemon, *Kan'ai no reika ni kagayaku mohan kōjō*, 95–148.

72. Uno Riemon, *Kan'ai no reika ni kagayaku mohan kōjō*, 139–140.

73. Ichikawa Kinuyo, "Jokō no te," *Hataraku fujin* 2, no. 1 (February 1933): 46.

74. Hōsei Daigaku Ōhara shakai mondai kenkyūjo and Sōdōmei gojūnenshi kankō iinkai, *Rōdō fujin*, vols. 2–4. For an example of the use of the term *mashu*, see vol. 2, 213.

75. *Rōdō fujin* (July 1929), reprinted in Hōsei Daigaku Ōhara shakai mondai kenkyūjo and Sōdōmei gojūnenshi kankō iinkai, *Rōdō fujin*, vol. 2, 230–231.

76. See for example articles in the February and June 1929 issues of *Rōdō fujin* reprinted in Hōsei Daigaku Ōhara shakai mondai kenkyūjo and Sōdōmei gojūnenshi kankō iinkai, *Rōdō fujin*, vol. 2.

77. *Rōdō fujin* (July 1929), reprinted in Hōsei Daigaku Ōhara shakai mondai kenkyūjo and Sōdōmei gojūnenshi kankō iinkai, *Rōdō fujin*, vol. 2, 248.

78. *Rōdō fujin* (July 1929), reprinted in Hōsei Daigaku Ōhara shakai mondai kenkyūjo and Sōdōmei gojūnenshi kankō iinkai, *Rōdō fujin*, vol. 2, 228–229.

79. *Rōdō fujin* (November 1930), reprinted in Hōsei Daigaku Ōhara shakai mondai kenkyūjo and Sōdōmei gojūnenshi kankō iinkai, *Rōdō fujin*, vol. 3, 331. Takahashi Hidemine has pointed out that radio calisthenics during this period were aimed particularly at members of the working class. Out of the dozens of venues in Tokyo that offered radio calisthenics programs on a daily basis in 1935, all of them were located in the wards that were part of *shitamachi*, or the "low city," where Tokyo's factory workers lived and worked, while there were no such venues located in the Yamanote district called home by much of the urban middle class. Takahashi, *Subarashiki rajio taisō*, 138–139.

80. Shūyōdan henshūbu, *Shūyōdan sanjūnenshi*, 231. On *gozoku kyōwa*, see Louise Young, "Imagined Empire: The Cultural Construction of Manchukuo," in *The Japanese Wartime Empire, 1931–1945*, ed. Peter Duus, Ramon H. Myers, and Mark R. Peattie (Princeton: Princeton University Press, 1996), 92–93.

81. Shūyōdan henshūbu, *Shūyōdan sanjūnenshi*, 236. A list of local branches compiled in 1940 shows them in every prefecture, plus in the colonies of Taiwan and Korea and in Manchuria, the Republic of China, and Brazil. Shūyōdan undō hachijūnenshi hensan iinkai, *Shūyōdan undō hachijūnenshi*, vol. 4, *Shiryō hen*, 92–108.

82. The Shūyōdan has enjoyed a continuous existence since its founding in 1906. The organization lost several of its buildings in Tokyo during the Allied air raids, but after World War II, occupation officials approved a petition from the Shūyōdan requesting that the organization be allowed to continue its activities and maintain its institutional structure. Since 1945 the Shūyōdan has built training centers in Kansai (1957) and Ise (1971) and a sixteen-story office building in downtown Tokyo (1996), and it continuously offers training retreats for new employees, for women, and for youth. For a list of the organization's current activities, see the Zaidan hōjin SYD home page, www.syd.or.jp/index2.html.

4. SEX, STRIKES, AND SOLIDARITY

1. On the development of the radical male student subculture at Tokyo Imperial University during this period with which Orimoto was involved, see Henry DeWitt Smith II, *Japan's First Student Radicals* (Cambridge, MA: Harvard University Press, 1972).

2. For a brief biography of Tatewaki that includes a discussion of her activity with the Workers' School for Women, see Rōdōshi kenkyū dōjinkai, ed., *Nihon rōdō undō no senkushatachi* (Tokyo: Keiō tsūshin, 1985), 293–328. See also her autobiography, Tatewaki Sadayo, *Aru henreki no jijōden* (Tokyo: Sōdō bunka, 1980).

3. For a brief biography of Sakai Magara and a description of her involvement with the Red Wave Society (Sekirankai, a socialist women's organization founded in 1921), see Mikiso Hane, *Reflections on the Way to the Gallows* (Berkeley: University of California Press, 1988), 125–131. For an institutional history of the All-Japan Women's Federation and the Proletarian Women's League, see Ishizuki Shizue, " 'Chūkanha' Fujin dōmei ni kan suru oboegaki: 1927-nen kara 1932-nen ni kakete," *Rekishi hyōron*, no. 337 (1978): 104–119. The split among leftist political parties in 1925 resulted in a trifurcation. The resulting factionalism created a cascade effect whereby labor unions and women workers' political organizations scrambled to reconfigure and align themselves with one of the three new parties representing the left, middle, and right of the socialist/proletarian movement. On these broader political developments (without mention of the relation of women's organizations to them), see Stephen S. Large, *Organized Workers and Socialist Politics in Interwar Japan* (Cambridge: Cambridge University Press, 1981). For a more detailed explanation of the way these new political configurations played out in the Tōyō Muslin strike, see Shiota Shōbe, *Sutoraiki no rekishi* (Tokyo: Shin Nihon shinsho, 1966), 182–183.

4. The Tokyo Imperial University Settlement House was disbanded by government order in 1939. For a brief description of the settlement house and its activities, see Henry Smith, *Japan's First Student Radicals,* 142–144. Japan's first settlement house was Katayama Sen's Kingsley Hall, modeled on London's Toynbee Hall and founded in 1897. Ikeda Yoshimasa, *Nihon shakai fukushishi* (Kyoto: Hōritsu bunkasha, 1986), 281–282. For an overview of the early settlement movement in Japan, see Kyōchōkai, ed., *Saikin no shakai undō: Sōritsu jisshūnen kinen shuppan* (Tokyo: Kyōchōkai, 1929), 946–948. For a more extended discussion from a Marxist perspective that focuses on the high point of the movement immediately following the Great Kantō Earthquake of 1923, see Ōbayashi Munetsugu, *Settsurumento no kenkyū* (Tokyo: Dōjinsha, 1926).

5. On the settlement's labor school, see Tōkyō-shi shakaikyoku, *Waga kuni ni okeru rōdō gakkō* (Tokyo: Tōkyō-shi shakaikyoku, 1925), 16–19.

6. The reference to Tatewaki's exposure to the settlement, and to another radical (male) student organization called the Waseda (University) Architects League (Waseda Kensetsusha Dōmei), can be found in Watanabe Etsuji and Suzuki Yūko, *Takakai ni ikite: Senzen fujin rōdō undō e no shōgen* (Tokyo: Domesu shuppan, 1980), 194.

7. Nihon rōnō shinbun, "Saisho no kaikyūteki Kyōai Jojuku Gunma Kyōdo

ni setsuritsu saru," in *Nihon josei undō shiryō shūsei*, vol. 4, *Seikatsu/Rōdō I*, ed. Suzuki Yūko (Tokyo: Fuji shuppan, 1994), 810. For a report on the school's opening ceremony, see Zenkoku Fujin Dōmei, "Zenkoku Fujin Dōmei nyūsu, dai-3 kaime," in *Nihon josei undō shiryō shūsei*, vol. 4, 799–802.

8. Tōkyō-shi shakaikyoku, *Waga kuni ni okeru rōdō gakkō*, 2–3.

9. Tōkyō-shi shakaikyoku, *Waga kuni ni okeru rōdō gakkō*, 32–34.

10. In addition to the Tokyo Social Bureau report—Tōkyō-shi shakaikyoku, *Waga kuni ni okeru rōdō gakkō*—which provides the most detailed contemporary information, the Kyōchōkai also included a study of labor schools in its comprehensive assessment of "recent social movements." See Kyōchōkai, *Saikin no shakai undō*, 960–966.

11. Nihon rōnō shinbun, "Saisho no kaikyūteki Kyōai Jojuku Gunma Kyōdo ni setsuritsu saru," 810.

12. Watanabe Etsuji and Suzuki Yūko, *Tatakai ni ikite*, 204.

13. W. Dean Kinzley, *Industrial Harmony in Modern Japan: The Invention of a Tradition* (New York: Routledge, 1991), 93.

14. Watanabe Etsuji and Suzuki Yūko, *Tatakai ni ikite*, 206.

15. Thomas C. Smith, "The Right to Benevolence: Dignity and Japanese Workers, 1890–1920," in *Native Sources of Japanese Industrialization, 1750–1920* (Berkeley: University of California Press, 1988), 246.

16. Quoted in Suzuki Yūko, *Jokō to rōdō sōgi: 1930 nen Yō Mosu sōgi* (Tokyo: Renga shobō shinsha, 1989), 59.

17. On the Meiji enlightenment movement and the leading role of a group of intellectuals known collectively as the Meirokusha, see Carmen Blacker, *The Japanese Enlightenment: A Study of the Writings of Fukuzawa Yukichi* (Cambridge: Cambridge University Press, 1964).

18. Hiratsuka Raichō, "Haha ni naru jokō no mondai," in *Rōdō mondai no shinzui*, ed. Segawa Genji (Tokyo: Hakuyūsha, 1919), 103.

19. Suzuki Yūko, *Jokō to rōdō sōgi*, 60–62, reproduces a flyer advertising the school and distributed by Tatewaki that lists the first three of these titles. According to Yamakawa's preface to the 1926 edition of his *Purorateria keizaigaku* (Proletarian Economics, which first appeared in 1923), the book was meant to be a primer on communist economics influenced by Bukharin's *ABC's of Communist Economics*. Yamakawa Hitoshi and Tadokoro Teruaki, *Purorateria keizaigaku* (Tokyo: Kagaku shisō fukyūkai, 1926). I have not been able to find full citations for the other titles. Nakamoto Takako remembers that the school also used another book by Yamakawa Hitoshi titled *Shihonshugi no karakuri* (The Farce of Capitalism) and a pamphlet by Nozaka Ryū titled *Fujin to seiji* (Women and Politics). Nakamoto Takako, *Waga sei wa kunō ni yakarete: Waga wakaki hi no ikigai* (Tokyo: Hakuseki shoten, 1973), 11. Rōdōshi kenkyū dōjinkai, *Nihon rōdō undō no senkushatachi*, 303, mentions both Yamakawa's *Shihonshugi no karakuri* and Tatewaki's small book *Rōdō fujin mondai* (The Working Woman Problem), which has been republished in Tatewaki Sadayo, *Nihon rōdō fujin mondai*, edited and with an introduction by Shiota Shōbe (Tokyo: Domesu shuppan, 1980).

20. The Kyōai Jojuku had two female full-time teachers, Ōtsubo Haruko and Mashita Kinu of the Working Women's Society (Shokugyō Fujinsha), and a male

teacher of ethics and national language (*shūshin* and *kokugo*) named Sanoma Ryūdō. Nihon rōnō shinbun, "Saisho no kaikyūteki Kyōai Jojuku Gunma Kyōdo ni setsuritsu saru," 810.

21. For discussions in English of *Nyonin geijutsu* (which ran from July 1928 through June 1932) and the women who contributed to it, see Miriam Silverberg, "The Modern Girl as Militant," in *Recreating Japanese Women, 1600–1945,* ed. Gail Lee Bernstein, 239–266 (Berkeley: University of California Press, 1991), 250–255; and Sarah Frederick, *Turning Pages: Reading and Writing Women's Magazines in Interwar Japan* (Honolulu: University of Hawai'i Press, 2006), chapter 4, which includes a brief analysis of "The Female Bell Cricket." Among the few works in English that treat Nakamoto's literature are a translation of her postwar short story "The Only One," in Grace Suzuki, trans. and ed., *Ukiyo: Eleven Short Stories of Post-War Japan* (Tokyo: Phoenix Books, 1954), 11–35; a translation of the 1929 short story "The Female Bell Cricket," preceded by a brief biographical sketch in Yukiko Tanaka, ed., *To Live and to Write: Selections by Japanese Women Writers, 1913–1938* (Seattle: Seal Press, 1987), 129–144; a treatment by Vera Mackie of Nakamoto's "Tōmosu dai-ni kōjo" (Tokyo Muslin No. 2 Factory), which originally appeared serially in *Nyonin geijutsu* in 1932, in Vera Mackie, "Narratives of Struggle: Writing and the Making of Socialist Women in Japan," in *Society and the State in Interwar Japan,* ed. Elise K. Tipton, 126–145 (New York: Routledge, 1997); Michael Molasky's analysis of Nakamoto's 1953 short story "Women of a Base Town" (Kichi no onna), in Michael S. Molasky, *The American Occupation of Japan and Okinawa: Literature and Memory* (New York: Routledge, 1999), 145–149; and a similarly brief examination of the same story (this time translated as "Military Base Women") in Douglas N. Slaymaker, *The Body in Postwar Japanese Fiction* (New York: RoutledgeCurzon, 2004), 145–149. Scant attention has been paid to Nakamoto in Japan until recently, with the republication of a number of her works in two volumes of the series Kindai josei sakka seisenshū (Selected Writings of Modern Women Authors): Nakamoto Takako, *Kyōkō,* with an introduction by Okada Takako (Tokyo: Yumani shobō, 1999); and Nakamoto Takako, *Nanbu tetsubinkō* (Tokyo: Yumani shobō, 1999).

22. Nakamoto discusses these influences in Nakamoto, *Waga sei wa kunō ni yakarete,* 8.

23. Kobayashi spelled out the purpose and method of his writing in a letter to his publisher, partially reproduced in Frank Motofuji, introduction to *"The Factory Ship" and "The Absentee Landlord,"* by Kobayashi Takiji (Tokyo: University of Tokyo Press, 1973), xvii–xviii. One of the ways Kobayashi employs this method in *Kani kōsen* (The Factory Ship) is by leaving unnamed almost all the working-class characters that collectively make up the novel's "protagonist." Most of the characters are known by appellations such as "the student" or "the stutterer." The only two characters who are named, except for the evil boss Asakawa, are Miyaguchi and Yamada, both workers who die on the ship from abuse. Kobayashi Takiji, *Kani kōsen, Tō-seikatsusha* (Tokyo: Shinchō bunko, 1991).

24. In 1973 Nakamoto was one of several established writers asked to name her favorite book in a special section of the magazine *Fujin kōron* (Women's

Forum). Unlike most of her colleagues, who chose famous works of literature by foreign authors such as Dostoevsky and Emily Brontë, Nakamoto named Hosoi's nonfiction book *Jokō aishi* (The Sorrowful History of Female Factory Workers) and described its influence on her when she first read it "in early Shōwa" (probably soon after it was published in 1925). Nakamoto Takako, "Hosoi Wakizō no *Jokō aishi*," *Fujin kōron*, no. 11 (November 1973): 178–179.

25. Mariko Asano Tamanoi, "Japanese Nationalism and the Female Body: A Critical Reassessment of the Discourse of Social Reformers on Factory Women," in *Women and Class in Japanese History*, ed. Hitomi Tonomura, Anne Walthall, and Haruko Wakita (Ann Arbor: Center for Japanese Studies, University of Michigan, 1999), 286. Cultivating a working-class consciousness among female factory workers was never part of Hosoi's intent. In fact, as he made clear in *Jokō aishi*, he believed factory women to be incapable of organizing effectively and in need of both leadership and protection: "In their strikes, female factory workers act very much like peevish lovers. They are, as Kagawa Toshihiko [the Christian social reformer] has said in *Research on the Psychology of the Poor*, extremely childlike. In truth their disputes are entirely unrelated to working conditions and devoid of any cultural meaning." Hosoi Wakizō, *Jokō aishi* (1925; Tokyo: Iwanami bunkō, 1993), 363.

26. Silverberg argues that in his later writings Nakano "would recognize the importance of examining the consciousness of the worker, its complexity, and its availability in language," but that such recognition is not apparent in his 1927 poem "Kisha" (Train) or in writings as late as 1931. Miriam Silverberg, *Changing Song: The Marxist Manifestos of Nakano Shigeharu* (Princeton: Princeton University Press, 1990), 101–111.

27. On Zenkyō, see Large, *Organized Workers and Socialist Politics in Interwar Japan*, 139–140. For an analysis of Zenkyō and its relationship to the two more moderate unions (Sōdōmei and Kumiai Dōmei) also involved in organizing at Tōyō Muslin, see Shiota, *Sutoraiki no rekishi*, 182–84.

28. A historical analysis of the phenomenon, either from the point of view of women's/feminist history or Marxist/communist movement history, has yet to be undertaken. For a brief mention of this system, see Suzuki Yūko, *Joseishi o hiraku*, vol. 1, *Haha to onna: Hiratsuka Raichō/Ichikawa Fusae o jaku ni* (Tokyo: Miraisha, 1989), 17–18.

29. Suzuki Yūko, ed., *Nihon josei undō shiryō shūsei*, vol. 3, *Shisō, seiji III* (Tokyo: Fuji shuppan, 1997), 456–460.

30. Suzuki Yūko, *Nihon josei undō shiryō shūsei*, vol. 11, *Bekkan, sakuin*, 720–721. Nakamoto wrote of her experiences of imprisonment during this period in a two-part essay. Nakamoto Takako, "Jukeiki, 1: Tōsō yori hakkyō made," in *Chūō kōron* 52, no. 6 (June 1937): 502–532; and "Jukeiki, 2: Tenkō e no shinro," *Chūō kōron* 52, no. 7 (July 1937): 358–385.

31. Nakamoto Takako, *Mosurin Yokochō* (Tokyo: Tōga shobō, 1950), 19.

32. Nakamoto, *Waga sei wa kunō ni yakarete*, 11–12.

33. Sherry B. Ortner, "Resistance and the Problem of Ethnographic Refusal," *Comparative Studies in Society and History* 37, no. 1 (1995): 173.

34. Nakamoto, *Mosurin Yokochō*, 16.

35. Hosoi, *Jokō aishi*, 323.

36. Nakamoto, *Mosurin Yokochō*, 105–106.

37. Vera Mackie has argued that "gaining in assertiveness was one aspect of the transformation of the identity of 'factory girls' into an identity which gave equal weighting to the fact that they were workers, members of the working class, and potential unionists." Vera Mackie, *Creating Socialist Women in Japan: Gender, Labour and Activism, 1900–1937* (New York: Cambridge University Press, 1997), 122. Notably absent from Mackie's list of identities are any that are gender-specific (woman, mother), though I agree with Mackie's observation, which Nakamoto's fiction similarly bears out.

38. The labor historian Shiota Shōbe has placed the number of Japanese textile industry strikes in the year 1930 at 231. See his introduction to Tatewaki, *Nihon rōdō fujin mondai,* 8. Elsewhere he places the total number of strikes for all industries during 1930 at 906. Shiota, *Sutoraiki no rekishi,* 8. Suzuki Yūko, discussing the influence of the Tōyō Muslin strike in precipitating a general strike in the Minami Katsushika (Nankatsu) region, lists ten other companies in the vicinity that experienced labor disputes during 1930. Suzuki Yūko, *Jokō to rōdō sōgi,* 48–49. Andrew Gordon puts the total number of labor disputes in Nankatsu, Tokyo's industrial zone, during 1930 at 64, more than double the number recorded for 1929. Andrew Gordon, *Labor and Imperial Democracy in Prewar Japan* (Berkeley: University of California Press, 1991), 190.

39. Shirai Taishirō, "Kantō daishinsai kara kinyū kyōkō e," in *Shōwa kyōkō,* ed. Sumiya Mikio (Tokyo: Yuhikaku, 1975), 1–78.

40. For an overview of the process of consolidation in the cotton industry, see Takamura Naosuke, *Nihon bōseki gyōshi josetsu* (Tokyo: Hanawa shobō, 1971). On the intensification of labor, see Orimoto Sadayo's "Kōjō rōdō fujin mondai" (in *Fujin daigaku: Fujin mondai hen,* 1932), cited in Suzuki Yūko, *Jokō to rōdō sōgi,* 12–13.

41. See the essays in Sumiya Mikio, ed., *Shōwa kyōkō* (Tokyo: Yuhikaku, 1975), for this trend. Peter Duus notes that the a significant burst of investment activity by Japanese textile industrialists in China occurred immediately after World War I, largely because of changing market conditions. Peter Duus, "Zaikabo: Japanese Cotton Mills in China, 1895–1937," in *The Japanese Informal Empire In China, 1895–1937,* ed. Peter Duus, Ramon H. Myers, and Mark R. Peattie, 65–100 (Princeton: Princeton University Press, 1989). Janet Hunter notes that Japanese investment in mills in China coincided with industry leaders' realization by the 1920s that a ban on night work in Japan was imminent. "Lower levels of worker protection" in China that allowed for night work were among the attractions of setting up operations on the continent. Janet Hunter, "Factory Legislation and Employer Resistance: The Abolition of Night Work in the Cotton-Spinning Industry," in *Japanese Management in Historical Perspective: The International Conference on Business History 15; Proceedings of the Fuji Conference,* ed. Yui Tsunehiko and Nakagawa Keiichirō (Tokyo: University of Tokyo Press, 1989), 253. By the time the recession of the late 1920s had hit the industry in Japan, most of the large firms already had factories in China to which they could transfer much of their operations.

42. Mark Metzler, *Lever of Empire: The International Gold Standard and*

the Crisis of Liberalism in Prewar Japan (Berkeley: University of California Press, 2005), 224–226.

43. See Gordon, *Labor and Imperial Democracy in Prewar Japan,* which takes Nankatsu as a case study to argue for changing manifestations of the sociopolitical movement Gordon calls "imperial democracy" in the prewar period. Suzuki Yūko also gives a slightly different list of companies in the Nankatsu region that experienced strikes. Suzuki Yūko, *Jokō to rōdō sōgi,* 48–49.

44. Gordon, *Labor and Imperial Democracy in Prewar Japan,* 176–181. Gordon also provides brief biographies of the victims of the Kameido Incident, 345–348.

45. Suzuki Yūko, *Jokō to rōdō sōgi,* 27. *Gaishutsu jiyū* is best rendered in English as "freedom to go out [of the factory compound]."

46. Suzuki Yūko, *Jokō to rōdō sōgi,* 34–35.

47. Matsuoka Komakichi, *Noda dai rōdō sōgi* (Nagareyama: Ronshobō, 1973), 150. A more recent book (more sensationalist than scholarly) on an organization called the Dai Nippon Seigidan and the Osaka *yakuza* wars of the 1960s and 1970s claims that the Justice League emerged in the 1950s and was inspired by Mishima Yukio's right-wing nationalism. Shūkan Asahi geinō henshūbu, ed., *Jitsuroku Ōsaka sensō: Dai Nippon Seigidan no uchimaku* (Tokyo: Tokuma shoten, 1979), 93.

48. Shimonaka Kunihiko, *Nihon jinmei daijiten* (Tokyo: Heibonsha, 1979), 344–345.

49. I draw the following chronology from Shiota Shōbe, *Sutoraiki no rekishi;* Suzuki Yūko, *Jokō to rōdō sōgi;* and the writings of Tatewaki Sadayo and other observers. In English the strike is discussed by Janet Hunter, *Women and the Labour Market in Japan's Industrializing Economy: The Textile Industry before the Pacific War* (London: RoutledgeCurzon, 2003), 261–264; and Gordon, *Labor and Imperial Democracy in Prewar Japan,* 225–228.

50. Shiota Shōbe, *Sutoraiki no rekishi,* 185–186.

51. Suzuki Yūko, *Jokō to rōdō sōgi,* 20. Such tactics were not unique to Tōyō Muslin. Matsuoka Komakichi, a Sōdōmei leader who played a key role in the Noda (the makers of Kikkoman soy sauce) strike of 1928–29, reported that the Noda management similarly wrote letters to workers, their families, and residents of the communities surrounding the striking factories and that the company "also mounted a vigorous media campaign, making sure that the families of the strike group all received the papers; they hung posters all over town; and they even employed 'sandwichman' billboards to walk around with their message." Matsuoka, *Noda dai rōdō sōgi,* 164. Janet Hunter describes letter-writing campaigns—including the one at Tōyō Muslin—in *Women and the Labour Market in Japan's Industrializing Economy,* 261–264.

52. Tatewaki, *Aru henreki no jijōden,* 88.

53. Watanabe Etsuji and Suzuki Yūko, *Tatakai ni ikite,* 197–202.

54. See for example Shiota, *Sutoraiki no rekishi,* 191; and Gordon, *Labor and Imperial Democracy in Prewar Japan,* 243.

55. Suzuki Yūko, *Nihon josei undō shiryō shūsei,* vol. 5, *Seikatsu/Rōdō II,* 739.

56. Suzuki Yūko, *Jokō to rōdō sōgi,* 21.

57. Shiota, *Sutoraiki no rekishi*, 188; Rōdōshi kenkyū dōjinkai, ed., *Nihon rōdō undō no senkushatachi*, 308.

58. The full texts of these twenty-one letters can be found in Suzuki Yūko, *Nihon josei undō shiryō shūsei*, vol. 5, 736–748.

59. All quotes from this letter are from Suzuki Yūko, *Nihon josei undō shiryō shūsei*, vol. 5, 742.

60. Suzuki Yūko, *Nihon josei undō shiryō shūsei*, vol. 5, 739–740.

61. Watanabe Etsuji and Suzuki Yūko, *Tatakai ni ikite*, 203.

62. While the factionalism of the left has not been a central part of my arguments here, labor historian Shiota Shōbe has read the Tōyō Muslin strike as a prime example of the failure of the socialist- and communist-affiliated labor unions of that era to work together. His assessment of the strike was written in part as an appeal to the Japanese left of the 1960s to unify and avoid repeating the mistakes of the past. Shiota, *Sutoraiki no rekishi*, 193.

5. COLONIAL LABOR

1. Here I follow economic historian Ha Myonsen in the use of the term "immigrant/migrant" to indicate the breadth of meaning associated with the Japanese word *imin*, which Ha argues can be translated as "migration," "emigration," or "immigration." Thus, Koreans in Japan consisted of both migrants, who planned only to work for a short time in the metropole before returning to Korea, and immigrants, who settled in Japan permanently. Ha Myonsen, *Kanjin Nihon imin shakai keizaishi: Zensen hen* (Tokyo: Akashi shoten, 1997), 1.

2. Mark Peattie has offered one of the earliest focused treatments of Japanese colonial culture in Mark R. Peattie, "Japanese Attitudes Toward Colonialism, 1895–1945," in *The Japanese Colonial Empire, 1895–1945*, ed. Ramon H. Myers and Mark R. Peattie (Princeton: Princeton University Press, 1984), 80–127; and an examination of the culture of colonialism in Mark R. Peattie, "Japanese Treaty Port Settlements in China, 1895–1937," in *The Japanese Informal Empire in China, 1895–1937*, ed. Peter Duus, Ramon H. Myers, and Mark R. Peattie (Princeton: Princeton University Press, 1989), 166–209. Miriam Silverberg has argued for the fluidity of both gender and national identity during Japan's "modern moment," a moment defined by colonial relations among Japanese, Koreans, Chinese, and others who inhabited the "interior" and "exterior" of Japan's imperium. Miriam Silverberg, "Remembering Pearl Harbor, Forgetting Charlie Chaplin, and the Case of the Disappearing Western Woman: A Picture Story," in *Formations of Colonial Modernity in East Asia*, ed. Tani E. Barlow (Durham, NC: Duke University Press, 1997), 249–294. Barbara Brooks's work examines changes in Japanese official policy with regard to the "national" status of Koreans living in Manchuria, and the role of gender in determining community among Japanese colonists in Manchuria and Korea. Barbara J. Brooks, "Peopling the Japanese Empire: The Koreans in Manchuria and the Rhetoric of Inclusion," in *Japan's Competing Modernities: Issues in Culture and Democracy, 1900–1930*, ed. Sharon A. Minichiello (Honolulu: University of Hawai'i Press, 1998), 25–44; Barbara J. Brooks, "Reading the Japanese Colonial Archive: Gender and Bourgeois Civility in Korea and Manchuria before 1932," in *Gendering*

Modern Japanese History, ed. Barbara Molony and Kathleen S. Uno (Cambridge, MA: Harvard University Asia Center, 2005), 295–325. Alan Christy has discussed how (lower) classed and feminized visions of Okinawan migrants to Taiwan drove Okinawan elites to support assimilation, and Tomiyama Ichirō has offered a compelling argument for how the pressures of colonial ideology contributed to the construction of an Okinawan (versus Ryūkyūan) identity that defined itself as Japanese. Alan S. Christy, "The Making of Imperial Subjects in Okinawa," in *Formations of Colonial Modernity in East Asia,* ed. Tani E. Barlow (Durham, NC: Duke University Press, 1997), 141–169; and Tomiyama Ichirō, *Kindai Nihon shakai to "Okinawajin"* (Tokyo: Nihon keizai hyōronsha, 1990). In his most recent study of the Korean community in prewar Japan, Michael Weiner attempts to "deconstruct the assumptions which underpin the myth of a Japanese race." Michael Weiner, *Race and Migration in Imperial Japan* (New York: Routledge, 1994). Ōguma Eiji's pathbreaking book delineates the "boundaries of the Japanese" via a study of colonial policy throughout the Japanese empire (including Okinawa, Ainu, Korea, and Taiwan) and how such policies defined the parameters of ethnicity as well as national citizenship/imperial subjecthood. Ōguma Eiji, *"Nihonjin" no kyōkai: Okinawa, Ainu, Taiwan, Chōsen, shokuminchi shihai kara fukki undō made* (Tokyo: Shinyōsha, 1998).

3. For an analysis of the Japanese discussion of what Kevin Doak calls "ethnic nationalism" in the 1930s and 1940s, see Kevin M. Doak, "What Is a Nation and Who Belongs? National Narratives and the Ethnic Imagination in Twentieth-Century Japan," *American Historical Review* 102, no. 2 (April 1997): 283–309.

4. The use of the ancient term "Yamatojin" to refer to ethnic Japanese also resonated with government and academic attempts to posit Okinawa as a "Japan of the past," which would account both for sameness (i.e., Okinawans are Japanese) and difference (explaining contemporary Okinawan linguistic and cultural practices as authentic traces of an ancient Japanese past no longer existing on the four main islands). See Julia Yonetani, "Ambiguous Traces and the Politics of Sameness: Placing Okinawa in Meiji Japan," in *Japanese Studies* 20, no. 1 (May 2000): 15–31; and Tomiyama Ichirō, "Kokumin no tanjō to 'Nihon jinshu,' " *Shisō* 845 (November 1994): 37–56.

5. Ōguma Eiji discusses the ascension, in the wake of Korea's annexation by Japan, of the mixed-nation theory of Japanese origins among Japanese intellectuals. One strand of this theory suggested that the Japanese imperial family came originally from Korea, thus making the case that assimilation of Koreans into the Japanese national polity should take place easily and naturally, since Koreans and Japanese were already the same. See his *Tan'itsu minzoku shinwa no kigen: "Nihonjin" no jigazō no keifu* (Tokyo: Shinyōsha, 1995), translated by David Askew as *A Geneology of "Japanese" Self-Images* (Melbourne: TransPacific Press, 2002), especially chapters 6 and 7.

6. For a brief summary of the details of the *Ryūkyū shobun,* see Koji Taira, "Troubled National Identity: The Ryukyuans/Okinawans," in *Japan's Minorities: The Illusion of Homogeneity,* ed. Michael Weiner (New York: Routledge, 1997), 153–157.

7. Taira, "Troubled National Identity," 156–157. Taira omits the Japanese

main islands from his list of migratory destinations for Ryūkyūans, but as Tomiyama Ichirō and others have noted, Okinawan immigration to industrial cities like Osaka was also part of the pattern of out-migration from Okinawa after the 1920 drop in sugar prices. See Tomiyama, *Kindai Nihon shakai to "Okinawajin";* and Fukuchi Hiroaki, *Okinawa jokō aishi* (Naha: Naha shuppansha, 1985).

8. For a detailed analysis of the relationship between the foreign and domestic prices of sugar leading up to and immediately after the 1920 drop in prices, and their impact on the Okinawan economy, see Tomiyama, *Kindai Nihon shakai to "Okinawajin,"* 78–82.

9. Fukuchi, *Okinawa jokō aishi,* 85.

10. Similar methods of deception were used by recruiters to lure Japanese girls to sites in China and Southeast Asia as prostitutes (referred to as *karayuki,* literally, "going to China") early in the twentieth century. See Yamazaki Tomoko, *Sandakan hachiban shokan* (Tokyo: Chikuma shobo, 1972), translated by Karen Colligan-Taylor as *Sandakan Brothel No. 8: An Episode in the History of Lower-Class Japanese Women* (Armonk, NY: M. E. Sharpe, 1999). In the 1930s and 1940s the same tactics were used to recruit Japanese, Korean, Filipina, and other Asians as military sexual slaves, or "comfort women." See Yoshimi Yoshiaki, *Jugun ianfu* (Tokyo: Iwanami shoten, 1995), translated by Suzanne O'Brien as *Comfort Women: Sexual Slavery in the Japanese Military During World War II* (New York: Columbia University Press, 2000); and Yuki Tanaka, *Japan's Comfort Women: Sexual Slavery and Prostitution during World War II and the U.S. Occupation* (New York: Routledge, 2001). In both cases, girls were often told they would be going to a well-paid factory job.

11. See Fukuchi, *Okinawa jokō aishi,* 78–79, 85, for several firsthand accounts from former Okinawan female factory workers who tell of the circumstances surrounding the deaths and repatriation of the bones and ashes of fellow Okinawan workers who had fallen ill and died.

12. Fukuchi, *Okinawa jokō aishi,* 11.

13. Fukuchi, *Okinawa jokō aishi,* 78.

14. G. H. Kerr, cited in Taira, "Troubled National Identity," 143.

15. Fukuchi, *Okinawa jokō aishi,* 117.

16. Higa Michiko, *Aii, piijaayo,* quoted in Tomiyama, *Kindai Nihon shakai to "Okinawajin,"* 150.

17. Tomiyama, *Kindai Nihon shakai to "Okinawajin,"* 151.

18. W. Donald Smith has documented a similar process in the coal industry whereby Koreans, originally hired in significant numbers at the Chikuhō Coal Mines as part of company efforts to dilute labor activism among Japanese workers, themselves came to be seen (and with good reason) as the most militant element of the labor force by the 1920s. W. Donald Smith, "Ethnicity, Class and Gender in the Mines: Korean Workers in Japan's Chikuhō Coal Field, 1917–1945" (Ph.D. diss., University of Washington, 1999), especially chapter 3.

19. Nittōsha, "Okinawa jokō ni seikō shite iru Fukubō Sakai kōjō," *Jokō kenkyū,* vol 1., no. 9 (September 1925), 99.

20. Peter Duus has referred to the result of these colonial policies as the "Korean land grab," in which Japanese colonists rushed in to take over previously

unregistered (and therefore "unowned") tracts of farmland. Peter Duus, *The Abacus and the Sword: The Japanese Penetration of Korea, 1895–1910* (Berkeley: University of California Press, 1995), 366–373. On the land survey and registration laws implemented by the colonial administration in Korea that led to this land grab, and their effect on Korea's farming population, see Ha, *Kanjin Nihon imin shakai keizaishi*, 2, 27–28; and Kim Ch'an-jong, *Chōsenjin jokō no uta* (Tokyo: Iwanami shoten, 1982), 17–20. On Japanese emigration to Manchuria, see Louise Young, "Imagined Empire: The Cultural Construction of Manchukuo," in *The Japanese Wartime Empire, 1931–1945,* ed. Peter Duus, Ramon H. Myers, and Mark R. Peattie (Princeton: Princeton University Press, 1996), 71–96; Louise Young, *Japan's Total Empire: Manchuria and the Culture of Wartime Imperialism* (Berkeley: University of California Press, 1998); and Mariko Asano Tamanoi, "Knowledge, Power, and Classifications: The 'Japanese' in 'Manchuria,' " *Journal of Asian Studies* 59, no. 2 (May 2000): 248–276.

21. Michael Weiner, *The Origins of the Korean Community in Japan, 1910–1923* (Atlantic Highlands, NJ: Humanities Press International, Inc., 1989), 74.

22. Ōhara shakai mondai kenkyūjo, ed., *Nihon rōdō nenkan* (1931; Tokyo: Hōsei Daigaku shuppankyoku, 1968), 75.

23. Duus, *The Abacus and the Sword,* 399–406.

24. Ōsaka-shi shakaibu chōsaka, ed. *Chōsenjin rōdōsha mondai* (Osaka: Kōbundō shobō, 1924), 88–89. See also Weiner, *The Origins of the Korean Community in Japan, 1910–1923,* 83.

25. Ishigami Kinji, "Chōsen jokō o tsukau kokoroe," *Jokō kenkyū,* no. 184 (May 1933): 1.

26. Watsuji's book *Fūdo* appeared in 1935, two years after Ishigami published his essay on Korean workers in *Jokō kenkyū* (Research on Female Factory Workers). However, Watsuji began publishing essays and lecturing on early drafts of sections of the book in late 1928. It is quite possible that Ishigami was influenced in his discussion of climate by Watsuji's ideas. Watsuji Tetsurō, *Fūdo* (1935; Tokyo: Iwanami bunkō, 1989). On Watsuji and his book *Fūdo,* see also Harry Harootunian and Tetsuo Najita, "Japanese Revolt against the West: Political and Cultural Criticism in the Twentieth Century," in *The Cambridge History of Japan,* vol. 6, *The Twentieth Century,* ed. Peter Duus (Cambridge: Cambridge University Press, 1988), 743–749; and Ōguma Eiji, *Tan'itsu minzoku shinwa no kigen,* translated by David Askew as *A Genealogy of "Japanese" Self-Images,* chapter 15. *Fūdo* has been translated into English by Geoffrey Bownas as *Climate and Culture: A Philosophical Study* (New York: Greenwood Press, 1988).

27. Ishigami, "Chōsen jokō o tsukau kokoroe," 1–11.

28. Weiner, *The Origins of the Korean Community in Japan, 1910–1923,* 65–66.

29. On Korean coal miners, see Kim Ch'an-jong, *Hi no dōkoku: Zainichi Chōsenjin kōfu no seikatsushi* (Tokyo: Tabatake shoten, 1980); W. Donald Smith, "Sorting Coal and Pickling Cabbage: Korean Women in the Japanese Mining Industry," in *Gendering Modern Japanese History,* ed. Barbara Molony and Kathleen S. Uno (Cambridge, MA: Harvard University Asia Center, 2005),

393–422. Sugihara Tōru notes that by 1930 Koreans made up approximately 32 percent of Osaka's rubber industry workforce. Sugihara Tōru, "Zaihan Chōsenjin no tōkō katei: Chōsen, Cheju-shima to no kanren de," in *Taishō Ōsaka suramu: Mō hitotsu no Nihon kindaishi*, ed. Sugihara Kaoru and Tamai Kingō (Tokyo: Shin hyōron, 1996), 14. For a study of Korean workers in the Higashi-nari area of the city of Osaka during the 1920s, see Sasaki Nobuaki, "1920 nendai ni okeru zaihan Chōsenjin no rōdō = seikatsu katei: Higashi-nari, shuju chiku o chūshin ni," in *Taishō Ōsaka suramu: Mō hitotsu no Nihon kindaishi*, ed. Sugihara Kaoru and Tamai Kingō (Tokyo: Shin hyōron, 1996), 161–212.

30. Michael Weiner has noted that most Korean migrants did not get hired in large factories, *except* for female workers in the textile industry. Weiner, *The Origins of the Korean Community in Japan, 1910–1923*, 80.

31. On the development of urban working-class ghettoes, see Jeffrey E. Hanes, *The City as Subject: Seki Hajime and the Reinvention of Modern Osaka* (Berkeley: University of California Press, 2002), especially chapters 5 and 6. Hanes does not refer to the growing population of Koreans in Osaka, but his study suggests the spatial arrangements of class in the new industrial cities to which the Korean (and Okinawan) population would also have been subject. On Korean workers in Osaka, and particularly the ghetto of the Ikaino district of the city, see Sasaki, "1920 nendai ni okeru zaihan Chōsenjin no rōdō = seikatsu katei"; and Sugihara, "Zaihan Chōsenjin no tōkō katei."

32. Louise Young has offered a compelling analysis of the operations of the family metaphor in the context of colonial policies of Japanese emigration to Manchuria in the 1930s. During this time, second and third sons of Japanese farming families were encouraged to go to Manchuria, and the whole project was described as setting up "branch families," a common practice of Japanese family organization involving inheritance and family headship. Within the logic of this metaphor, Japan itself became the stem family and Manchuria the branch. Young demonstrates how this metaphor was used in conjunction with the policy of *gozoku kyōwa*, the "harmony of the five races." Louise Young, "Imagined Empire," 92.

33. Japanese critics of assimilation such as Yanaihara Tadao used essentially this argument: that colonial peoples should not and could not become Japanese, but rather should be treated fairly within a hierarchy of races with Japanese at the top. See Oguma, *"Nihonjin" no kyōkai*, chapter 7.

34. Brooks, "Peopling the Japanese Empire," 30. In the 1920s a group of Korean political activists formed an organization called the Futei Senjinsha (Society of Korean Malcontents), clearly a tongue-in-cheek reference to the way much public and official discourse named Koreans and Korean activities after the failure of the independence movement. The anarchist-leaning Futei Senjinsha advocated the overthrow of the state through direct action. Weiner, *The Origins of the Korean Community in Japan, 1910–1923*, 111, 151.

35. The death toll of the 1923 Korean massacre ranges from as low as 231 in a report issued by the Home Ministry Police Affairs Bureau not long after the event, up to 6,000, the number arrived at by several scholars studying the massacre in more recent years. For a useful summary of the death toll issue and debates on it, see Weiner, *The Origins of the Korean Community in Japan,*

1910–1923, 181–182. Kim Ch'an-jong, a scholar of resident-Korean history, believes the number may be closer to 7,000. Kim Ch'an-jong, *Zainichi Korian hyakunenshi* (Tokyo: Sangokan, 1997), 51.

36. Hosoi Wakizō, *Jokō aishi* (1925; Tokyo: Iwanami bunkō, 1993), 244.

37. Fukuchi, *Okinawa jokō aishi*, 86.

38. On the Otaru Incident, see Weiner, *Race and Migration in Imperial Japan*, 119–120. Ironically, the celebrated author of arguably the proletarian literature movement's most influential novel, Kobayashi Takiji, who wrote *Kani kōsen* (The Factory Ship), had graduated from Otaru Higher Commercial School only a year earlier. Frank Motofuji, introduction to *"The Factory Ship" and "The Absentee Landlord,"* by Kobayashi Takiji (Tokyo: University of Tokyo Press, 1973), xiii–xiv. Kobayashi, a member of the Japan Communist Party, died at the hands of the Special Higher Police in 1933.

39. Weiner, *Race and Migration in Imperial Japan*, 156.

40. For the testimony of a woman recruited by the Sōaikai in Korea to work in a silk mill in Toyohashi (Aichi Prefecture), see Chōsenjin kyōsei renkō shinsō chōsadan, ed., *Chōsenjin kyōsei renkō chōsa no kioku: Chūbu/Tōkai* (Tokyo: Kashiwa shobō, 1997), 260–262; and Kim Ch'an-jong, *Maboroshi no shinbun: "Minshū jihō"* (Tokyo: Sangokan, 2001), 159–160.

41. Kim Ch'an-jong, *Chōsenjin jokō no uta*, 101, 104.

42. Kim Ch'an-jong, *Maboroshi no shinbun*, 159–160.

43. Sōaikai Izumi honbu, ed., *Sōaikai jigyō kōgai* (Kishiwada: Sōaikai Izumi honbu, 1927), 5.

44. Sally Ann Hastings, *Neighborhood and Nation in Tokyo, 1905–1937* (Pittsburgh: University of Pittsburgh Press, 1995), 63.

45. Sōaikai sōhonbu, *Sōaikai jigyō kōgai* (Tokyo: Sōaikai sōhonbu, 1923), 28–36; Sōaikai Izumi honbu, *Sōaikai jigyō kōgai*, 29–32.

46. Sōaikai sōhonbu, *Sōaikai jigyō kōgai*, 69.

47. Ōhara shakai mondai kenkyūjo, *Nihon rōdō nekan*, 78–80. Pak Kyongsik, *Zainichi Chōsenjin undōshi: 8.15 kaihōzen* (Tokyo: San'ichi shobō, 1979), 61–63.

48. Sōaikai sōhonbu, *Sōaikai jigyō kōgai*, 71–72.

49. Sōaikai sōhonbu, *Sōaikai jigyō kōgai*, 48–49.

50. Quoted in Kim Ch'an-jong, *Maboroshi no shinbun*, 155–156.

51. Saitō Makoto served as governor-general of Korea from 1919 until 1927. A high-ranking naval officer, he also served as prime minister of Japan from 1932 to 1934.

52. Weiner, *The Origins of the Korean Community in Japan, 1910–1923*, 179–181; Kim Ch'an-jong, *Zainichi Korian hyakunenshi*, 53.

53. Kim Ch'an-jong, *Zainichi Korian hyakunenshi*, 53.

54. Nishinarita Yutaka, *Zainichi Chōsenjin no "sekai" to "teikoku" kokka* (Tokyo: Tōkyō Daigaku shuppan, 1997), 176–177.

55. Manfred Ringhoffer, "Sōaikai: Chōsenjin dōka dantai no ayumi," in *Zainichi Chōsenjinshi kenkyū*, no. 9 (December 1981): 54.

56. Koyama Hitoshi, *Sensō, sabetsu, kōgai* (Osaka: Kaihō shuppansha, 1995), 119.

57. For membership numbers and founding dates for some of the most im-

portant Sōaikai regional offices, see Nishinarita, *Zainichi Chōsenjin no "sekai" to "teikoku" kokka*, 177–178.

58. Sōaikai Izumi honbu, *Sōaikai jigyō kōgai*, 23–28.

59. Matsushita Matsutsugu, *Shiryō Kishiwada Bōseki no sōgi* (Osaka: Yuniusu, 1980), 15–16.

60. Koji Taira has argued persuasively that by 1920 Japanese industry had absorbed most of the country's available labor supply. Koji Taira, "Economic Development, Labor Markets, and Industrial Relations in Japan, 1905–1955," in *The Cambridge History of Japan*, vol. 6, *The Twentieth Century*, ed. Peter Duus (Cambridge: Cambridge University Press, 1988), especially 613–615. For further discussion of trends in the early twentieth-century textile industry labor market, see also Koji Taira, *Economic Development and the Labor Market in Japan* (New York: Columbia University Press, 1970). The classic discussion of changing patterns of labor recruitment in the cotton industry up to 1925 is Hosoi, *Jokō aishi*.

61. Ōsaka shakai rōdō undōshi henshu iinkai, ed., *Ōsaka shakai rōdō undōshi (dai-1-maki): Senzenhen, jō* (Tokyo: Yūhikaku, 1986), 949; Weiner, *The Origins of the Korean Community in Japan, 1910–1923*, 56–58.

62. This support waned by the late 1920s as the government restricted the emigration of Koreans from Pusan to the metropole and began to promote the northward migration of poor Korean workers to Manchuria. Brooks, "Peopling the Japanese Empire," 28.

63. Chōsen Sōtokufu shomubu chōsaka, "Hanshin Keihin chihō no Chōsenjin rōdōsha" (1924), in *Zainichi Chōsenjin kankei shiryō shūsei*, vol. 1, ed. Pak Kyong-sik (Tokyo: San'ichi shobō, 1975), 412.

64. The migrant workers arriving in Japan in the 1920s would not have been subject to the Korean Government General's most extreme efforts to promote assimilation on the peninsula, which made the exclusive use of the Japanese language at all Korean schools compulsory by 1941. Wan-you Chou, "The *Kominka* Movement in Taiwan and Korea: Comparisons and Interpretations," in *The Japanese Wartime Empire, 1931–1945*, ed. Peter Duus, Ramon H. Myers, and Mark R. Peattie (Princeton: Princeton University Press, 1996), 40–68. For a personal account of the policy of mandated Japanese-language use and its effects on a family, see the memoir by Richard E. Kim, *Lost Names: Scenes from a Korean Boyhood* (Berkeley: University of California Press, 1998).

65. Tonomura Masaru, "Senjiki Zainichi Chōsenjin ni okeru shakaiteki jōshō," *Shakai kagaku tōkyū* 43, no. 3 (March 1998), 634.

66. Kishiwada shiritsu josei senta, Kishiwada no joseishi hensan iinkai, eds., *Shimin ga tsuzutta joseishi: Kishiwada no onna-tachi* (Tokyo: Domesu shuppan, 1999), 73.

67. Kishiwada-shi shi hensan iinkai, ed., *Kishiwada-shi shi*, vol. 4, *Kindai hen* (Kishiwada: Kishiwada-shi, 2005), 39.

68. Matsushita, *Shiryō Kishiwada Bōseki no sōgi*, 20, 99–100. Kishiwada-shi shi hensan iinkai, *Kishiwada-shi shi*, vol. 4, 30.

69. The union was initially called the Yūaikai and changed its name to Sōdōmei in 1919. Stephen S. Large, *The Rise of Labor in Japan: The Yūaikai, 1912–19* (Tokyo: Sophia University Press, 1972), 44; Andrew Gordon, *The Evo-*

lution of Labor Relations in Japan: Heavy Industry, 1853–1955 (Cambridge, MA: Harvard Council on East Asian Studies, 1988), 71–72.

70. Kishiwada-shi shi hensan iinkai, *Kishiwada-shi shi*, vol. 4, 33.

71. Janet Hunter, *Women and the Labour Market in Japan's Industrialising Economy: The Textile Industry before the Pacific War* (London: RoutledgeCurzon, 2003), 253.

72. Suzuki Yūko, *Josei to rōdō kumiai (jō): Rōdō kumiai fujinbu no rekishi* (Tokyo: Renga shobō shinsha, 1990), 18–20.

73. Hunter, *Women and the Labour Market in Japan's Industrialising Economy*, 251. On the debate that led to the creation of the Hyōgikai Women's Section, see Itō Akira, *Nihon Rōdō Kumiai Hyōgikai no kenkyū: 1920 nendai rōdō undō no kōbō* (Tokyo: Shakai hyōronsha, 2001), 289–302.

74. Weiner, *The Origins of the Korean Community in Japan, 1910–1923*, 102.

75. Weiner, *The Origins of the Korean Community in Japan, 1910–1923*, 107; Pak Kyong-sik, *Zainichi Chōsenjin undōshi*, 122–123.

76. Kim Ch'an-jong, *Chōsenjin jokō no uta*, 141–146.

77. "Kishiwada Bō Haruki kōjo tatsu," *Rōdō fujin*, no. 22 (September 1929), reprinted in Hōsei Daigaku Ōhara shakai mondai kenkyūjo and Sōdōmei gojūnenshi kankō iinkai, eds., *Rōdō fujin*, vol. 2 (Tokyo: Hōsei Daigaku shuppankyoku, 1978), 318.

78. Matsushita, *Shiryō Kishiwada Bōseki no sōgi*, 17–18. See also Kim Ch'an-jong, *Chōsenjin jokō no uta*, 43.

79. Kim Ch'an-jong, *Chōsenjin jokō no uta*, 147–148.

80. *Ōsaka Asahi*, "Kishibō no jokō hyakumei ga dasshutsu, Sakaibun kōjo no Senjin-tachi kojin nesage o fufuku to shi" [One hundred female factory workers escape Kishibō, Koreans at the Sakai factory protest wage cut] (May 4, 1930), reprinted in Matsushita, *Shiryō Kishiwada Bōseki no sōgi*, 52–53. The newspaper article does not specify whether the number 539 refers to the total number of workers at the Sakai factory or to the number of those attending the rally. One Korean woman who took part in the event claimed that the factory employed approximately 530 female factory workers and over 100 male factory hands at the time of the strike. Hirabayashi Hisae, "Kiroku: Ito o tsuida onna-tachi," *Kikan sanzen-ri* 5 (Spring 1976): 105.

81. For a detailed list of these demands, see Kim Ch'an-jong, *Kaze no dōkoku: Zainichi Chōsenjin jokō no seikatsu* (Tokyo: Tabatake shoten, 1977), 174–176.

82. See for example Weiner, *Race and Migration in Imperial Japan*, 171.

83. Naimushō shakaikyoku, "Chōsenjin rōdōsha ni kan suru jōkyō" (1924), charts reprinted in Ha, *Kanjin Nihon imin shakai keizaishi*, 177–178.

84. Kim Ch'an-jong, *Chōsenjin jokō no uta*, 100–101.

85. The Korean Female Factory Worker Protection League was established by the Korean Labor Association (Chōsen Rōdō Dōshikai) in early 1925 with the purpose of improving the poor conditions of Korean textile-factory workers in the Senshū region. Ōsaka shakai rōdō undōshi henshū iinkai, *Ōsaka shakai rōdō undōshi (dai-1-kan)*, 851.

86. Weiner, *Race and Migration in Imperial Japan*, 172.

87. This is the assertion of one of several former Korean female factory workers at Kishibō interviewed by Kim Ch'an-jong in the 1980s. In his book on Korean female factory workers and the Kishibō strike, Kim claims he could not find any former Korean worker who had actually participated in the 1930 strike to interview, because after the strike the company fired all Korean participants and provided them with a transportation fee to send them back to Korea. Kim Ch'an-jong, *Chōsenjin jokō no uta*, 149–151.

88. Michael Weiner notes that Sōaikai "goon squads" were used in 1929 to break up a strike in Kawasaki. Weiner, *Race and Migration in Imperial Japan*, 172.

89. Hirabayashi, "Kiroku," 106.

90. Kim Ch'an-jong, *Kaze no dōkoku*, 191–194.

91. *Naimushō Shōwa 4-nen nenpō*, cited in Kim Ch'an-jong, *Chōsenjin jokō no uta*, 140.

92. Ōhara shakai mondai kenkyūjo, ed., *Nihon rōdō nenkan*, 80.

93. Martin Kaneko, "Senzenki sen'i sangyō ni okeru hisabetsu shūdan shusshin no josei rōdōsha," *Rekishigaku kenkyū*, no. 664 (October 1994): 139–140.

94. Ishigami, "Chōsen jokō o tsukau kokoroe," 10.

95. On the Okinawa Kenjinkai in Osaka, see Tomiyama, *Kindai Nihon shakai to "Okinawajin."*

96. Kishiwada-shi shi hensan iinkai, ed. *Kishiwada-shi shi*, vol. 4, 50; Weiner, *Race and Migration in Imperial Japan*, 171.

97. Kishiwada-shi shi hensan iinkai, *Kishiwada-shi shi*, vol. 4, 50.

EPILOGUE

1. The Ōhara Institute for Social Research records the highest number of strikes (984) in all industries occurring in 1931. Hōsei Daigaku Ōhara shakai mondai kenkyūjo, *Shakai/rōdō undō dai nenpyō* [Timeline of Social and Labor Movements] (Tokyo: Rōdō junpōsha, 1995), 278.

2. "Jokō-san tachi no Manshū kengaku miyagebanashi," *Ie no hikari* (September, 1933), 128.

3. On Japan's colonial and settler project in Manchuria, see Mariko Asano Tamanoi, "Knowledge, Power, and Classifications: The 'Japanese' in 'Manchuria,' " *Journal of Asian Studies* 59, no. 2 (May 2000): 248–276; and Louise Young, *Japan's Total Empire: Manchuria and the Culture of Wartime Imperialism* (Berkeley: University of California Press, 1998).

4. The major works that deal with women and work during wartime are Thomas R. H. Havens, "Women and War in Japan, 1937–1945," *The American Historical Review* 80, no. 4 (October 1975): 913–934; Janet Hunter, "An Absence of Change: Women in the Japanese Labour Force, 1937–45," in *Conflict and Amity in East Asia: Essays in Honour of Ian Nish,* ed. T. J. Fraser and Peter Lowe (London: Macmillan Academic and Professional Ltd., 1992), 59–76; and Regine Mathias, "Women and the War Economy in Japan," in *Japan's War Economy,* ed. Erich Pauer (New York: Routledge, 1999), 65–84.

5. These percentages remained fairly consistent throughout the first four

decades of the twentieth century. Irene B. Taeuber, "Population and Labor Force in The Industrialization of Japan, 1850–1950," in *Economic Growth: Brazil, India, Japan*, ed. Simon Kuznets, Wilbert E. Moore, and Joseph J. Spengler (Durham, NC: Duke University Press, 1955), 352.

6. Among the previously existing seventy-seven member companies, at least half had under fifty thousand spindles, and 65 percent had under twenty thousand. Tōyō Bōseki kabushiki kaisha and "Tōyō bōseki shichijū nenshi" henshū iinkai, eds., *Tōyō Bōseki shichijū nenshi* (Tokyo: Tōyō bōseki kabushiki kaisha, 1953), 408–409.

7. Tōyō Bōseki kabushiki kaisha and "Tōyō bōseki shichijū nenshi" henshū iinkai, eds., *Tōyō Bōseki shichijū nenshi*, 411.

8. Until 1937 the United States and India supplied 90 percent of Japan's raw cotton imports. After Pearl Harbor, Japan was forced to rely exclusively on inferior-quality imports from China and Manchuria. Jerome B. Cohen, *Japan's Economy in War and Reconstruction* (Minneapolis: University of Minnesota Press, 1949), 391.

9. The Big Ten consisted of the following companies: Tōyō Cotton Spinning, Dai Nippon Cotton Spinning, Shikishima Cotton Spinning, Kurashiki Cotton Spinning, Nisshin Cotton Spinning, Daiken Sangyō, Kanegafuchi Cotton Spinning, Daiwa Cotton Spinning, Fuji Cotton Spinning, and Nittō Cotton Spinning. Tōyō Bōseki kabushiki kaisha and "Tōyō Bōseki shichijū nenshi" henshū iinkai, *Tōyō Bōseki shichijū nenshi*, 412–415.

10. Cohen, *Japan's Economy in War and Reconstruction*, 389–390.

11. The population in 1940 was just under 72 million. Census figures for 1960 put the population at 94,302,000—not far from the wartime goal for that year.

12. Suzuki Yūko, *Feminizumu to sensō: Fujin undōka no sensō kyōryoku* (1986; Tokyo: Marujusha, 1997), 203.

13. Cohen, *Japan's Economy in War and Reconstruction*, 292. See also Hunter, "An Absence of Change: Women in the Japanese Labour Force, 1937–45," 59–76.

14. Quoted in Suzuki Yūko, *Feminizumu to sensō*, 194–195.

15. *Rōmu jihō*, no. 227 (July 15, 1943), reprinted in Suzuki Yūko, ed., *Nihon josei undō shiryō shūsei*, vol. 6, *Seikatsu/Rodo III* (Tokyo: Fuji shuppan, 1993), 497.

16. *Rōmu jihō*, no. 227 (July 15, 1945), reprinted in Suzuki Yūko, *Nihon josei undō shiryō shūsei*, vol. 6, 497.

17. *Rōmu jihō*, no. 227 (July 15, 1945), reprinted in Suzuki Yūko, *Nihon josei undō shiryō shūsei*, vol. 6, 498.

18. *Rōmu jihō*, no. 227 (July 15, 1945), reprinted in Suzuki Yūko, *Nihon josei undō shiryō shūsei*, vol. 6, 502.

19. *Rōmu jihō*, no. 227 (July 15, 1945), reprinted in Suzuki Yūko, *Nihon josei undō shiryō shūsei*, vol. 6, 499–500.

20. Higuchi Yūichi, "Chōsenjin shojo no Nihon e no kyōsei renkō ni tsuite," *Zainichi Chōsenjin-shi kenkyū*, no. 20 (October 1990): 2. Higuchi asserts that these exhortations had little effect on Korean women; they were more invested than Korean men in upholding culture and tradition and were also saddled with

the household and farming work in the absence of their husbands, who had been mobilized as factory workers and soldiers.

21. Nihon rōdō kenkyū kiko, ed., *Labour Standards Law (Law No. 49 of April 7, 1947)* (Tokyo: Japan Institute of Labor, 2002), 64.

22. On the popularization of democratic principles, see John Dower, *Embracing Defeat: Japan in the Wake of World War II* (New York: W. W. Norton & Company, 1999), chapter 7.

23. Despite the significance of this strike there has been very little written about it in English. For one of the most extensive accounts, see Helen Macnaughtan, *Women, Work, and the Japanese Economic Miracle: The Case of the Cotton Textie Industry, 1945–1975* (London: RoutledgeCurzon, 2005), 40–43.

24. Cohen, *Japan's Economy in War and Reconstruction,* 484.

25. Cohen, *Japan's Economy in War and Reconstruction,* 486.

26. Young-il Park and Kym Anderson, "The Rise and Demise of Textiles and Clothing in Economic Development: The Case of Japan," in *Japanese Economic History, 1600–1960: The Textile Industry and the Rise of the Japanese Economy,* ed. Michael Smitka (New York: Garland Publishing, Inc., 1998), 165–182; Yutaka Kōsai, "The Postwar Japanese Economy, 1945–1973," trans. Andrew Goble in *The Cambridge History of Japan,* vol. 6, *The Twentieth Century,* ed. Peter Duus (New York: Cambridge University Press, 1988), 516–522.

27. Simon Partner, *Assembled in Japan: Electrical Goods and the Making of the Japanese Consumer* (Berkeley: University of California Press, 1999), 207–212.

28. Kishiwada shiritsu josei senta, Kishiwada no joseishi hensan iinkai, eds., *Shimin ga tsuzutta joseishi: Kishiwada no onna-tachi* (Tokyo: Domesu shuppan, 1999), 168.

29. Cohen, *Japan's Economy in War and Reconstruction,* 486. The Big Ten, consolidated under government order during the war, formed the backbone of the postwar textile industry.

30. Hata Seikō, *Ōmi Kenshi rōdō sōgi no shinsō* (Tokyo: Bonyūsha, 1954), 151–152.

31. Kishiwada shiritsu josei senta, Kishiwada no joseishi hensan iinkai, *Shimin ga tsuzutta joseishi,* 170.

32. Hata, *Ōmi Kenshi rōdō sōgi no shinsō,*128.

33. In addition to requirements for paid holidays, overtime pay, and limits on working hours, the law also stipulated that "when a woman for whom work during menstrual periods would be especially difficult has requested leave, the employer shall not have the said woman work on days of the menstrual period." Nihon rōdō kenkyū kiko, *Labour Standards Law,* 52. For a list of specific violations at each factory, see Kishiwada shiritsu josei senta, Kishiwada no joseishi hensan iinkai, *Shimin ga tsuzutta joseishi,* 17.

34. The list of twenty-two demands is reproduced in Kishiwada shiritsu josei senta, Kishiwada no joseishi hensan iinkai, *Shimin ga tsuzutta joseishi,* 170. An English translation of the demands can be found in Hirosuke Kawanishi, ed., *The Human Face of Industrial Conflict in Post-war Japan* (New York: Kegan Paul International, 1999), 179–181.

35. Kishiwada shiritsu josei senta, Kishiwada no joseishi hensan iinkai, *Shimin ga tsuzutta joseishi*, 169; Hata, *Ōmi Kenshi rōdō sōgi no shinsō*, 147.

36. Miyake Yoshiko, "Nihon no shakai kagaku to jenda: 'Jokō aishi gensetsu' o megutte," in *Nihon shakai to jenda*, ed. Miyake Yoshiko and Muta Kazue (Tokyo: Akashi shoten, 2001), 15–18.

37. Hirosuke Kawanishi, editor's introduction to Minoru Takita, "The Labour Conflict of the Omi-Kenshi Silk Mills, 1954," in Hirosuke Kawanishi, ed., *The Human Face of Industrial Conflict in Post-war Japan* (New York: Kegan Paul International, 1999), 177.

38. Yukio Mishima, *Silk and Insight*, translated and with an introduction by Hiroaki Sato (Armonk, NY: M. E. Sharpe, 1998), 165–166.

39. Miyajima Hisashi, *Jinken sōgi: Ōmi Kenshi rōdōsha no tatakai* (Kyoto: Hōritsu bunkasha, 1955), 117–118. This is my own translation from the actual Ōmi Kenshi flyer. Mishima's version of the flyer is only slightly modified from the original. Yukio Mishima, *Silk and Insight*, 166.

40. Black-and-white television ownership stood at 44.7 percent for non-farming households in 1960, but jumped to 95 percent by 1965. Yutaka Kōsai, "The Postwar Japanese Economy, 1945–1973," 515. Many Japanese families purchased their first television set in order to watch the live broadcasts of the Tokyo Olympics. Several events, including volleyball, were selected to be broadcast in color—the first color broadcasts of any Olympic games. Very few Japanese, however, owned color television sets at this time. Nihon hōsō kyōkai, *Broadcasting in Japan: Twentieth Century Journey from Radio to Multimedia* (Tokyo: NHK, 2002), 137, 180–181, 204.

41. Nihon hōsō kyōkai, *Broadcasting in Japan*, 182.

42. Yoshikuni Igarashi, *Bodies of Memory: Narratives of War in Postwar Japanese Culture, 1945–1970* (Princeton: Princeton University Press), 162.

43. During the 1976 Olympic Games in Montreal most of Japan's women's basketball team, which took fifth place, were employees of Unitika, the new name of the company after Nichibō merged with Nihon Rayon in 1969. This was the first year Japan had sent a women's basketball team to play in the Olympics. Yunichika shashi henshū iinkai, ed., *Yunichika hyakunenshi, ge* (Osaka: Yunichika kabushiki kaisha, 1991), 544–545.

44. The Soviet press had been calling the team the "Typhoon of the Orient" in the early 1960s until a journalist there noticed that, unlike a typhoon, their strength never seemed to subside. He dubbed them instead the "Witches of the Orient," indicating their superhuman powers. This name was picked up by the Japanese press, which continued to use the moniker well after the team's Olympic victory. Daimatsu Hirofumi, *Ore ni tsuite koi! Watashi no shōbu konjō* (Tokyo: Kōdansha, 1963), 187–188.

45. Nichibō kabushiki kaisha shashi hensan iinkai, ed., *Nichibō 75 nenshi* (Osaka: Nichibō kabushiki kaisha, 1966), 561.

46. Nichibō kabushiki kaisha shashi hensan iinkai, *Nichibō 75 nenshi*, 564.

47. Daimatsu Hirofumi, *Tōyō no majo no gonenkan: Nichibō Kaizuka barechimu no namida to hokori no monogatari* (Tokyo: Jiyū kokuminsha, 1963), 10.

48. Details about Daimatsu Hirofumi's life up to the time he coached the

gold-medal Olympic team can be found in his books, *Tōyō no majo no go-nenkan*, 9–104 and *Ore ni tsuite koi!*, and in Igarashi, *Bodies of Memory*, 155–162.

49. Daimatsu, *Tōyō no majo no gonenkan*, 138–142.

50. Daimatsu, *Tōyō no majo no gonenkan*, 7. Ishihara has become a prominent and sometimes controversial conservative politician since his early days as a novelist. He coauthored *The Japan That Can Say No* with Sony chairman Morita Akio in 1989—a book that advocated Japan loosening the bonds of dependence it has had with the United States—and is well-known for his racist remarks regarding people from Japan's former colonies in Asia. He has held the position of governor of Tokyo since 1999 and has made the city's bid for the 2016 Olympics the cornerstone of his current term in office and his reelection campaign.

51. Okuno Takeo, "Daimatsu kantoku ni miru otoko no kenkyū," *Fujin kōron* (December 1964): 118, quoted and translated in Yoshikuni Igarashi, *Bodies of Memory*, 159.

52. Kataoka Yasuko, ed., *Joshi taiiku kihon bunkenshū*, vol. 12, *Nihon joshi Orimupikku nenkan* (Tokyo: Ōzorasha, 1995), 85.

53. Yunichika shashi henshū iinkai, *Yunichika hyakunenshi, ge*, 530.

54. Yunichika shashi henshū iinkai, *Yunichika hyakunenshi, jō*, 244.

55. Sakuta Keiichi, *Haji no bunka saikō* (Tokyo: Chikuma shobō, 1967), 274.

56. Daimatsu, *Tōyō no majo no gonenkan*, 153–156.

57. Daimatsu, *Tōyō no majo no gonenkan*, 149.

58. Daimatsu, *Tōyō no majo no gonenkan*, 143–144.

59. See for example Yuko Ogasawara, *Office Ladies and Salaried Men: Power, Gender, and Work in Japanese Companies* (Berkeley: University of California Press, 1998).

Bibliography

Aihara Takeo. "Gojin wa ika ni susumu beki ka." *Jokō kenkyū* 5, no. 7 (July 1929): 11–24.

Akamatsu Keisuke. *Yobai no minzokugaku.* Tokyo: Akashi shoten, 1994.

———. *Yobai no seiairon.* Tokyo: Akashi shoten, 1994.

Amano Fujio. *Nōson shojokai no soshiki oyobi shidō,* with an introduction by Chino Yōichi. Tokyo: Nihon tosho senta, 1984.

Ambaras, David R. *Bad Youth: Juvenile Delinquency and the Politics of Everyday Life in Modern Japan.* Berkeley: University of California Press, 2006.

Ayusawa, Iwao F. *A History of Labor in Modern Japan.* Honolulu: East-West Center Press, 1946.

Barlow, Tani E. "Theorizing Woman: *Funü, Guojia, Jiating* (Chinese Woman, Chinese State, Chinese Family)." In *Body, Subject and Power in China,* edited by Angela Zito and Tani E. Barlow, 253–289. Chicago: University of Chicago Press, 1994.

Blacker, Carmen. *The Japanese Enlightenment: A Study of the Writings of Fukuzawa Yukichi.* Cambridge: Cambridge University Press, 1964.

Brady, Robert A. *The Rationalization Movement in German Industry: A Study in the Evolution of Economic Planning.* Berkeley: University of California Press, 1933.

Brooks, Barbara J. "Peopling the Japanese Empire: The Koreans in Manchuria and the Rhetoric of Inclusion." In *Japan's Competing Modernities: Issues in Culture and Democracy, 1900–1930,* edited by Sharon A. Minichiello, 25–44. Honolulu: University of Hawai'i Press, 1998.

———. "Reading the Japanese Colonial Archive: Gender and Bourgeois Civility in Korea and Manchuria before 1932." In *Gendering Modern Japanese History,* edited by Barbara Molony and Kathleen S. Uno, 295–325. Cambridge, MA: Harvard University Asia Center, 2005.

Chōsenjin kyōsei renkō shinsō chōsadan, ed. *Chōsenjin kyōsei renkō chōsa no kioku: Chūbu/Tōkai.* Tokyo: Kashiwa shobō, 1997.

Chōsen Sōtokufu shomubu chōsaka. "Hanshin Keihin chihō no Chōsenjin rō-dōsha." 1924. In *Zainichi Chōsenjin kankei shiryō shūsei.* Vol. 1, edited by Pak Kyong-sik. Tokyo: San'ichi shobō, 1975.

Chou, Wan-you. "The *Kominka* Movement in Taiwan and Korea: Comparisons and Interpretations." In *The Japanese Wartime Empire, 1931–1945,* edited by Peter Duus, Ramon H. Myers, and Mark R. Peattie, 40–68. Princeton: Princeton University Press, 1996.

Christy, Alan S. "The Making of Imperial Subjects in Okinawa." In *Formations of Colonial Modernity in East Asia,* edited by Tani E. Barlow, 141–169. Durham, NC: Duke University Press, 1997.

Clark, Anna. *The Struggle for the Breeches: Gender and the Making of the British Working Class.* Berkeley: University of California Press, 1995.

Cohen, Jerome B. *Japan's Economy in War and Reconstruction.* Minneapolis: University of Minnesota Press, 1949.

Daimatsu Hirofumi. *Ore ni tsuite koi! Watashi no shōbu konjō.* Tokyo: Kōdansha, 1963.

———. *Tōyō no majo no gonenkan: Nichibō Kaizuka barechiimu no namida to hokori no monogatari.* Tokyo: Jiyū kokuminsha, 1963.

Doak, Kevin M. "What Is a Nation and Who Belongs? National Narratives and the Ethnic Imagination in Twentieth-Century Japan." *American Historical Review* 102, no. 2 (April 1997): 283–309.

———. "Building National Identity Through Ethnicity: Ethnology in Wartime Japan and After." *Journal of Japanese Studies* 27, no. 1 (2001): 1–39.

Dore, R. P. "The Modernizer as a Special Case: Japanese Factory Legislation, 1882–1911." In *Comparative Studies in Society and History* 11, no. 4 (October 1969): 433–450.

Dower, John. *Embracing Defeat: Japan in the Wake of World War II.* New York: W. W. Norton & Company, 1999.

Dublin, Thomas. *Women at Work: The Transformation of Work and Community in Lowell, Massachusetts, 1926–1860.* New York: Columbia University Press, 1979.

Duus, Peter. "Zaikabo: Japanese Cotton Mills in China, 1895–1937." In *The Japanese Informal Empire In China, 1895–1937,* edited by Peter Duus, Ramon H. Myers, and Mark R. Peattie, 65–100. Princeton: Princeton University Press, 1989.

———. *The Abacus and the Sword: The Japanese Penetration of Korea, 1895–1910.* Berkeley: University of California Press, 1995.

Ericson, Steven J. *The Sound of the Whistle: Railroads and the State in Meiji Japan.* Cambridge, MA: Council on East Asian Studies, Harvard University, 1996.

Fletcher, W. Miles, III. "The Japan Spinners Association: Creating Industrial Policy in Meiji Japan." *The Journal of Japanese Studies* 22, no. 1 (Winter 1996): 49–75.

———. "Co-operation and Competition in the Rise of the Japanese Cotton Spinning Industry, 1890–1926." *Asia Pacific Business Review* 5, no. 1 (Autumn 1998): 45–70.

———. "Economic Power and Political Influence: The Japan Spinners Association and National Policy, 1900–1930." *Asia Pacific Business Review* 7, no. 2 (Winter 2000): 39–62.

———. "The Impact of the Great Depression: The Japan Spinners Association, 1927–1936." In *Building a Modern Japan,* edited by Morris Low, 207–232. New York: Palgrave Macmillan, 2005.

Ford, Henry. *My Life and Work.* In collaboration with Samuel Crowther. Garden City, NY: Doubleday, Page and Company, 1922.

Frederick, Sarah. *Turning Pages: Reading and Writing Women's Magazines in Interwar Japan.* Honolulu: University of Hawai'i Press, 2006.

Fujime, Yuki. "The Licensed Prostitution System and the Prostitution Abolition Movement in Modern Japan." *Positions: East Asia Cultures Critique* 5, no. 1 (1997): 135–170.

———. *Sei no rekishigaku.* Tokyo: Fuji shuppan, 1999.

Fujitani, Takashi. *Splendid Monarchy: Power and Pageantry in Modern Japan.* Berkeley: University of California Press, 1996.

Fukuchi Hiroaki. *Okinawa jokō aishi.* Naha: Naha shuppansha, 1985.

Furukawa, Makoto. "The Changing Nature of Sexuality: The Three Codes Framing Homosexuality in Modern Japan," translated by Angus Lockyer. *U.S.-Japan Women's Journal,* no. 7 (1994): 98–127.

Garon, Sheldon M. *The State and Labor in Modern Japan.* Berkeley: University of California Press, 1987.

———. *Molding Japanese Minds: The State in Everyday Life.* Princeton: Princeton University Press, 1997.

Gluck, Carol. *Japan's Modern Myths: Ideology in the Late Meiji Period.* Princeton: Princeton University Press, 1985.

Gordon, Andrew. *The Evolution of Labor Relations in Japan: Heavy Industry, 1853–1955.* Cambridge, MA: Harvard Council on East Asian Studies, 1985.

———. *Labor and Imperial Democracy in Prewar Japan.* Berkeley: University of California Press, 1991.

———. "The Invention of Japanese-Style Labor Management." In *Mirror of Modernity: Invented Traditons of Modern Japan,* edited by Stephen Vlastos, 19–36. Berkeley: University of California Press, 1998.

———. *The Wages of Affluence: Labor and Management in Postwar Japan.* Cambridge, MA: Harvard University Press, 1998.

Ha Myonsen. *Kanjin Nihon imin shakai keizaishi: Zensen hen.* Tokyo: Akashi shoten, 1997.

Hadley, Eleanor. *Antitrust in Japan.* Princeton: Princeton University Press, 1970.

Hammitzsch, Horst. *Shūyōdan: Die Erneuerungsbewegung des gegenwärtigen Japans.* Tokyo: Deutsche Gesellschaft für Natur- und Völkerkunde Ostasiens, 1939.

Hane, Mikiso. *Peasants, Rebels, and Outcastes: The Underside of Modern Japan.* New York: Pantheon Books, 1982.

———, trans. and ed. *Reflections on the Way to the Gallows.* Berkeley: University of California Press, 1988.

Hanes, Jeffrey E. "Media Culture in Taisho Osaka." In *Japan's Competing*

Modernities: Issues in Culture and Democracy, 1900–1930, edited by Sharon A. Minichiello, 267–287. Honolulu: University of Hawai'i Press, 1999.

———. *The City as Subject: Seki Hajime and the Reinvention of Modern Osaka.* Berkeley: University of California Press, 2002.

Hara Tetsuo. *Kanebō zaiaku shi.* With an introduction by Tōjō Yukihiko. Tokyo: Kyūzansha, 1998.

Hastings, Sally Ann. *Neighborhood and Nation in Tokyo, 1905–1937.* Pittsburgh: University of Pittsburgh Press, 1995.

Harootunian, Harry. *Overcome by Modernity: History, Culture and Community in Interwar Japan.* Princeton: Princeton University Press, 2000.

Harootunian, Harry, and Tetsuo Najita. "Japanese Revolt against the West: Political and Cultural Criticism in the Twentieth Century." In *The Cambridge History of Japan.* Vol. 6, *The Twentieth Century,* edited by Peter Duus, 711–774. Cambridge: Cambridge University Press, 1988.

Harvey, David. *The Condition of Postmodernity: An Enquiry into the Origins of Cultural Change.* Cambridge, MA: Blackwell, 1989.

Hata Seikō. *Ōmi Kenshi rōdō sōgi no shinsō.* Tokyo: Bonyūsha, 1954.

Havens, Thomas R. H. "Women and War in Japan, 1937–1945." *The American Historical Review* 80, no. 4 (October 1975): 913–934.

Hazama, Hiroshi. *The History of Labour Management in Japan.* Translated by Mari Sako and Eri Sako. New York: St. Martin's Press, 1997.

Hazama Hiroshi. *Nihon rōmu kanri shi kenkyū.* Tokyo: Daiyamondosha, 1964.

———. *Nihon ni okeru rōshi kyōchō no teiryū: Uno Riemon to Kōgyō Kyōikukai no katsudō.* Tokyo: Waseda Daigaku shuppanbu, 1978.

———, ed. *Nihon rōmu kanrishi shiryōshū, dai-2-ki, dai-9-kan: Uno Riemon chosakusen; Mohan kōjōshū.* Tokyo: Gozandō shoten, 1989.

Higuchi Yūichi. "Chōsenjin shojo no Nihon e no kyōsei renkō ni tsuite." *Zainichi Chōsenjin-shi kenkyū,* no. 20 (October 1990): 1–16.

Hirabayashi Hisae. "Kiroku: Ito o tsuida onna-tachi." *Kikan sanzen-ri* 5 (Spring 1976): 97–106.

Hiratsuka Raichō. "Haha ni naru jokō no mondai." In *Rōdō mondai no shinzui,* edited by Segawa Genji, 79–120. Tokyo: Hakuyūsha, 1919.

Hirayama Kazuhiko. *Seinen shūdanshi kenkyū josetsu.* 2 vols. Tokyo: Shinsensha, 1978.

Horiuchi Ryō. *Dai Nippon Hōtokusha shōshi.* Nagoya: Dai Nippon Hōtokusha, 1997.

Hōsei Daigaku Ōhara shakai mondai kenkyūjo, ed. *Shakai/rōdō undō dai nenpyō.* Tokyo: Rōdō junpōsha, 1995.

Hōsei Daigaku Ōhara shakai mondai kenkyūjo and Sōdōmei gojūnenshi kankō iinkai, eds. *Rōdō fujin.* 1927–34. Reprinted in 6 vols. Tokyo: Hōsei Daigaku shuppankyoku, 1978.

Hosoi Wakizō. *Jokō aishi.* 1925. Tokyo: Iwanami bunkō, 1993.

———. *Hosoi Wakizō zenshū.* 4 vols. Tokyo: San'ichi shobō, 1955–56.

Hunter, Janet. "Factory Legislation and Employer Resistance: The Abolition of Night Work in the Cotton-Spinning Industry." In *Japanese Management in Historical Perspective: The International Conference on Business History 15;*

Proceedings of the Fuji Conference, edited by Yui Tsunehiko and Nakagawa Keiichirō, 243–272. Tokyo: University of Tokyo Press, 1989.

———. "An Absence of Change: Women in the Japanese Labour Force, 1937–45." In *Conflict and Amity in East Asia: Essays in Honour of Ian Nish,* edited by T. J. Fraser and Peter Lowe, 59–76. London: Macmillan Academic and Professional Ltd., 1992.

———. "Textile Factories, Tuberculosis, and the Quality of Life in Industrializing Japan." In *Japanese Women Working,* edited by Janet Hunter, 69–97. New York: Routledge, 1993.

———. *Women and the Labour Market in Japan's Industrialising Economy: The Textile Industry before the Pacific War.* London: RoutledgeCurzon, 2003.

Ichikawa Kinuyo. "Jokō no te." *Hataraku fujin* 2, no. 1 (February 1933): 46–47.

Igarashi, Yoshikuni. *Bodies of Memory: Narratives of War in Postwar Japanese Culture, 1945–1970.* Princeton: Princeton University Press, 2000.

Ikeda Yoshimasa. *Nihon shakai fukushishi.* Kyoto: Hōritsu bunkasha, 1986.

Inoue, Kyoko. *Individual Dignity in Modern Japanese Thought: The Evolution of the Concept of Jinkaku in Moral and Educational Discourse.* Ann Arbor: Center for Japanese Studies, University of Michigan, 2001.

Irokawa, Daikichi. *The Culture of the Meiji Period.* Edited and translated by Marius B. Jansen. Princeton: Princeton University Press, 1985.

Ishibashi Takehiko and Satō Tomohisa. *Nihon no taisō: Hyakunen no ayumi to jitsugi.* Tokyo: Fumaidō shoten, 1966.

Ishigami Kinji. "Shinyagyō haishi ni sai shite." *Jokō kenkyū* 5, no. 7 (July 1929): 2–3.

———. "Yoka zenyō to kun'iku gengyō." *Jokō kenkyū,* no. 56 (August 1929): 1–19.

———. "Kinshuku setsuyaku to kinrō kyōiku (ge)." *Jokō kenkyū,* no. 62 (October 1929): 1–16.

———. "Jokō no taiiku to hōshō taisō." *Jokō kenkyū,* no. 89 (July 1930): 1–7.

———. "Chōsen jokō o tsukau kokoroe." *Jokō kenkyū,* no. 184 (May 1933): 1–11.

———. *Jokō no shitsukekata to kyōiku.* 1921. Tokyo: Nihon tosho senta, 1984.

Ishihara Osamu. *Jokō to kekkaku.* Edited and with an introduction by Kagoyama Takashi. Tokyo: Kōseikan, 1970.

Ishizuki Shizue. " 'Chūkanha' Fujin dōmei ni kan suru oboegaki: 1927-nen kara 1932-nen ni kakete." *Rekishi hyōron,* no. 337 (1978): 104–119.

Itō Akira. *Nihon Rōdō Kumiai Hyōgikai no kenkyū: 1920 nendai rōdō undō no kōbō.* Tokyo: Shakai hyōronsha, 2001

Johnson, Chalmers. *MITI and the Japanese Miracle: The Growth of Industrial Policy, 1925–1975.* Stanford: Stanford University Press, 1982.

Johnston, William. *The Modern Epidemic: A History of Tuberculosis in Japan.* Cambridge, MA: Harvard Council on East Asian Studies, 1995.

"Jokō-san tachi no Manshū kengaku miyagebanashi." *Ie no hikari* (September 1933): 128–133.

Kagoyama Takashi. Introduction to *Jokō to kekkaku,* by Ishihara Osamu, 3–46. Tokyo: Kōseikan, 1970.

Kanebō kabushiki kaisha shashi hensanshitsu, ed. *Kanebō hyakunenshi*. Osaka: Kanebō kabushiki kaisha, 1988.

Kaneko, Martin. "Senzen-ki sen'i sangyō ni okeru Hyōgō-ken hisabetsu buraku no josei rōdōsha: Okinawa, Chōsen kara no degasegi rōdōsha to no kanren de (jō)." *Hyōgō buraku kaihō*, no. 33 (December 1988): 87–116.

———. "Senzen-ki sen'i sangyō ni okeru Hyōgō-ken hisabetsu buraku no josei rōdōsha: Okinawa, Chōsen kara no degasegi rōdōsha to no kanren de (ge)." *Hyōgō buraku kaihō*, no. 34 (March 1989): 81–98.

———. "Senzenki sen'i sangyō ni okeru hisabetsu shūdan shusshin no josei rōdōsha." *Rekishigaku kenkyū*, no. 664 (October 1994): 134–140.

Kashiwazaki, Chikako. "The Politics of Legal Status: The Equation of Nationality with Ethnonational Identity." In *Koreans in Japan: Critical Voices From the Margin*, edited by Sonia Ryang, 13–31. New York: Routledge, 2000.

Kataoka Yasuko, ed. *Joshi taiiku kihon bunkenshū*. Vol. 12, *Nihon joshi Orimupikku nenkan*. Tokyo: Ōzorasha, 1995.

Katō Tomomasa. *Kōjo kun*. Tokyo: Katō Tomomasa, 1910.

Kawada Shirō. "Kachōsei kazoku soshiki no hōkai no kiun." In *Nihon fujin mondai shiryō shūsei*. Vol. 5, *Kazoku seido*, edited by Yūzawa Yasuhiko, 438–453. Tokyo: Domesu shuppan, 1976.

Kawanishi, Hirosuke. Editor's introduction to Minoru Takita, "The Labour Conflict of the Omi-Kenshi Silk Mills, 1954." In *The Human Face of Industrial Conflict in Post-war Japan*, ed. Hirosuke Kawanishi, 176–181. New York: Kegan Paul International, 1999.

———, ed. *The Human Face of Industrial Conflict in Post-war Japan*. New York: Kegan Paul International, 1999.

Kevles, Daniel J. *In the Name of Eugenics: Genetics and the Uses of Human Heredity*. Berkeley: University of California Press, 1985.

Kidd, Yasue Aoki. *Women Workers in the Japanese Cotton Mills, 1880–1920*. Ithaca, NY: China-Japan Program, Cornell University, 1978.

Kim, Richard E. *Lost Names: Scenes from a Korean Boyhood*. Berkeley: University of California Press, 1998.

Kim Ch'an-jong. *Kaze no dōkoku: Zainichi Chōsenjin jokō no seikatsu*. Tokyo: Tabatake shoten, 1977.

———. *Hi no dōkoku: Zainichi Chōsenjin kōfu no seikatsushi*. Tokyo: Tabatake shoten, 1980.

———. *Chōsenjin jokō no uta*. Tokyo: Iwanami shoten, 1982.

———. *Zainichi Korian hyakunenshi*. Tokyo: Sangokan, 1997.

———. *Maboroshi no shinbun: "Minshū jihō."* Tokyo: Sangokan, 2001.

Kindai josei bunkashi kenkyūkai, ed. *Taishōki no josei zasshi*. Tokyo: Ōzorasha, 1996.

Kinmonth, Earl H. *The Self-Made Man in Meiji Japanese Thought: From Samurai to Salary Man*. Berkeley: University of California Press, 1981.

Kinzley, W. Dean. *Industrial Harmony in Modern Japan: The Invention of a Tradition*. New York: Routledge, 1991.

Kishiwada shiritsu josei senta, Kishiwada no joseishi hensan iinkai, eds., *Shimin ga tsuzutta joseishi: Kishiwada no onna-tachi*. Tokyo: Domesu shuppan, 1999.

Kishiwada-shi shi hensan iinkai, ed. *Kishiwada-shi shi.* Vol. 4, *Kindai hen.* Kishiwada: Kishiwada-shi, 2005.

Kobayashi Takiji. *"The Factory Ship" and "The Absentee Landlord."* Translated and with an introduction by Frank Motofuji. Tokyo: University of Tokyo Press, 1973.

———. *Kani kōsen, Tō-seikatsusha.* Tokyo: Shinchō bunkō, 1991.

Komine Shigeyuki and Minami Takao. *Dōseiai to dōsei shinjū no kenkyū.* Tokyo: Komine kenkyūjo, 1985.

Kondo, Dorinne K. *Crafting Selves: Power, Gender, and Discourses of Identity in a Japanese Workplace.* Chicago: University of Chicago Press, 1990.

Kōsai, Yutaka. "The Postwar Japanese Economy, 1945–1973." Translated by Andrew Goble. In *The Cambridge History of Japan.* Vol. 6, *The Twentieth Century,* edited by Peter Duus, 494–537. New York: Cambridge University Press, 1988.

Koyama Hitoshi. *Sensō, sabetsu, kōgai.* Osaka: Kaihō shuppansha, 1995.

Koyama, Shizuko. "The 'Good Wife and Wise Mother' Ideology in Post–World War I Japan." In *U.S.-Japan Women's Journal, English Supplement,* no. 7 (1994): 31–52.

Koyama Shizuko. *Ryōsai kenbo to iu kihan.* Tokyo: Keisō shobō, 1991.

Kyōchōkai, ed. *Saikin no shakai undō: Sōritsu jisshūnen kinen shuppan.* Tokyo: Kyōchōkai, 1929.

Large, Stephen S. *The Rise of Labor in Japan: The Yūaikai, 1912–19.* Tokyo: Sophia University Press, 1972.

———. *Organized Workers and Socialist Politics in Interwar Japan.* Cambridge: Cambridge University Press, 1981.

Mackie, Vera. *Creating Socialist Women in Japan: Gender, Labour and Activism, 1900–1937.* New York: Cambridge University Press, 1997.

———. "Narratives of Struggle: Writing and the Making of Socialist Women in Japan." In *Society and the State in Interwar Japan,* edited by Elise K. Tipton, 126–145. New York: Routledge, 1997.

Macnaughtan, Helen. *Women, Work and the Japanese Economic Miracle: The Case of the Cotton Textile Industry, 1945–1975.* London: RoutledgeCurzon, 2005.

Maeda Ai. *Maeda Ai chosakushū, dai-2-kan: Kindai dokusha no seiritsu.* Tokyo: Chikuma shobō, 1989.

Mathias, Regine. "Women and the War Economy in Japan." In *Japan's War Economy,* edited by Erich Pauer, 65–84. New York: Routledge, 1999.

Matsuoka Komakichi. *Noda dai rōdō sōgi.* Nagareyama: Ronshobō, 1973.

Matsushita Matsutsugu. *Shiryō Kishiwada Bōseki no sōgi.* Osaka: Yuniusu, 1980.

McClintock, Anne. *Imperial Leather: Race, Gender and Sexuality in the Colonial Contest.* New York: Routledge, 1995.

Metzler, Mark. *Lever of Empire: The International Gold Standard and the Crisis of Liberalism in Prewar Japan.* Berkeley: University of California Press, 2005.

Miki Hiroko. "Kindai fujin zasshi kankei nenpyō." In *Nihon no fujin zasshi, kaisetsu hen,* edited by Nakajima Kuni, 171–222. Tokyo: Ōzorasha, 1994.

———. "Taishōki no josei zasshi: Hataraku onna no kikanshi o chūshin ni." In *Taishōki no josei zasshi,* edited by Kindai josei bunkashi kenkyūkai, 3–53. Tokyo: Ōzorasha, 1996.

Minami Hiroshi. *Taishō bunka.* Tokyo: Keisō shobō, 1965.

———, ed. *Kindai shomin seikatsushi.* Vol. 2, *Sakariba, uramichi.* Tokyo: San'ichi shobō, 1984.

Mishima, Yukio. *Silk and Insight.* Translated and with an introduction by Hiroaki Sato. Armonk, NY: M. E. Sharpe, 1998.

Miwa Yasushi. "Bōseki rōdōsha no shakai ishiki." In *Kindai Ōsaka no gyōsei, shakai, keizai,* edited by Hirokawa Tadahide, 200–242. Tokyo: Aoki shoten, 1998.

Miyachi Masato. *Nichi-Ro sengo seijishi no kenkyū: Teikokushugi keiseiki no toshi to nōson.* Tokyo: Tōkyō Daigaku shuppankai, 1973.

Miyajima Hisashi. *Jinken sōgi: Ōmi Kenshi rōdōsha no tatakai.* Kyoto: Hōritsu bunkasha, 1955.

Miyake, Yoshiko. "Doubling Expectations: Motherhood and Women's Factory Work Under State Management in the 1930s and 1940s." In *Recreating Japanese Women, 1600–1945,* edited by Gail Lee Bernstein, 267–295. Berkeley: University of California Press, 1991.

Miyake Yoshiko. "Nihon no shakai kagaku to jenda: 'Jokō aishi gensetsu' o megutte." In *Nihon shakai to jenda,* edited by Miyake Yoshiko and Muta Kazue, 15–45. Tokyo: Akashi shoten, 2001.

Miyoshi Nobuhiro. *Nihon no josei to sangyō kyōiku: Kindai sangyō shakai ni okeru josei no yakuwari.* Tokyo: Toshindō, 2000.

Molasky, Michael S. *The American Occupation of Japan and Okinawa: Literature and Memory.* New York: Routledge, 1999.

Molony, Barbara. "Activism Among Women in the Taisho Cotton Textile Industry." In *Recreating Japanese Women, 1600–1945,* edited by Gail Lee Bernstein, 217–238. Berkeley: University of California Press, 1991.

Morito Tatsuo. "Nihon ni okeru joshi shokugyō mondai." In *Fujin rōdō mondai: Dai jūnikai taikai kiji,* edited by Shakai Seisaku Gakkai, 123–226. Tokyo: Dōbunkan, 1919.

Morris-Suzuki, Tessa. *Re-Inventing Japan: Time, Space, Nation.* Armonk, NY: M. E. Sharpe, 1998.

Motofuji, Frank. Introduction to *"The Factory Ship" and "The Absentee Landlord,"* by Kobayashi Takiji, xvii–xviii. Tokyo: University of Tokyo Press, 1973.

Murakami Nobuhiko. *Taishōki no shokugyō fujin.* Tokyo: Domesu shuppan, 1983.

Muta Kazue. *Senryaku to shite no kazoku: Kindai Nihon no kokumin kokka keisei to josei.* Tokyo: Shinyōsha, 1996.

Nagamine Shigetoshi. *Zasshi to dokusha no kindai.* Tokyo: Nihon editaa sukūru shuppan-bu, 1997.

Nakagawa Keiichirō and Yui Tsunehiko, eds. *Keiei tetsugaku keiei rinen.* 2 vols. Tokyo: Daiyamondosha, 1969–70.

Nakajima Kuni, ed. *Nihon no fujin zasshi, kaisetsu hen.* Tokyo: Ōzorasha, 1994.

Nakamoto Takako. "Jukeiki, 1: Tōsō yori hakkyō made." *Chūō kōron* 52, no. 6 (June 1937): 502–532.

———. "Jukeiki, 2: Tenkō e no shinro." In *Chūō kōron* 52, no. 7 (July 1937): 358–385.

———. "Shokufu." In *Hikari kuraku*. Tokyo: San'ichi shobō, 1947.

———. *Mosurin Yokochō*. Tokyo: Tōga shobō, 1950.

———. "Hosoi Wakizō no *Jokō aishi*" *Fujin kōron*, no. 11 (November 1973): 178–179.

———. *Waga sei wa kunō ni yakarete: Waga wakaki hi no ikigai*. Tokyo: Hakuseki shoten, 1973.

———. *Kyōkō*. With an introduction by Okada Takako. Tokyo: Yumani shobō, 1999.

———. *Nanbu tetsubinkō*. Tokyo: Yumani shobō, 1999.

National Industrial Conference Board. *Rationalization of German Industry*. New York: National Industrial Conference Board, Inc., 1931.

Nichibō kabushiki kaisha shashi hensan iinkai, ed. *Nichibō 75 nenshi*. Osaka: Nichibō kabushiki kaisha, 1966.

Nihon hōsō kyōkai, ed. *Broadcasting in Japan: Twentieth Century Journey from Radio to Multimedia*. Tokyo: NHK, 2002.

Nihon rōdō kenkyū kikō, ed. *Labour Standards Law (Law No. 49 of April 7, 1947)*. Tokyo: Japan Institute of Labor, 2002.

Nihon rōnō shinbun. "Saisho no kaikyūteki Kyōai Jojuku Gunma Kyōdo ni setsuritsu saru." In *Nihon josei undō shiryō shūsei*. Vol. 4, *Seikatsu/Rōdō I*, edited by Suzuki Yūko, 810. Tokyo: Fuji shuppan, 1994.

Nimura Kazuo. *Ashio bōdō no shiteki bunseki: Kōzan rōdōsha no shakaishi*. Tokyo: Tōkyō Daigaku shuppankai, 1988.

———. *The Ashio Riot of 1907: A Social History of Mining in Japan*. Edited by Andrew Gordon. Translated by Andrew Gordon and Terry Boardman. Durham, NC: Duke University Press, 1997.

Nishikawa Hiroshi. "1920 nendai no Nihon menshi bōsekigyō no 'gōrika' to dokusen taisei." *Tochi seido shigaku* 62, no. 2 (1974): 17–35.

Nishikawa, Yuko. "The Changing Form of Dwellings and the Establishment of the *Katei* (Home) in Modern Japan," translated by Mariko Muro Yokokawa. *U.S.-Japan Women's Journal, English Supplement* 8 (1995): 3–36.

Nishikawa Yūko. *Kindai kokka to kazoku moderu*. Tokyo: Yoshikawa kōbunkan, 2000.

———. "Sumai no henyō to 'katei' no seiritsu." In *Nihon josei seikatsushi*. Vol. 4, *Kindai*, edited by Joseishi sōgō kenkyūkai, 1–49. Tokyo: Tōkyō Daigaku shuppankai, 1990.

Nishinarita Yutaka. *Zainichi Chōsenjin no "sekai" to "teikoku" kokka*. Tokyo: Tōkyō Daigaku shuppan, 1997.

Nittōsha. "Okinawa jokō ni seikō shite iru Fukubō Sakai kōjō." *Jokō kenkyū*, vol 1., no. 9 (September 1925): 99–101.

———. "Shinyagyō haishi ni tomonau yoka zenyō no mondai." *Jokō kenkyū* 5, no. 3 (March 1929): 61–83.

———. "Jokō no sei ni kan suru mondai." *Jokō kenkyū* 5, no. 7 (July 1929): 69–101.

———. "Enjin no chimata o sakete: Kantei ni jinji jikyoku o danzuru danchōro." *Jokō kenkyū*, no. 54 (August 1929): 1–29.

———. "Rōdō sōgi o chūshin toshite (jō)." *Jokō kenkyū*, no. 101 (November 1930): 1–20.

———. "Rōdō sōgi o chūshin toshite (ge)." *Jokō kenkyū*, no. 104 (December 1930): 1–16.

Nolan, Mary. *Visions of Modernity: American Business and the Modernization of Germany*. New York: Oxford University Press, 1994.

Nolte, Sharon H., and Sally Ann Hastings. "The Meiji State's Policy Toward Women, 1890–1910." In *Recreating Japanese Women, 1600–1945*, edited by Gail Lee Bernstein, 151–174. Berkeley: University of California Press, 1991.

Nōshōmushō Shōkōkyoku, ed. *Shokkō jijō*. With an introduction by Okouchi Kazuo. Tokyo: Kōseikan, 1971.

Notehelfer, F. G. "Rethinking the Meiji Restoration." First Inamoto Lecture, University of Southern California, December 2, 1997.

Ōbayashi Munetsugu. *Minshū goraku no jissai kenkyū: Ōsaka-shi no minshū goraku chōsa*. Tokyo: Ōhara shakai mondai kenkyūjo, 1922.

———. *Settsurumento no kenkyū*. Tokyo: Dōjinsha, 1926.

Ochiai, Emiko. *The Japanese Family System in Transition: A Sociological Analysis of Family Change in Postwar Japan*. Tokyo: LTCB International Library Foundation, 1997.

Ochiai Emiko. *21-seiki kazoku e*. Tokyo: Yūhikaku, 1994.

Ogasawara, Yuko. *Office Ladies and Salaried Men: Power, Gender and Work in Japanese Companies*. Berkeley: University of California Press, 1998.

Ōguma Eiji. *Tan'itsu minzoku shinwa no kigen: "Nihonjin" no jigazō no keifu*. Tokyo: Shinyōsha, 1995.

———. *"Nihonjin" no kyōkai: Okinawa, Ainu, Taiwan, Chōsen, shokuminchi shihai kara fukki undō made*. Tokyo: Shinyōsha, 1998.

———. *A Genealogy of "Japanese" Self-Images*. Translated by David Askew. Melbourne: TransPacific Press, 2002.

Ōhara shakai mondai kenkyūjo, ed. *Nihon rōdō nenkan*. 1931. Tokyo: Hōsei Daigaku shuppankyoku, 1968.

Oka Minoru. *Kōjōhō ron*. Tokyo: Yūhikaku shobō, 1917.

Okuda Akiko. "Shokugyō fujin no tanjō." In *Mainoritei toshite no joseishi*, edited by Okuda Akiko, 235–270. Tokyo: San'ichi shobō, 1997.

Orimoto Sadayo. "Ashita no josei: jokō o kataru." In *Nihon fujin mondai shiryō shūsei*. Vol. 3, *Rōdō*, edited by Akamatsu Yoshiko, 239–243. Tokyo: Domesu shuppan, 1977.

Ortner, Sherry B. "Resistance and the Problem of Ethnographic Refusal." *Comparative Studies in Society and History* 37, no.1 (1995): 173–193.

Ōsaka shakai rōdō undōshi henshū iinkai, ed. *Ōsaka shakai rōdō undōshi, dai-1-kan: Senzenhen, jō*. Tokyo: Yūhikaku, 1986.

Ōsaka shōgyō kaigisho shokikyoku, ed. *Ōsaka-fu ka ni okeru saikin no rōdō sōgi*. Osaka: Ōsaka shōgyō kaigijo shokikyoku, 1930.

Ōsaka-shi shakaibu chōsaka, ed. *Chōsenjin rōdōsha mondai*. Osaka: Kōbundō shobō, 1924.

Ōshima Eiko. "Ryō taisenkan no joshi rōdō: Bōseki, seishi jokō o chūshin ni." In *Nihon joseishi*, edited by Joseishi sōgō kenkyūkai, 1–38. Tokyo: Tōkyō Daigaku shuppankai, 1982.

Otsubo, Sumiko. "The Female Body and Eugenic Thought in Meiji Japan." In *Building a Modern Japan: Science, Technology, and Medicine in the Meiji Era and Beyond*, edited by Morris Low, 61–81. New York: Palgrave Macmillan, 2005.

Pak Kyong-sik, ed. *Zainichi Chōsenjin kankei shiryō shūsei*. Vol. 1. Tokyo: San'ichi shobō, 1975.

———. *Zainichi Chōsenjin undōshi: 8.15 kaihōzen*. Tokyo: San'ichi shobō, 1979.

Park, Young-il, and Kym Anderson. "The Rise and Demise of Textiles and Clothing in Economic Development: The Case of Japan." In *Japanese Economic History, 1600–1960: The Textile Industry and the Rise of the Japanese Economy*, edited by Michael Smitka, 165–182. New York: Garland Publishing, Inc., 1998.

Partner, Simon. *Assembled in Japan: Electrical Goods and the Making of the Japanese Consumer*. Berkeley: University of California Press, 1999.

Peattie, Mark R. "Japanese Attitudes Toward Colonialism, 1895–1945." In *The Japanese Colonial Empire, 1895–1945*, edited by Ramon H. Myers and Mark R. Peattie, 80–127. Princeton: Princeton University Press, 1984.

———. "Japanese Treaty Port Settlements in China, 1895–1937." In *The Japanese Informal Empire In China, 1895–1937*, edited by Peter Duus, Ramon H. Myers, and Mark R. Peattie, 166–209. Princeton: Princeton University Press, 1989.

Pflugfelder, Gregory M. *Cartographies of Desire: Male-Male Sexuality in Japanese Discourse, 1600–1950*. Berkeley: University of California Press, 1999.

———. " 'S' Is for Sister: Schoolgirl Intimacy and 'Same-Sex Love' in Early Twentieth-Century Japan." In *Gendering Modern Japanese History*, edited by Barbara Molony and Kathleen S. Uno, 133–190. Cambridge, MA: Harvard University Asia Center, 2005.

Price, John. *Japan Works: Power and Paradox in Postwar Industrial Relations*. Ithaca, NY: Cornell University Press, 1997.

Pyle, Kenneth B. *The New Generation in Meiji Japan: Problems of Cultural Identity, 1885–1895*. Stanford: Stanford University Press, 1969.

———. "The Technology of Japanese Nationalism: The Local Improvement Movement, 1900–1918." *Journal of Asian Studies* 33, no. 1 (1973): 51–65.

Riley, Denise. *Am I That Name? Feminism and the Category of 'Women' in History*. Minneapolis: University of Minnesota Press, 1990.

Ringhoffer, Manfred. "Sōaikai: Chōsenjin dōka dantai no ayumi." In *Zainichi Chōsenjinshi kenkyū*, no. 9 (December 1981): 45–69.

Robertson, Jennifer. *Takarazuka: Sexual Politics and Popular Culture in Modern Japan*. Berkeley: University of California Press, 1998.

———. "Dying to Tell: Sexuality and Suicide in Imperial Japan." In *Queer Diasporas*, edited by Cindy Patton and Benigno Sanchez-Eppler, 38–70. Durham, NC: Duke University Press, 2000.

Roden, Donald. *Schooldays in Imperial Japan: A Study in the Culture of a Student Elite*. Berkeley: University of California Press, 1980.

Rōdō fujin. 1927–34. Reprinted in 6 vols., edited by Hōsei Daigaku Ōhara shakai mondai kenkyūjo and Sōdōmei gojūnenshi kankō iinkai. Tokyo: Hōsei Daigaku shuppankyoku, 1978.

Rōdōshi kenkyū dōjinkai, ed. *Nihon rōdō undō no senkushatachi.* Tokyo: Keiō tsūshin, 1985.

Rose, Barbara. *Tsuda Umeko and Women's Education in Japan.* New Haven: Yale University Press, 1992.

Rosenthal, Michael. *The Character Factory: Baden-Powell and the Origins of the Boy Scout Movement.* New York: Pantheon, 1986.

Rosenzweig, Roy. *Eight Hours for What We Will: Workers and Leisure in an Industrial City, 1870–1920.* New York: Cambridge University Press, 1983.

Saguchi, Kazuro. "The Historical Significance of the Industrial Patriotic Association: Labor Relations in the Total-War State." In *Total War and "Modernization,"* edited by Yasushi Yamanouchi, J. Victor Koschmann, and Ryuichi Narita, 261–287. Ithaca, NY: Cornell University East Asia Program, 1998.

Sakisaka Itsurō and Iwai Akira, eds. *'Gōrika' to wa nani ka.* Tokyo: Kawade shobō shinsha, 1974.

Sakura Takuji. *Seishi jokō gyakutaishi.* 1927. Tokyo: Kaihōsha, 1981.

Sakuta Keiichi. *Haji no bunka saikō.* Tokyo: Chikuma shobō, 1967.

Sand, Jordan. "At Home in the Meiji Period: Inventing Japanese Domesticity." In *Mirror of Modernity: Invented Traditions of Modern Japan,* edited by Stephen Vlastos, 191–207. Berkeley: University of California Press, 1998.

———. *House and Home in Modern Japan: Architecture, Domestic Space, and Bourgeois Culture, 1880–1930.* Cambridge, MA: Harvard University Asia Center, 2003.

Sangyō fukuri kyōkai, ed. *Kekkaku yobō dokuhon.* Tokyo: Sangyō fukuri kyōkai, 1930.

Sasaki Nobuaki. "1920 nendai ni okeru zaihan Chōsenjin no rōdō = seikatsu katei: Higashi-nari, shūjū chiku o chūshin ni." In *Taishō Ōsaka suramu: Mō hitotsu no Nihon kindaishi,* edited by Sugihara Kaoru and Tamai Kingō, 161–212. Tokyo: Shin hyōron, 1996.

Sato, Barbara. *The New Japanese Woman: Modernity, Media, and Women in Interwar Japan.* Durham, NC: Duke University Press, 2003.

Saxonhouse, Gary, and Gustav Ranis. "Technology Choice and the Quality Dimension in the Japanese Cotton Textitle Industry." In *Japan and the Developing Countries: A Comparative Analysis,* ed. Kazushi Ohkawa and Gustave Ranis, 155–176. New York: Blackwell, 1985.

Scott, Joan Wallach. *Gender and the Politics of History.* New York: Columbia University Press, 1988.

Seishi orimono shinpōsha, ed. *Shūshin kunwa: Kōjo no kagami.* Tokyo: Seishi orimono shinpōsha, 1912.

Shakaikyoku rōdōbu. "Shinyagyō haishi no yoka riyō to fukuri shisetsu (ge)." *Jokō kenkyū,* no. 118 (May 1931): 1–16.

Shearer, J. Ronald. "Talking about Efficiency: Politics and the Industrial Rationalization Movement in the Weimar Republic." In *Central European History* 28, no. 4 (1995): 483–506.

Shimomura Torarokurō. *Wakamono seido no kenkyū: Wakamono jōmoku o tsūjite mitaru wakamono seido.* Tokyo: Dai Nippon Rengō Seinendan, 1936.
———. *Seinendan: Young Men's Leagues of Japan.* Translated by Kaizo Matsuda. Tokyo: Dai Nippon Rengō Seinendan, 1937.
Shimonaka Kunihiko. *Nihon jinmei daijiten.* Tokyo: Heibonsha, 1979.
Shiota Shōbe. *Sutoraiki no rekishi.* Tokyo: Shin Nihon shinshō, 1966.
Shirai Taishirō. "Kantō daishinsai kara kinyū kyōkō e." In *Shōwa kyōkō*, edited by Sumiya Mikio, 1–78. Tokyo: Yūhikaku, 1975.
Shūkan Asahi geinō henshūbu, ed. *Jitsuroku Ōsaka sensō: Dai Nippon Seigidan no uchimaku.* Tokyo: Tokuma shoten, 1979.
Shūyōdan henshūbu, ed. *Shūyōdan sanjūnenshi.* Tokyo: Nihon tosho senta, 1991.
Shūyōdan undō hachijūnenshi hensan iinkai, ed. *Shūyōdan undō hachijūnenshi: Waga kuni shakai kyōiku no genryū.* 4 vols. Tokyo: Shūyōdan, 1985.
Sievers, Sharon L. *Flowers in Salt: The Beginnings of Feminist Consciousness in Modern Japan.* Stanford: Stanford University Press, 1983.
Silverberg, Miriam. *Changing Song: The Marxist Manifestos of Nakano Shigeharu.* Princeton: Princeton University Press, 1990.
———. "The Modern Girl as Militant." In *Recreating Japanese Women, 1600–1945,* edited by Gail Lee Bernstein, 239–266. Berkeley: University of California Press, 1991.
———. "Constructing the Japanese Ethnography of Modernity." *Journal of Asian Studies* 51, no. 1 (February 1992): 30–54.
———. "Remembering Pearl Harbor, Forgetting Charlie Chaplin, and the Case of the Disappearing Western Woman: A Picture Story." In *Formations of Colonial Modernity in East Asia,* edited by Tani E. Barlow, 249–294. Durham: Duke University Press, 1997.
———. *Erotic Grotesque Nonsense: The Mass Culture of Japanese Modern Times.* Berkeley: University of California Press, 2006.
Slaymaker, Douglas N. *The Body in Postwar Japanese Fiction.* New York: RoutledgeCurzon, 2004.
Smethurst, Richard J. *A Social Basis for Prewar Japanese Militarism: The Army and the Rural Community.* Berkeley: University of California Press, 1974.
Smith, Henry DeWitt, II. *Japan's First Student Radicals.* Cambridge, MA: Harvard University Press, 1972.
Smith, Kerry. *A Time of Crisis: Japan, The Great Depression, and Rural Revitalization.* Cambridge, MA: Harvard University Asia Center, 2001.
Smith, Thomas C. *Political Change and Industrial Development in Japan: Government Enterprise, 1868–1880.* Stanford: Stanford University Press, 1965.
———. "The Right to Benevolence: Dignity and Japanese Workers, 1890–1920." In *Native Sources of Japanese Industrialization, 1750–1920,* 236–270. Berkeley: University of California Press, 1988.
Smith, W. Donald. "Ethnicity, Class and Gender in the Mines: Korean Workers in Japan's Chikuhō Coal Field, 1917–1945." Ph.D. diss., University of Washington, 1999.
———. "Sorting Coal and Pickling Cabbage: Korean Women in the Japanese Mining Industry." In *Gendering Modern Japanese History,* edited by Barbara

Molony and Kathleen S. Uno, 393–422. Cambridge, MA: Harvard University Asia Center, 2005.

Sōaikai Izumi honbu, ed. *Sōaikai jigyō kōgai*. Kishiwada: Sōaikai Izumi honbu, 1927.

Sōaikai sōhonbu, *Sōaikai jigyō kōgai*. Tokyo: Sōaikai sōhonbu, 1923.

Stansell, Christine. *City of Women: Sex and Class in New York, 1789–1860*. Chicago: University of Illinois Press, 1987.

Sugihara, Kaoru. "The Transformation of Social Values of Young Country Girls: Towards a Reinterpretation of the Japanese Migrant (Dekasegi) Industrial Labour Force." In *Aspects of the Relationship Between Agriculture and Industrialisation in Japan*, edited by Janet Hunter, 32–51. London: Suntory Toyota International Centre for Economics and Related Disciplines, London School of Economics and Political Science, 1986.

Sugihara Kaoru. "Nihon ni okeru kindaiteki rōdō = seikatsu kateizō no seiritsu: Uno Riemon to Kōgyō Kyōikukai no shisō." In *Taishō Ōsaka suramu: Mō hitotsu no Nihon kindaishi*, edited by Sugihara Kaoru and Tamai Kingō, 29–58. Tokyo: Shin hyōron, 1996.

Sugihara Tōru. "Zaihan Chōsenjin no tōkō katei: Chōsen, Cheju-shima to no kanren de." In *Taishō Ōsaka suramu: Mō hitotsu no Nihon kindaishi*, edited by Sugihara Kaoru and Tamai Kingō, 213–248. Tokyo: Shin hyōron, 1996.

Sumiya Mikio, ed. *Shōwa kyōkō*. Tokyo: Yūhikaku, 1975.

———. "Kōjōhō taisei to rōshi kankei." In *Nihon rōshi kankeishi ron*, edited by Sumiya Mikio, 1–40. Tokyo: Tōkyō Daigaku shuppan, 1977.

Suzuki, Grace, trans. and ed. *Ukiyo: Eleven Short Stories of Post-War Japan*. Tokyo: Phoenix Books, 1954.

Suzuki Yūko. *Feminizumu to sensō: Fujin undōka no sensō kyōryoku. 1986*. Tokyo: Marujusha, 1997.

———. *Joseishi o hiraku*. Vol. 1, *Haha to onna: Hiratsuka Raichō/Ichikawa Fusae o jaku ni*. Tokyo: Miraisha, 1989.

———. *Jokō to rōdō sōgi: 1930 nen Yō Mosu sōgi*. Tokyo: Renga shobō shinsha, 1989.

———. *Josei to rōdō kumiai (jō): Rōdō kumiai fujinbu no rekishi*. Tokyo: Renga shobō shinsha, 1990.

———, ed. *Nihon josei undō shiryō shūsei*. 11 vols. Tokyo: Fuji shuppan, 1993–98.

Tachibana Yūichi. *Hyōden — Yokoyama Gennosuke*. Tokyo: Sōkisha, 1979.

Taeuber, Irene B. "Population and Labor Force in the Industrialization of Japan, 1850–1950." In *Economic Growth: Brazil, India, Japan*, edited by Simon Kuznets, Wilbert E. Moore, and Joseph J. Spengler. Durham, NC: Duke University Press, 1955.

Taigakai, ed. *Naimushō shi*. Tokyo: Chihō zaimu kyōkai, 1971.

Taira, Koji. *Economic Development and the Labor Market in Japan*. New York: Columbia University Press, 1970.

———. "Economic Development, Labor Markets, and Industrial Relations in Japan, 1905–1955." In *The Cambridge History of Japan*. Vol. 6, *The Twentieth Century*, edited by Peter Duus, 606–653. Cambridge: Cambridge University Press, 1988.

———. "Troubled National Identity: The Ryukyuans/Okinawans." In *Japan's Minorities: The Illusion of Homogeneity*, edited by Michael Weiner, 140–177. New York: Routledge, 1997.

Takahashi Hidemine. *Subarashiki rajio taisō*. Tokyo: Shōgakkan, 1998.

Takamura, Naosuke. "The Cotton Spinning Industry in Japan During the Pre–World War I Period: Its Growth and Essential Conditions." In *Innovation, Know How, Rationalization and Investment in the German and Japanese Economies, 1868/1871–1930/1980*, edited by Hans Pohl, 207–230. Wiesbaden, Germany: Franz Steiner Verlag GmbH, 1982.

Takamura Naosuke. *Nihon bōseki gyōshi josetsu*. Tokyo: Hanawa shobō, 1971.

Takasaki Sōji, ed. *Kindai Nihon to shokuminchi: Shochō suru teikoku no jinryū*. Tokyo: Iwanami shoten, 1993.

Takebe Yoshito. *Ōsaka sangyōshi: Fukken e no michi*. Tokyo: Yūhikaku sensho, 1982.

Takenobu Toshihiko, ed. *Jokō tokuhon*. Tokyo: Jitsugyō kokumin kyōkai, 1911.

Takita, Minoru. "The Labour Conflict of the Omi-Kenshi Silk Mills, 1954." In *The Human Face of Industrial Conflict in Post-war Japan*, edited by Hirosuke Kawanishi, 175–201. New York: Kegan Paul International, 1999.

Tamanoi, Mariko Asano. "The City and the Countryside: Competing Taisho 'Modernities' on Gender." In *Japan's Competing Modernities: Issues in Culture and Democracy, 1900–1930*, edited by Sharon Minichiello, 91–113. Honolulu: University of Hawai'i Press, 1998.

———. *Under the Shadow of Nationalism: Politics and Poetics of Rural Japanese Women*. Honolulu: University of Hawai'i Press, 1998.

———. "Japanese Nationalism and the Female Body: A Critical Reassessment of the Discourse of Social Reformers on Factory Women." In *Women and Class in Japanese History*, edited by Hitomi Tonomura, Anne Walthall, and Haruko Wakita, 275–298. Ann Arbor: Center for Japanese Studies, University of Michigan, 1999.

———. "Knowledge, Power, and Classifications: The 'Japanese' in 'Manchuria.' " *Journal of Asian Studies* 59, no. 2 (May 2000): 248–276.

Tanaka, Yuki. *Japan's Comfort Women: Sexual Slavery and Prostitution during World War II and the U.S. Occupation*. New York: Routledge, 2001.

Tanaka, Yukiko, ed. *To Live and to Write: Selections by Japanese Women Writers, 1913–1938*. Seattle: Seal Press, 1987.

Tatewaki Sadayo. *Aru henreki no jijōden*. Tokyo: Sōdō bunka, 1980.

———. *Nihon rōdō fujin mondai*. Edited and with an introduction by Shiota Shōbe. Tokyo: Domesu shuppan, 1980.

Taylor, Frederick Winslow. *The Principles of Scientific Management*. New York: Harper & Brothers, 1911.

Tazawa Yoshiharu. "Seinen undō." In *Shakai seisaku taikei*, ed. Hasegawa Yoshinobu, 1–74. Tokyo: Daitō shuppansha, 1927.

Thompson, E. P. *The Making of the English Working Class*. New York: Vintage, 1966.

Tōjō Yukihiko. *Seishi dōmei no jokō tōroku seidō: Nihon kindai no hen'yō to jokō no 'jinkaku.'* Tokyo: Tōkyō Daigaku shuppansha, 1990.

Tōkyō-shi shakaikyoku. *Waga kuni ni okeru rōdō gakkō.* Tokyo: Tōkyō-shi shakaikyoku, 1925.

Tomita, Kokei. *A Peasant Sage of Japan: The Life and Work of Sontoku Ninomiya.* Translated by Tadasu Yoshimoto. New York: Longmans, Green and Co., 1912.

Tomiyama Ichirō. *Kindai Nihon shakai to "Okinawajin."* Tokyo: Nihon keizai hyōronsha, 1990.

————. "Kokumin no tanjō to 'Nihon jinshu' " *Shisō* 845 (November 1994): 37–56.

Tonomura Masaru. "Senjiki Zainichi Chōsenjin ni okeru shakaiteki jōshō." *Shakai kagaku tōkyū* 43, no. 3 (March 1998): 37–67.

Tōyō Bōseki kabushiki kaisha and "Tōyō Bōseki shichijū nenshi" henshū iinkai, eds. *Tōyō Bōseki shichijū nenshi.* Tokyo: Tōyō Bōseki kabushiki kaisha, 1953.

Tōyō Mosurin kabushiki kaisha. "Tōyō Mosurin kabushiki kaisha ni okeru jokō no shisō chōsa." In *Jokō kenkyū* 1 (January 1925): 69–102.

Tsurumi, E. Patricia. "Problem Consciousness and Modern Japanese History: Female Textile Workers of Meiji and Taisho." *Bulletin of Concerned Asian Scholars* 18, no. 4 (October 1986–December 1986): 41–48.

————. *Factory Girls: Women in the Thread Mills of Meiji Japan.* Princeton: Princeton University Press, 1990.

Tsūshō sangyōshō, Chōsa tōkeibu, ed. *Kōgyō tōkei gojūnenshi = History of the Census of Manufactures for 1909–1958.* 3 vols. Tokyo: Ōkurashō insatsukyoku, 1961–63.

Tsutsui, William M. *Manufacturing Ideology: Scientific Management in Twentieth-Century Japan.* Princeton: Princeton University Press, 1998.

Tsutsui Kiyotada. "Kindai Nihon no kyōyōshugi to shūyōshugi." *Shisō,* no. 812 (February 1992): 151–173.

Ujihara Shōjirō, ed. *Yoka seikatsu no kenkyū.* Tokyo: Kōseikan, 1970.

Umemura Mataji, Akasaka Keiko, Minami Ryōshin, Takamatsu Nobukiyo, Arai Kurotake, and Itō Shigeru. *Rōdōryoku.* Tokyo: Tōyō keizai shinpōsha, 1988.

Uno, Kathleen S. "Women and Changes in the Household Division of Labor." In *Recreating Japanese Women, 1600–1945,* edited by Gail Lee Bernstein, 17–41. Berkeley: University of California Press, 1991.

Uno Riemon. *Kōjo risshindan.* Tokyo: Kōgyō Kyōikukai, 1910.

————. *Shokkō yūgu ron.* 1915. Edited and with an introduction by Hazama Hiroshi. Tokyo: Gozandō shoten, 1989.

————. *Teikoku seima Ōsaka seihin kōjō.* 1922. Edited and with an introduction by Hazama Hiroshi in *Nihon rōmu kanrishi shiryōshū, dai-2-ki, dai-9-kan: Uno Riemon chosakusen; Mohan kōjōshū.* Tokyo: Gozandō shoten, 1989.

————. *Kan'ai no reika ni kagayaku mohan kōjō: Tōyō Bōseki Himeji kōjō.* 1927. Edited and with an introduction by Hazama Hiroshi in *Nihon rōmu kanrishi shiryōshū, dai-2-ki, dai-9-kan: Uno Riemon chosakusen; Mohan kōjōshū.* Tokyo: Gozandō shoten, 1989.

Wagner, Edward W. *The Korean Minority in Japan, 1904–1950.* New York: Institute of Pacific Relations, 1951.

Watanabe Etsuji and Suzuki Yūko. *Tatakai ni ikite: Senzen fujin rōdō undō e no shōgen.* Tokyo: Domesu shuppan, 1980.

Watanabe Yōko. *Kindai Nihon joshi shakai kyōiku seiritsushi: Shojokai no zenkoku sōshikika to shidō shisō.* Tokyo: Akashi shoten, 1997.

Watsuji Tetsurō. *Fūdo.* 1935. Tokyo: Iwanami bunkō, 1989.

———. *Climate and Culture: A Philosophical Study.* Translated by Geoffrey Bownas. New York: Greenwood Press, 1988.

Weeks, Jeffrey. *Sex, Politics, and Society: The Regulation of Sexuality Since 1800.* New York: Longman, 1989.

Weiner, Michael. *The Origins of the Korean Community in Japan, 1910–1923.* Atlantic Highlands, NJ: Humanities Press International, Inc., 1989.

———. *Race and Migration in Imperial Japan.* New York: Routledge, 1994.

Wilson, Sandra. "Angry Young Men and the Japanese State: Nagano Prefecture, 1930–33." In *Society and the State in Interwar Japan,* edited by Elise K. Tipton, 100–125. New York: Routledge, 1997.

Wittner, David. "Iron and Silk: Progress and Ideology in the Technological Transformation of Japan, 1850–1895." Ph.D. diss., Ohio State University, 1999.

Yamakawa Hitoshi. *Shihonshugi no karakuri.* Tokyo: Kensetsusha, 1926.

Yamakawa Hitoshi and Tadokoro Teruaki. *Purorateria keizaigaku.* Tokyo: Kagaku shisō fukyōkai, 1926.

Yamamoto Shigemi. *Aa Nomugi tōge.* 1979. Tokyo: Kadokawa bunkō, 1994.

Yamanouchi Mina. *Yamanouchi Mina jiden: Jūnisai no bōseki jokō kara no shōgai.* With an introduction by Ichikawa Fusae. Tokyo: Shinjuku shobō, 1975.

Yamazaki Tomoko. *Sandakan hachiban shokan.* Tokyo: Chikuma shobō, 1972.

———. *Sandakan Brothel No. 8: An Episode in the History of Lower-Class Japanese Women.* Translated and with an introduction by Karen Colligan-Taylor. Armonk, NY: M. E. Sharpe, 1999.

Yasko, Richard. "Hiranuma Kiichirō and Conservative Politics in Pre-War Japan." Ph.D. diss., University of Chicago, 1973.

Yokoyama Gennosuke. *Naichi zakkyōgo no Nihon.* 1899. Tokyo: Iwanami shoten, 1954.

———. *Nihon no kasō shakai.* 1899. Tokyo: Iwanami bunkō, 1995.

Yokusan undōshi kankōkai, ed. *Yokusan kokumin undōshi.* With an introduction by Kitagawa Keiji. Tokyo: Yumani shobō, 1998.

Yoneda Sayoko. "Shufu to shokugyō fujin." In *Nihon tsūshi,* edited by Iwanami kōza. Tokyo: Iwanami shoten, 1994.

Yonetani, Julia. "Ambiguous Traces and the Politics of Sameness: Placing Okinawa in Meiji Japan." *Japanese Studies* 20, no. 1 (May 2000): 15–31.

Yoshimi Yoshiaki. *Jugun ianfu.* Tokyo: Iwanami shoten, 1995.

Yoshimi, Yoshiaki. *Comfort Women: Sexual Slavery in the Japanese Military During World War II.* Translated and with an introduction by Suzanne O'Brien. New York: Columbia University Press, 2000.

Young, Louise. "Imagined Empire: The Cultural Construction of Manchukuo." In *The Japanese Wartime Empire, 1931–1945,* edited by Peter Duus, Ramon H. Myers, and Mark R. Peattie, 71–96. Princeton: Princeton University Press, 1996.

————. *Japan's Total Empire: Manchuria and the Culture of Wartime Imperialism.* Berkeley: University of California Press, 1998.

Yunichika shashi henshū iinkai, ed. *Yunichika hyakunenshi, jō/ge.* Osaka: Yunichika kabushiki kaisha, 1991.

Yutani, Eiji. "*Nihon no kaso shakai* of Gennosuke Yokoyama." Ph.D. diss., University of California, 1985.

Zaidan hōjin SYD. Zaidan hōjin SYD home page. www.syd.or.jp/index2.html (accessed October 8, 2006).

Zenkoku Fujin Dōmei. "Zenkoku Fujin Dōmei nyūsu, dai-3 kaime." In *Nihon josei undō shiryō shūsei.* Vol. 4, *Seikatsu/Rōdō I,* ed. Suzuki Yūko, 799–802. Tokyo: Fuji shuppan, 1994.

Index

Abe Isō, 83
Aichi Prefecture, 116, 124
Akamatsu Tsuneko, 64, 79
Allied occupation. *See* occupation of Japan
All-Japan Women's Federation (Zenkoku Fujin Dōmei), 82–84
Amagasaki Cotton Spinning, 31
Amano Fujio, 58, 60, 62–63
America. *See* United States
anarchism, 119
"Aru jokō no shuki" (Notes from a Female Factory Worker), 42–43
assimilation, 116–117, 120, 122, 134–136, 159

Big Five, 31
Big Six, 169n14
Big Ten, 140, 147, 198n9
Bolshevik Revolution, 30
Boy Scouts, 176n17
Brady, Robert, 171n27
Buddhism, 55, 66, 79, 86

café waitresses, 44
calisthenics, 28, 47–49, 92, 158; factory, 48–49, 72; national, 47, 48, 65, 72, 74, 76, 79, 181n69; radio, 181n69, 182n79
Chiba Prefecture, 96, 121
China, 32, 94, 111, 159
Chōsenjin, 110
Chōsenjin rōdōsha ni kan suru jōkyō (The Condition of Korean Workers), 132

"Chōsen jokō o tsukau kokoroe" (Methods for Using Korean Female Factory Workers), 116
chūseiteki shinri (neutered psyche), 44
cities, 10, 38, 40, 41, 42–43, 45, 60–61, 63, 68, 79, 101, 193n31
Citizens' Labor Patriotic Cooperation Order, 143
Civil Code, 67
"civilization and enlightenment," 8, 41, 164n2
civil rights, 6, 7, 149, 157. *See also* human rights
Clark, Anna, 163n6
class consciousness, 3, 83, 87, 88, 89, 129–130
climate (*fudō*), 116–117
coal mines, 117–118, 191n18
comfort women, 191n10
Comintern, 135
Communist Party. *See* Japan Communist Party
compassionism (*onjōshugi*), 15, 19, 22, 157
consumers, 35–36, 42, 54
consumption, 44, 157
Cotton and Staple Fiber Control Association (Men Sufu Tōseikai), 140
counting songs, 60–61, 112–113
countryside, 2, 5, 20, 23, 38, 40, 45, 51, 56, 63, 67, 76, 80, 100, 101, 103, 105, 125, 138–139, 151, 160
cultivation groups, 28, 37, 48, 51–53, 76, 77, 79, 84, 101, 108, 136, 158
Cultivation Hall, 80

Text: 10/13 Sabon
Display: Sabon
Compositor: Binghamton Valley Composition, LLC
Printer and binder: Maple-Vail Manufacturing Group